INDIAN DALIT LITERATURE
Critical Ruminations

INDIAN DALIT LITERATURE

Critical Ruminations

Edited by
Bijender Singh

AUTHORSPRESS

Worldwide Circulation through Authorspress Global Network

First Published 2015

by

Authorspress

Q-2A Hauz Khas Enclave, New Delhi-110 016 (India)

Phone : (0) 9818049852

WordTree

2306, Snug Harbor NE, Marietta, GA 30066 (USA)

Phone : +1-720-360-8270

e-mails: authorspress@rediffmail.com; authorspress@hotmail.com

Website: www.authorspressbooks.com

Indian Dalit Literature: Critical Ruminations

ISBN 978-81-7273-965-2

Printed in India at Thomson Press (India) Limited

Foreword

> Why do you play with that boy? Is there no one else in the whole village to play with? Don't give him water in that vessel. If he touches it, he'll defile it. Go away." I was upset because I couldn't give water to a friend. Is one's caste more important than one's friend? Is caste more important than thirst? Wasn't Arjya a human being? If so, how could he make water impure by merely touching it?" (Limbale 2003: 20)

Marginalization has emerged as a complex phenomenon in this era of globalization where people of the low class or with poor economic status and politically marginalized are pushed to the peripheral positions and the social mobility of these people has become a challenge. Much effort has been done by the Government through constitutional laws, reservation policies and five-year plans to enhance the socio-economic status of these marginalized people. Though there is a considerable improvement in their socio-economic position yet desired result is still awaited; that is due to large-scale corruption, improper implementation of plans, lack of strategic efforts and disinterestedness of people to work for them. Our idea behind the book is to map a lighted discourse: a trajectory of emancipation.

One of the aims of writing Dalit literature has been to reveal to the readers the injustice, helplessness, tyrannies, oppressions and struggles of many of the disadvantaged populations under the social machine of stratification in India. Caste politics in India are unique and culture specific. A powerful tool that aids the Dalit writers in doing so is the language used—militant, socially rooted and blunt. The language is mostly colloquial and jarring to elite aesthetics defined by the upper caste and upper class citizens in India. Unconventionally militant similes, metaphors and analogies used seem to befittingly paint specific social experiences, experience of the self, as well as that of fellow subaltern populations, as devoid of dignity, frustrating, repulsive and torturous. Speaking as an inmate of the cage describes how on being tortured as Manoranjan Byapari, a Dalit refugee writer from Bengal in Itibritte *Chandal Jiban* says: "Skull would crack and brain fluid would sprinkle out. There will be downpour of blood. Turning humans into lumps of giddy flesh...." (translation mine, 230). Dalit writers are involved in literary Movement in India conceiving the ideology of Dr. B. R. Ambedkar: "Educate, agitate, organize". Contemporary Dalit voices register a corpus of resistance to mark a journey from *nothing* to at least *something*! Arjun Dangle defining Dalit literature, says: "Dalit literature is not simply literature... (it) is associated with a movement to bring about change... it (is) strongly evident that there is no established critical theory behind (Dalit writings); instead there is a new thinking and a new point of view" (Dangle 1994: vii-viii). But this new outlook which is intended to give a new society, its new literature and aesthetics, has many fresh concerns. The first one is whether the Dalit writers really have their own language other than the language which they call Brahmanical. One should not forget that in India language has regional variations, not only class variations. They use ordinary, day to day life language to share their experience. It seems that those who claim for a Dalit language, they confuse the language with the Dalit experience. The Dalits are determined to narrate the Dalit agony, resistance, strengths and path of liberation. It is important to note here that while responding to the past experience, the Dalit writers are conscious of the present and give hint of the future prosperity. These make a fervent plea for a complete overhaul of society by questioning prevailing practices of caste and identity in different parts of India. Like Aboriginal literature in Australia, there is a collective spirit that governs Dalit literary tradition in India. Manohar Mouli Biswas' following lines, translated from Bangla by Jaydeep Sarangi beautifully explain this strand:

> The age of twenty four
> She gun fired all
> Against exploitation.

Her determination registered
Oh! Phoolan, you have come from
The lowest caste
From a remote and unknown village.
Oppressors of women, be aware of it—
She cannot be unnoticed.

(Biswas 2014: 'Phoolan Devi', 31)

We must not forget that Dalit is not a caste but a realization and is related to the experience of joys and sorrows and struggle of those in the lowest stratum of the society. Dalit literary corpus is window on culture—a Dalit culture that is the culture of exclusion and exploitation. Those who shoulder Dalit poetics walk through long corridors of ignited discourse through which there is often no return; but returns with the coloured wings of successive images and idioms. Let me proclaim, my grail is Dalit. No one can deny the Sun rising. 'Right' is a euphonious equivalent of the word 'might.'

This book entitled *Indian Dalit Literature: Critical Ruminations* is a collection of twenty-nine articles scholarly written by erudite contributors. All contributors have infused their full intellectual energy to contribute some new knowledge on the Dalit themes. The book contains articles on three Dalit genres—autobiographies, novels and short-stories—written by both Dalit and non-Dalit writers.

Present anthology, edited by Bijender Singh, is a unique voluminous work that endeavours to touch and explore some salient themes related to Dalit issues and it encompasses some of the seminal issues related to Dalit aesthetics in India. I'm confident that the book will create a new space in Dalit Literature in India and break the age-old stereotypes. Happy reading!

Dr. Jaydeep Sarangi
Bilingual Poet, Critic & Expert in Dalit Criticism
Associate Professor, Department of English
Jogesh Chandra Chaudhuri College, (Calcutta University)
Kolkata, West Bengal, India

Preface

> Get as much education as you can. Take away this accursed bread from the mouths of the Mahars. This poisonous bread will finally kill the very humanness of man. (Dangle 1992: 153)

Indian Dalit Literature is replete with some authentic bitter and excruciating experiences; and it always remains an interesting and contentious topic in the scholarly circle due to decadent propensities of Dalits and narrow-mindedness of so-called elite classes who consider themselves at the apex of caste-hegemony. Epistemologically, the word 'Dalit' or 'untouchable' is as old as history of human-beings and our mundane world has witnessed several conflicts between superior dominating groups and so-called inferior exploited classes. We have illustrations of it in many Greco-Roman books, great classics, Greek and Indian epics; but who made this superior and inferior differentiation, cannot be explicitly explained. This caste system is a complex phenomenon and there is no certainty of its genesis how this caste-system originated in India. It was in practice with its circumscribed rules even before imperial India.

Resurgent India is considered as a land of unity in diversity; and people of different castes, creeds, religions and sects inhabit on vast Indian landscape. Since time immemorial, living standard and the mentality of the people have been changing and there has been a considerable change in their occupations with the pace of time and tide. Thus, the society bifurcated in upper and lower classes on the basis of nature of their work. Anthropocentric facts reveal that upper caste people insinuate and humiliate the low caste people and sometimes even oust the people living in grinding poverty. In the very last resort when everything else fails, these poverty-stricken and economically backward people have to resort reformative movements to work hand in hand on equal platform.

Historians say that the *varna* system was initiated by the Aryans when they settled in the Indo-Gangetic Plains. According to ancient Hindu scriptures, the quadruple division of society was in the form of Brahmins (priests, teachers and preachers), Kshatriyas (kings, ministers, warriors and soldiers), Vaishyas (businessmen, merchants, cattle-herders and agriculturists) and Shudras (labourers, workers and servants). This tripartite society namely the priestly class, warrior class and the class of commoners excluded the fourth class of serfs. In that time these Shudras were considered the most degraded, ignored, suppressed, oppressed and exploited. These people are known as Dalits who are partially segregated from the society till today.

Etymologically speaking, the word 'Dalit' is derived from Sanskrit, where 'dal' means 'to break, crack or split'. Other people have idea that Dalit comes from the word 'padadalit' which means 'slaves at one's feet' or 'underclass'. The word 'Dalits' denotes 'broken people' who have been exploited and subjugated by so-called superior classes. Whenever we take Dalit Literature for discussion, we deal with the inferior group of people who are crushed, suppressed, underprivileged, down-trodden and outcasts. Dalits were called 'broken people' for the first time by B. R. Ambedkar in his book *The Untouchables*. Mahatma Jyotirao Phule also called 'Dalits' the victim of our caste-ridden society. Dalit Literature term was used in Mumbai in 1958 for the first time in Maharashtra Dalit Sahitya Sangha. The English called them 'the Depressed Classes' and 'the Scheduled Castes' and Mahatma Gandhi elevated them to a high level when he called them 'Harijans' which means 'Children of God'.

The literary phenomenon which we now call Dalit literature in India emerged in 1960s. Dalit literature aims at the liberation and socio-economic equality of Dalits in India. The aim of Dalit literature is to protest against the established system which is based on injustice and exposes the evil and hypocrisy of the upper castes. Dalit caucus has to start a ceaseless struggle to come out of the chains of untouchability and exploitation. Dalit literature is based on experiences rather than speculations. Dalit Literature, more or less, is essentially expression of the degraded human life and this great piece of literature depicts that reality in communicable lucid language in facilitating narrative with readers' aesthetic, comprehensive and literary sense. Dalit autobiographies are the storehouses of pains, afflictions, ignominies and pathos. Dalit authors penned their soul-numbing and heart-rending survival stories which remind us to American slave narratives. Dalit writers have depicted the reality of their lives in their autobiographies which are considered as the epoch-making documents in the human history. These writings based on marginalization proved milestones in shaping the future of the Indian Dalit literature. Thus, Dalit literature not only speaks the bitter past of Dalit people but also envisages and prospects the bright future and smooth life of Dalits.

Caste-discrimination, exploitation, suppression and gender-violence are dominant themes in almost all Indian Dalit texts written by Dalit or non-Dalit writers in Indian or other regional languages. Dr. B. R. Ambedkar envisaged an egalitarian society and to fulfill this dream he introduced Hindu Code Bill in the Parliament. Dalit Literature expositarily unravels both gray areas and sparkling strands how the marginalized classes have to live a miserable life. This marginalization is everywhere and both the developed and developing countries are unable to solve the issues of caste discrimination absolutely. Untouchability still pervades in this era also where every country claims to solve the economical, gender and caste-based discriminations. The sorrows of the Dalits were unheard and untold history up to around one and half century back but Dalit writers brought a revolution by writing autobiographies, biographies, short-stories, poetry, novels etc. They abjured the slavery of the sophisticated people. Thus, through these Dalit writings this unexplored subject gained some momentum and spread to the wide circle of readers. Now Dalit literature is a powerful and strong weapon to fight for the cause of Dalits, marginalized, downtrodden and underprivileged people. It is being nurtured and flourished properly as it has been written in many Indian regional languages and much part of it has been translated into English.

The book is a collection of twenty-nine scholarly articles and a critical survey of different texts. It assays and analyses the Dalit aesthetics very systematically and beautifully. It is hoped that this book will be very helpful to teachers and scholars equally who want to pursue research on this less explored field of Indian Literature. Every condign effort has been made to establish concinnity in this book and give it a coadunate form. Some papers have been included in this anthology from Indian English Literature because they have strong Dalit themes. This book, it is hoped, will work as a catalyst and it will definitely add a new critical chapter in the field of Indian Dalit Literature. The book is one of its kinds and it tries to offer contextually a new direction to Indian Dalit literature.

The book has seen the light of the days with so many painstaking efforts of our diligent and erudite contributors who have infested their intellectual skills to give a weighty and fruitful critical survey on different themes from Indian Dalit Literature. Without their assiduous assistance, my dream of such a grand book on Dalit theme could never be fulfilled. I am highly grateful to Mr. Sudarshan Kcherry, Managing Director, Authorspress, New Delhi who established friendly rapport with me during the whole course of publishing. My gratitude is due to whole team members who showed professional zeal and worked on the manuscript tirelessly and consistently and improved it and reworked on the framework of the manuscript.

Last but not the least; let me introduce you a key person in Dalit criticism—Dr. Jaydeep Sarangi—who is a leading scholar, poet, critic and an authority on marginal literatures and Indian Writing in English with thirty books and hundred research-articles in his credit. Widely anthologized and reviewed as a poet and translator, Dr. Sarangi has delivered talks on Dalit criticism and translation studies in several countries and conducted workshops. He has translated Bengali Dalit poems/stories into English as well as edited a number of anthologies of translations of Bengali Dalit writings. I owe my heart-felt gratitude to Dr. Jaydeep Sarangi who co-operated and motivated me throughout the work and spent his valuable moments for us in writing the foreword for this book.

Bijender Singh
Mob: 91-9992873801, 9068814739
Email:drbijendersingh@india.com

Contents

1

Pains and Pathos of the Underdogs in *The God of Small Things*

Dr. Sigma G R

Dalit literature has become a debated subject in the present century and it has received a greater attention. Throughout the centuries, Dalit's were regarded as downtrodden and are treated as animals by upper class. Dalit's struggled a lot against caste system and they raised slogans for their liberation. This subaltern group underwent suppression, hatred and exploitation and were trapped by the society, by the government and by the religion. And the genre Dalit Literature gives us the picture of wicked exploitation and struggles faced by these poor people. The status of Dalits has undergone some changes and no doubt, they are in the process of liberation, but they are not given rightful place in society.

In the evolution of Dalit literature, it is certain that Dalit writers cry out the sufferings and shocking status of untouchable human beings in the Indian society. Dalit writers can be compared to the Black writers who always want to write about the world they experienced. C. D. Narasimhaiah analyses so in "India and the literature of common wealth":

> Not long ago there were Negro women who were ashamed to say their race created it. They didn't care for Negro paintings because they were 'too Negro'. I want to be a poet, not a Negro poet was what one heard. And today they have gone so far in asserting their identity that without it they have nothing to stand up to the white man. And some of their rebels rightly assert that Negro children are born into a white world and if they are to survive in it they need to achieve blackness. The black writer shouts 'The Statue of Liberty must go', the bitch must vacate our minds'. He says, 'it is more important to know how to cry, sob, laugh, stare and startle than to learn how to smile, grimace archly and wink'. The writers want to define the world in their own terms. (Narasimhaiah 33)

In India, Dalit literature has been flourished in almost all the Indian languages. Dalit writers contributed poems, articles, essays, fiction, and biographies etc. which enable the readers to view the social, cultural and religious heritages of Dalit community that created a Dalit consciousness about their identity. Dalit literature produced literary giants like Mahasweta Devi, Mangal Rathod, C. K Janu, C. Ayyappan, Thirumanavalan, Imayam, Raghavan, Neerav Patel, Rabi Singh, Basudev Sunani and others. Dalit writers have an urge to write like others for the betterment of humanity. There are several little magazines which exhibits genuine problems of untouchables. As written in *No Alphabet in Sight: A New Dalit Writing From South India*:

> Many old Dalit writers say that their early writings were published by Left literary and cultural magazines such as: Manavosai (a CPI-ML journal); Pirachanai, edited by Shanmugham (CPM); Manithan, edited by Rajendra Cholan (CPI-ML).... Journals entirely devoted to the circulation of Dalit writings appeared in the mid- to late 1990s. Among them are Dalit Murasu, Puthiya Kodangi, Dalit, Bodhi, Manusanga, Thaiman and Adi Tamizhan. (Narayana and Susie Tharu 27)

In the wake of Dalit writings, untouchables have come to realize their status and identity and now are aware that they have been suppressed and denied human rights. In fact, the concept of Dalit Identity had a certain congruency on the social level. It held out a promise of social transformation because our society is caste oriented. As M. Rajasekhar Rao wrote: "Super-ego too seems to be weakly differentiated and insufficiently idealized in Indians... He explains that communal conscience which comprises family and jati norms is a social rather than an individual formation : it is not inside psyche..." (Rao 24)

Apart From Dalit literature, Indian English Literature also deals with the issues of Untouchables. Like Arundhati Roy and many non-Dalit writers like Mulkraj Anand, R. K. Narayan, U. R. Ananthamurthy, Anita Desai, Rohinton Mistry, Raja Rao, Arvind Adiga and others took Dalit themes for their pronouncements. A Dalit issue in Indian Literature has received greater attention and it always successfully transplants the social, religious, psychic, educational and cultural experiences of the society. After reading the analyses of Dalit writers' one can trace the history of Dalits. Do Dalits have a natural inclination towards lower strata of society? Do our societies follow a set of beliefs and practices which helps to shape the social life in this way? M. Rajasekhar Rao points out: "Indians continue to be governed by group or jati norms. In other words, Indian society has not yet become an individualistic society. People are still viewed in relation to society rather than as separate entities in India." (Rao 26)

When the role of society in Dalit oppression is clear, idea about Dalit writings got publicity with alarming frequency that served to make the problem public. The accounts of Mulkraj Anand in his novel *Untouchable* referred to the temperamental traits and beliefs of the society. The character Bakha was an eye opener. K. Satchidananadan observes:

> Anand brought to fictional life Bakha, his boyhood companion, the untouchable sweeper boy in *The Untouchable.* Anand's mother abused Bakha for 'polluting' her son when Bakha carried home a bleeding Anand, hurt by a stone. Bakha is reviled by caste Hindus as he cleans latrines; but Anand capture Bakha's pride in his work: The novel was not only a powerful social tract, but a remarkable technical feat as in single day's action the author builds round his hero a spiritual crisis broad enough to embrace the whole of India. Foster wrote in its introduction: "It has gone straight to the heart of its subject and purified it." (Satchidanandan 86)

If Anand made the protagonist Bakha to spoke about a day in his life, Arundhati Roy took one step further. She examined the whole Life of Dalit victim Velutha and made him the mouth piece of Dalit victims. Arundhati Roy's *The God of Small Things* is a curious mixture of individual talent, history, politics and family. It has many major themes like quest for love, question of identity, fear, wanting for love, waiting for love, family, society etc. Roy witnessed vast political and social changes after independence. But in society certain group of class, caste and tribes are still dependents. Several incidents shook the society and it takes place off and on, but only few writers highlight the cause, problem, psychological motivations of the incidents. Arundhati Roy directed not only the love between a Syrian catholic and an untouchable, but also the evils in the Indian society. Roy skilfully woven each and every character in a way that family relationships are confusing, but in different ways they stick as a part of the family.

The re-examination of Dalit life took a new direction with Arundhati Roy's *The God of Small Things* which receives wider recognition and popularity, because the portrait of Velutha (untouchable) is very much real. Roy did not identify herself specifically as a Dalit, but this Indian English writer, social and political activist discussed the crisis faced by untouchables in her Booker Prize winning novel. *The God of Small Things* is a semi autobiographic novel portrays Roy's experiences at Ayemenam in Kerala. Roy presents the public and private life of Syrian Catholic divorcee Ammu Ipe and her relationship with a Paravan (Dalit) named Velutha. He is a carpenter and mechanic at Paradise Pickles and Preserves which is run by Ipe family. In appropriating the term 'Dalit', Roy portrayed the oppression and suffering of the hero. Velutha was at the root of all other oppressions pointed by Razi Abedi:

> Their suffering is not just the suffering of the individual, and there is nothing romantic about. Their problem is neither ideological nor philosophical. They do not seek poetic beauty. Similes, metaphors and symbols are not important. The reality of their life is too hideously shocking, beyond the capacity of fantasy or imagination. Their tragedy is universal, trampling them down and disfiguring their humanity. (Abedi 3)

Arundhati Roy intended to further the Dalit life style by showing the love affair between Ammu and Velutha. When it is discovered, Ammu is imprisoned at home and Velutha is a prisoner in jail and a victim to the cruel imprisonment. AmmuIpe is a divorcee who fights for her and for the dizygotic twins, Rahel and Estha. Both Rahel and Estha find comfort, love and protection from Velutha despite his status as a Dalit. The bond between Children and Velutha forced Ammu to make her love a reality. When she learned the news of Velutha's being arrested, Ammu goes to the police station and told the truth to the police, but police threaten her. She forgets her high caste status for love. Arundhati Roy reinforces the idea that there is no caste, no religion and nothing untouchable between a man and woman if there is love, trust and respect between two individuals and here it is the social conditions forced both of them to unite. In an Interview with Out-caste Arundhati makes clear her views on Ammu and Velutha affair:

> In fact I'm little sceptical about some Dalit writing which goes to great lengths to describe victimhood with gratuitous description of smell and

> stink and humiliation.... I believe in finding beauty in the saddest places, and honing into a weapon of war. It is not compassion or pity that attracts Ammu to Velutha. It's not subservience that delivers Velutha to Ammu. It is Ammu's anger at society she lives in and is shaped by that seeks out and recognizes Velutha's anger. They are united in anger as much in love. (Out-Caste 2)

Arundhati Roy wanted the readers to become convinced of the need for radical change in the current society. The social evils that Arundhati has projected are still afflictions of the untouchables. Rahel and Estha decided to run away, but their cousin Sophie Mol convinced the twins, but that night when the children's were trying to reach an abandoned house, their boat capsized and Sophie died. Baby Kochamma goes to police station and complained that Velutha is behind the death of Sophie. Like that Velutha never questions the administration of Paradise Pickles, even though he is not paid well for the work he does. At the same time Vellaya Papan always shows gratitude to the touchable class and he is against his son when he made inter-caste sexual affair. The prevalent social condition of Dalits in independent India which never allows them to enjoy his freedom is clearly stated in this novel, and readers can find that Paravan's (untouchables) are tormented not only by Hindus but also from other caste like Syrian catholic.

> Paravans were expected to crawl backwards with a broom, sway their footprints so that Brahmins or Syrian Christians would not defile themselves by accidentally stepping into Paravan's footprint. In Mammachi's time Paravan's like other untouchables, were not allowed to walk on public roads, or allowed to cover their upper bodies, not allowed to carry umbrellas. They had to put their hands over their mouths when they spoke, to divert their polluted breath away from those whom they address. (Roy 74)

In this context, it will be apt to quote the experience of Dalit's in a passage from *Untouchable:* "The outcastes were not allowed to mount the platform surrounding the well, because if they were ever draw water from it, the Hindu of the upper castes would consider water polluted." (Anand 14) From a political and historical point of view the above said Dalit experiences show that untouchables are treated equally in all parts of India before independence and in the late twentieth century.

In the reaction against the social suppression, Dalits were ready to give up the identity as an untouchable to get an identity and status in the society as the personality of the untouchables is overwhelmingly swamped by the dominating upper class society. In a curious way Arundhati portrayed Dalit's conversion towards Christianity in the pre and post-independence society. Here, in the novel Velutha's grandfather Kelan was converted to Christianity to get a noble status in the society. But they did not get any fortune or wealth and they remain again as the same old poverty stricken human beings.

> It did not take them long to realize that they had jumped from the frying pan into fire they were made to have separate churches, with separate services and separate priest. After independence they found they were not titled to any government benefits like job reservation or bank loans at low interest rates, because officially in paper, they were Christians, and therefore casteless. (Roy 74)

The contemporary Dalit experience is bad and any Dalit can be tortured at police station. By this type of marginalisation normally people should know how to spark and how to question the authorities, but in Roy novel Dalit's never has questioned the authorities. The Dalit victim Velutha did not get any human consideration at police station. When the love affair between Ammu and Velutha is on air, Baby Kochamma influenced the police inspector and put Velutha in Jail and beaten to death:

> He was semi-conscious, but was not moving. His skull was fractured in three places. His nose and both his cheek bones were smashed, leaving his face pulpy, undefined. The blow to his mouth had split open his upper lip and broken six teeth, three of which were embedded in his lower lip, hideously inverting his beautiful smile. Four of his ribs were splintered; one had pierced his left lung which was made him bleed from his mouth... His lower intestine was ruptured and haemorrhaged, the blood collected in the abdominal cavity. (Roy 310)

Velutha was buried in a pauper's pit and Ammu realises her responsibility for the death of her lover. She dies in a lodge and church disagrees to bury her in their cemetery. At last her body is buried in a crematorium for beggars. In fact, this incident gives a warning to other common people who want to break the conventions of the society. Roy is a staunch defender of human values and she wants people to come out from the shackles of untouchability. The experiences and incidents in this Dalit fiction is not illusionary or imagination. It says the life, grief, anger, sorrow and shameful incidents in the life of the victim Velutha. Dr. Jugal Kishore Mishra observes:

> Dalit Literature is experience based. This 'anubhava' (experience) takes precedence over 'anumana' (speculation). Thus to Dalit writers, history is not illusionary or unreal as Hindu metaphysical theory may make one to believe. That is why authenticity and liveliness have become hallmarks of Dalit Literature. These writers make use of the language of the out caste and underprivileged in Indian society, Shame, anger, sorrow and indomitable hope are the stuff of Dalit literature. Because of the anger against the age-old oppression, the expression of the Dalit writers has become sharp. (Mishra 2-3)

If *The God of Small Things* is one source of Dalit perspective; another was about the social and related subjects. Recently, Arundhati was in the news when she made Mahatma Ayyankali speech at Kerala University in a three day international seminar "Reimagining Struggles at the Margins: A History of the Unconquered and Oppressed" on July 17th in 2014. Here, she made an excellent focus on the Dalit style, the Dalit conditions of being subordinated by the society before and after independence, and how Dalit's successfully played their roles in the society. Arundhati Roy asked openly: "Do we need to name our universities after Gandhi or Ayyankali" and this speech stirred a lot of controversies. Similarly, Roy reacted in many places against the problems in differently organized society. Chad Bauman pointed out Roy's views on missionary activities: "And more recently, Arundhati Roy, the activist and novelist whose literary abilities I admire a great deal, drew upon the strength of popular sentiments against "missionary" activities when she called the forces of globalization..." (Bauman 1) Not only did she focus on Dalits and downtrodden, she took the condition of people displaced by industry, by dam, Maoist rebels, global war on terrorism and many other social issues.

Above all, *The God of Small Things* expanded her vision of life, on the one hand, wide appreciation—with the issues of Dalit, society, love, fear, guilt and on the other side criticism. Arundhati Roy's ideologies are packed up with fundamental attachment to the marginalised people, their existence and experiences. Her fiction arouses the process of Dalit consciousness. Now this fiction is being explored and developed as an important source of untouchables and their identity. Thus, the Dalit perspective of *The God of Small Things* contributed a lot to Dalit consciousness and this stance is much linked to the past, present and future of Dalits and this topic remain unexplored and it needs more scholastic analysis.

Works Cited

Abedi Razi. "Dalit Literature: The Voice of the Downtrodden". http://www.gowanusbooks.com/dalit.htm, 8/12/2014.

Anand, Mulkraj. *Untouchable.* Delhi: Penguin Books, 2001. Print.

Bauman, Chad. *Christian Identity and Dalit Religion in Hindu India.* USA: Wm. B Eerdman's Publishing, 2008. Print.

Mishra, Kishore Jugal. "A Critical Study of Dalit Literature in India" http://litteritt.blogspot.in/2012/09/dalit-literature-readinghtml.

Naik, M. K., Desai, S. K., & Amur G. S. *Critical Essays on Indian Writing in English.* S S Wodeyar. Karnataka University, Dharwar: Macmillan ISSD Press Madras, 1972. Print.

Narasimhaiah C. D. *Moving Frontiers of English Studies in India.* New Delhi: S. Chand and Company, 1997. Print.

Narayana, K Satya & Susie, Tharu. *No Alphabet in Sight: New Dalit Writing from South India.* Dossier-1 Tamil and Malayalam, Penguin Books, 2011. Print.

Out-Caste. "Interview with Arundhati Roy". http//out-caste.blogspot.in/2008/04 interview-with-roy.html/ Hyderabad, Andrapradesh, India. Dalit Studies Course Initiatives. English and Foreign Languages University.

Rao, Visweswara C. R. *Indian Writing Today.* M Rajasekhar. "Psychoanalysis and Indian Writing in English, Promises and Possibilities." Published by Indian Association for English Studies. Mehra Offset Press, 1999. Print.

Roy, Arundhati. *The God of Small Things.* New Delhi: Penguin, 1997. Print.

Satchidananadan, K. *Readings in Indian Literature and Beyond* "Mulkraj Anand: A Writer with Social Concern." Delhi: Yash Publications, 2009. Print.

2

Invincible Resistance: An Appraisal of the Indefatigable Female in Mahasweta Devi's "Draupadi"

Dr. Sony Jalarajan Raj and Dr. Soumya Jose

> If we must die—let it not be like hogs
> Hunted and penned in an inglorious spot,
> While round us bark the mad and hungry dogs.
> Making their mock at our accursed lot.
> If we must die—oh, let us nobly die,
> So that our precious blood may not be shed
> In vain; then even the monsters we defy
> Shall be constrained to honor us though dead!
> (Claude McKay, "If We Must Die" 1-9)

Dalit literature or literature of the marginalized underdog has gained its currency in India post 1950s. Dalit literature that depicts the life and miseries of Dalits gives voice to the people who have been silenced by the age old hegemonic doctrines. In the glossary of the book entitled *Growing up Untouchable in India: A Dalit Autobiography,* the term "Dalit" is defined as, "Downtrodden, oppressed. Used first by Jyotiba Phule in the mid-nineteenth century. The word gained currency as a self-chosen, proud name with the early 1970s development of the Dalit Panthers and Dalit literature. Today it has replaced most other names in the vocabulary of the politically aware ex-Untouchables and the press" (Moon, 181). The term "Dalit" instils self confidence and self-esteem among the people who were once shunned by the so called elite people of the upper-caste. According to Dangle: "Dalit literature is marked by revolt and negativism, since it is negatively associated with hopes for the freedom of a group of people, who, as untouchables, are victims of social, economic and cultural inequality" (qtd. in Misra 275).

Dalit literature empowers the Dalit community, and it equips them to voice their protest and defy the humiliations inflicted on them. Mahasweta Devi, when interviewed by Pankaj Singh voices the oppression that the tribes face in India. She explicitly states the reasons that have drawn her to the marginalized tribal groups. She points out:

> I was drawn towards the so-called criminal tribes quite logically. I was greatly shocked to realise that nobody ever felt concerned about them. I was much surprised when I translated the book called 'Mind of Mahatma Gandhi' into Bengali with the title 'Gandhi Manas' for the National Book Trust. In this voluminous book the word 'tribe' has figured once or twice... or perhaps nowhere. Gandhi came, Ambedkar, Jyoti Prasad Phule and so many other great national leaders... so many communist movements were launched, the socialists came on the scene... the communists got divided... CPI and CPI (M) came into existence... the new generation started the Naxalite movement which spread to the villages... their movement is still on... but … they never said even once that the so-called criminal tribes are the most oppressed. They have suffered the most brutal oppression.... There is this belief that each human being is born for some purpose. If I were to subscribe to this belief then about my own self I reckon that I am born to do what I am doing for these so-called 'criminal' tribes. (7)

She is greatly moved, as she could understand that the social reformers of India and even the national father of India could not do much to uplift the downtrodden tribes. She believes that it is her moral obligation to work and write on behalf of the tribal groups who have found a helping hand in her. She remarks: "I think a creative writer should have a social conscience. I have a duty towards society. Yet I don't really know why I do these things. The sense of duty is an obsession. I must remain accountable to myself" (Emory). Pankaj Singh in "Mahasweta Devi: An Intimate View" remarks on her close association with the tribal groups and the Dalit community. Singh points out:

> The most important fact about Mahashveta is that in the latter half of this century she has not only fought against the forces of darkness and exploitation in the semi-feudal and semi-colonial Indian society with the tools of language, but during her wandering in the villages, forests, and

> small and big cities alike, she has also spread the consciousness of the necessity of struggle among the exploited and suppressed poor people for the attainment of their dignity and human rights. To hundreds of thousands of such people she has become their 'Didi' (elder sister) and 'Maan' (Mother) as a beacon of inspiration and hope. (1)

Mahasweta Devi gives true accounts of the sufferings of Dalits and she ardently proclaimed her commitment to the Dalit community when she received Ramon Magsaysay Award in 1997, for her selfless crusade for the tribals. Mahasweta Devi dreams of an India where all Indians are treated equally irrespective of their castes. She is an advocate of the Dalit community and she reiterates it quite often. When interviewed by Pankaj Singh, she details about her recognition and acceptance among the tribals far and wide the country. She also talks about her association with the Naxalites:

> I was attached to the so-called criminal tribes, but when I wrote 'Aranyer Adhikar' I got real acceptance among them as they felt that what I wrote was their voice.... When 'Shri Shri Ganesh Mahima' and other books of mine were translated into the Telugu language and my sympathy for the Naxalite movement became known I got wider recognition. I also had contact with those tribals who were active Naxalites. In India's history it was the first time that the tribals began to get recognition. They drummed up support from every village and began to visit me. It was in 1979. Since then I had an easy access to tribal society. (An Intimate View, 6-7)

In the introduction to *Bitter Soil*, Mahasweta Devi expresses contempt for the ruling class who cannot safeguard the rights and privileges of the marginalized people. She remarks on her mission as a writer: "The sole purpose of my writing is to expose the many faces of the exploiting agencies: The feudal minded landowner, his henchmen, so-called religious head, all of whom as a combined force are out for lower-caste blood" (ix). Many a time Mahasweta Devi has expressed her unhappiness with the government which does not do anything for the upliftment of the marginalized community.

> I find my people still groaning under hunger, landlessness, indebtedness and bonded labour... All the parties to the Left as well as those to the Right have failed to keep their commitment to the common people. I

> do not hope to see in my lifetime any reason to change this conviction of mine. Hence, I go on writing to the best of my abilities about the people, so that I can face myself without any sense of guilt or shame. For a writer faces judgement in his lifetime and remains answerable. (qtd. in Nazneen)

The reception of Dalit literature among the litterateur increases its reach and readership. The present chapter gives an in-depth reading of the character of "Dopdi" in Darupadi, which portrays the indescribable miseries of a Dalit woman and her indefatigable resistance to the male hegemony. Dopdi is doubly marginalized on account of her gender and caste.

"Draupadi" powerfully presents the resistance and resilience of a tribal woman named Dopdi, a name very uncommon among the tribals. The story behind her name is expounded in the beginning of Draupadi as the two policemen exchange dialogues:

> FIRST MEDLLION. What is this, a tribal called Dopdi?
>
> ....
>
> SECOND MEDALLION. Draupadi Mejhan. Born the year her mother threshed rice at
>
> Surja Sahu (killed)'s at Bakuli. Surja Sahu's wife gave her the name. (19)

The low caste Hindus in India were not allowed to use certain names from the scriptures and if at all the untouchables want to choose a name from the scriptures they need to change the name a little bit which sounds different from the original name. Draupadi, the rebel tribal woman is brutally raped after her husband is killed in an encounter with the police force. Rape is used as a tactic to silence militant women.

> Sexual violence takes place in every region of the world and includes rape, sexual slavery, forced prostitution, mutilation, forced pregnancy and sterilization. Reasons for the use of sexual violence vary from region to region and conflict to conflict. It has been used as a tactic to terrorize communities suspected of supporting guerrilla forces, as a way of forcing populations off their lands and it has been used to punish political activism. (Women Forging A New Security 6)

Rape as a tactic of war has been used many a time and it causes indescribable hurt to the morale of the victim and the community as a whole. In "Sexual Violence as a Weapon of War" published in UNICEF State of the World's Children, it is mentioned that rape is the most intrusive of all traumatic events. The review elaborates on the gravity of this sexual violence:

> Sexual violation of women erodes the fabric of a community in a way that few weapons can. Rape's damage can be devastating because of the strong communal reaction to the violation and pain stamped on entire families. The harm inflicted in such cases on a woman by a rapist is an attack on her family and culture, as in many societies women are viewed as repositories of a community's cultural and spiritual values. (UNICEF)

There is a reference to "rape as a tactic of war" in Draupadi. Dopdi remarks that the tribals born out of forced rape by the American soldiers do not have the sincerity and loyalty that the real tribals have for their clan. Robin May Shott in "War, rape, natality and genocide" observes that war time rape was mentioned even in the Bible and Homer's Iliad:

> Sexual violence in wartime is not new to the twentieth century. We find references to it in Homer's Iliad, as well as references to capturing women in war in the Hebrew Bible. Not until the fourteenth century did European leaders announce standards of chivalry to forbid rape, though these rules were rarely enforced. The license to rape was considered a major incentive for being a soldier. (6)

In Draupadi, Devi mentions about the unfortunate rape victims who bore the children fathered by American soldiers. Dopdi is contemptuous of the "half-breeds" (31). She says: "Shomai and Budhna are half-breeds. The fruits of the war. Contributions to Radhabhumi by the American soldiers stationed at Shian-dange. Otherwise crow would eat crow's flesh before Santhal would betray Santhal" (32). Her fidelity to her group and her trust in her kinsmen are very well expressed in her words:

> Dopdi has a fighting spirit that has not ceased even after her beloved husband's death. When she comes to know that police has stuck look out notice for her, she immediately thinks of the safety of her fellow comrades. Mahasweta Devi pen pictures the thoughts that pass through Dopdi's mind. "She must let them know that the police have set up

notices for her again. Must tell them that that bastard Sahib has appeared again. Must change hideouts" (31).

Mahasweta Devi explicitly portrays the hardships that Dopdi faces as she moves towards her hiding place, determined not to betray her fellow naxalites. She reminds herself that her husband Dulna was loyal to his tribe till his last breath. "Dulna died, but let me tell you, he didn't lose anyone else's life. Because this was not in our heads to begin with, one was countered for the other's trouble" (33). She reiterates her loyalty to her tribe and takes a firm decision that she will never betray her people if at all they capture her. Mushai's wife, who gave her shelter and hiding place is afraid whether she will tell their name if Dopdi is taken by police. Dopdi assures her that she "won't tell anybody's name" (28). She knows very well how to keep secrets. "Dopdi knows, has learned by hearing so often and so long, how one can come to terms with torture. If mind and body give way under torture, Dopdi will bite off her tongue.... When they counter you, your hands are tied behind you. All your bones are crushed, your sex is terribly wounded" (28-29).

The reader can easily visualize the path Dopdi traverses. The description of the terrain is photographic. "These three and a half miles of land and rocky ground are the best way to enter the forest.... A little level ground ahead. Then rocks again. … this area is quite enough. It's like a maze, every hump looks like every other" (33).

When Dopdi is captured by the soldiers, she does give verbal signal to her fellow comrades to inform them to be more cautious. "Now Dopdi spreads her arms, raises her face to the sky, turns towards the forest, and ululates with the force of her entire being. Once twice, three times. At the third burst the birds in the trees at the outskirts of the forest awake and flap their wings. The echo of the calls travels far." (34)

Dopdi is brutally raped after the interrogation. She falls unconscious and as she wakes up she realizes that she is raped multiple times by the soldiers. "Trying to move, she feels her arms and legs still tied to four posts. Something sticky under her ass and waist. Her own blood. Only the gag has been removed. Incredible thirst. In case she says 'water' she catches her lower lip in her teeth. She senses that her vagina is bleeding.... Her breasts are bitten raw, the nipples torn" (35).

Dopdi manifests her indomitable and daunting spirit when she is asked to go to the tent to meet the Burra Sahib. She does not express any apprehension and instead she "tears her piece of cloth with her teeth" (36). Dopdi deconstructs the myth that rape shatters the morale of a woman. She walks forward like a victorious queen with her head high. She is not ashamed of her nakedness. She stands before Senanayak with her "thigh and pubic hair matted with dry blood. Two breasts, two wounds" (36). Dopdi's invincible resistance is echoed as she says: "You can strip me, but how can you clothe me again? Are you a man?" (37). The words of this daunting tribal woman is sufficient to make the all powerful and haughty Senanayak diffident. She no longer considers him as a human being and she humiliates him as she spits "a bloody gob" on his white bush shirt (37). Mahasweta Devi's characterization of Draupadi is a clarion call to all the tribal women who undergo various kinds of oppression from the soldiers and the elite class. Draupadi's character will stay as a powerful source of valour to the dispossessed tribal women. Draupadi's resistance makes the Senanayak honour the courage of an "unarmed target" (37). Though she is "hunted and penned in an inglorious spot" ("If We Must Die" 2) she makes Senanayak unarmed with her invincible resistance.

Works Cited

Chakravarothy, Saumitra. "The Image of Woman in Mahasweta Devi's Novels. *The Image of Woman in Indian Literature*. Ed. Yashoda Bhat and Yamuna Raja Rao. Delhi. B.R. Publishing, 1993.

Dangle, Arjun. Introduction. *New Entry for the New Sun*. Ed. Arjun Dangle. Bombay: Disha Books, 1992.

Devi, Mahasweta. *Bitter Soil*. Calcutta: Segull, 1998.

Devi's "The Hunt." Contemporary Literary Review India. 2014.

Devi, Mahasweta. Postcolonial Studies @ Emory http://postcolonialstudies.emory.edu/mahsweta-devi

Khan, Nazneen. "Women Resisting Patriarchy and Colonial Oppression: A Study of Mahasweta

Misra, Kamal Kant. Ed. *Anthropology, New Global Order, and Other Essays*. New Delhi: Concept Publishing Company, 2005.

Moon, Vasant. *Growing Up Untouchable in India: A Dalit Autobiography*. Trans. Gail Omvedt. New York: Rowman and Little field, 2000.

Schott, Robin May. "War rape, natality and genocide." *Journal of Genocide Research.* (2011):5-21.

Singh, Pankaj. "Mahaswetha Devi: An Intimate View." http://revolutionary democracy.org/rdv5n2/devi.htm

Women Forging a New Security: Ending Sexual Violence in Conflict. Montebello, Canada. May 23-25, 2011. http://issuu.com/nobelwomen/docs/forging-a-new-security-web

3

Visceral Impact of Caste-Discrimination in Arvind Adiga's *The White Tiger*

DR. ANAND KUMAR

Dalit literature is one of the most powerful forms of literary genre today and it has acquired a prestigious position in modern English fiction. Dalit literature is essentially a strong reaction against exploitation and use of writing as a vehicle of agitation. Dalits literature encapsulates the pain, suffering, humiliation, and poverty of this community. Dalit literature focuses on the description of plight situation of the Dalit includes Dalit characters and life. The first rank of Indian English non-Dalit trio writers Mulk Raj Anand, R. K. Narayan and Raja Rao, at the earlier stage of the fictional works were mainly concerned with the down-trodden and depressed section of the society, the middle class life and the expression of traditional cultural ethos of India.

India is a county of different castes, creed and religions. It is socially divided into higher and lowers classes. Here, we have pointed out that which caste one belongs depends on the person's occupation. As in the ancient time caste was decided according to the profession of the individual but later it became rigged and based on blood theory as can be seen in present scenario. Dalits, even form birth suppress and humiliated, never treated as a human beings, feels themselves alienated from the other segment of the society. The caste ridden society never worried about their entity and treated them as untouchables.

So many non-Dalits writers, before and after independence, colonial and post-colonial writing, presented Dalits in different shades and flavors. Even few Dalit writers also tried to penetrate the realistic aspect of Dalits.

Many movements were started for upheaval of the Dalits. The second generation of Indian English writers like Kamala Markandaya, Bhabani Bhattacharya and Khushwant Singh wrote about the themes related to this social evil. The third generation of Indian English writers including Amitav Ghosh, Arundhati Roy, Vikram Seth, Rohinton Mistry, Anita Desai, Sharankumar Limbale, U. R. Anathamurthy and Arvind Adiga, a Brahmin from coastal Karnataka.

Aravind Adiga's *The White Tiger (*2008), his debut novel and main Booker Prize winning work is epoch making piece in modern English fiction writing. This novel heralded a new era in the history of Indian English Fiction. It breaks out of the hindermost darkness of the caste ridden society. Caste system is a complex phenomenon and always a key factor in Indian society. The underclass is the result of our poverty system, caste and culture conflict, economic disparity, feudal system, superstitions and rigged social thinking.

Most of the part of this book is described the India's caste system. Arvind Adiga directly attacks on contemporary Indian caste-ridden society. Dalits are not allowed to get basic facilities like clean water, hygienic food, and proper education as Adiga says, through the voice of Balram Halwai:

> Me, and thousands of others in this country like me, are half-baked, because we were never allowed to complete our schooling (10). Here he links Indian education system with poverty "A school where you won't be allowed to corrupt anyone's head with prayers and stories about God and Gandhi—nothing but the facts of life for these kids. A school full of White Tigers. (319)

Balram was pulled out of the school and started working at tea shop where he got better education than at any school. "*The whole education system is governed by the crowd of thugs and idiots*". (35) Even the in the profession of prostitution, the price was depends on *"High class or low class? Virgin or non-virgin?"* (227) The novel gives the detailed accounts of the Indian society—rural as well as urban life. Illiteracy, poverty, caste and culture conflict, dowry, economic disparity and superstition are the marginal elements in Indian society. Balram's cousin-sister Reena's lavish marriage and lavish dowry compelled them to borrow big loan:

> It was one of the good marriages. We had the boy, and we crewed the girl's family hard. I remember exactly what we got in dowry... five thousand rupees in cash, all crisp new unsoiled notes resh from the bank, plus a Hero bicycle, plus a thick gold necklace or Kishan. (51)

Balram's English pronunciation was not perfect and he was asked to say the word 'pizza'. But instead of this he always says 'pijja' and they laughed and humiliated him in front of other people. He also wears a funny dress for the enjoyment of Pinky Madam and further as a worst incident Ashok's wife kills a man in drunken driving, Balram was forced to accept this crime. Balram says:

> Jails of Delhi are full of drivers who are there behind the bars because they are taking the blame for their good, solid middle-class masters. We have left the villages, but the masters still own us, body, soul, and ares (170).

Adiga very cunningly presents a brutal view of the class struggles in India. Simon Jenkins, former chairman of the Booker prize jury commented: "Indian writers in English face a peculiar problem—they write about India but their readership is mostly in other countries. Because of this paradox they create an image of India that is exotic and doesn't show the real India. I worry about this." (*Sunday Times of India*, Oct 19, 2008).

Adiga tries to unravel the underlying reasons of the continuing casteism in India. Everywhere underclass is trapped in struggling to come out of the cage caste. The novel, *White Tiger* describes the life of a Dalit man from north India and his triumphs over the slavery to the feudal upper caste and how he becomes an entrepreneur in the IT Company. This novel represents the struggle of a Dalit Man and his salvation. '*The White Tiger*' symbolizes power, freedom and individuality. The novel justifies all kind of trick to succeed in life. Social and political systems set up, according to the novel refer to the darkest areas of our country which breed, "*rottenness and corruption*". (50) An innocent and rustic man becomes a selfish, opportunist and criminal which is the greatest harm to humanity.

It is about the journey of Balram Halwai, a Dalit and the protagonist of the novel and how he worked his way out of his low caste and overcame the social obstacles. Born in a low caste, Balram gets a break when he is hired as a driver by the wealthiest man of the village. The mean mentality of the rich people is shown through the lost coin episode. "*Get down on your knees. Look for it on the floor of the car.' I got down on my knees. I sniffed in between the mats like a doe, all in search of that one rupee.*" (139) This is our real India where people, particular Dalit, are treated as animals. Adiga says that in the old times there were thousand[s] of castes but now only two "Men with Big Bellies, and Men with Small Bellies. And only two destinies: eat—or get eaten up". (64)

Although it is said that some extent casteism is disappeared in urban India but the caste system still remains in rural India. The Dalits, mostly living in villages, are still waiting for their salvation and another revolution in the country for their upheaval as Balram Halwai remarks:

> "...in any city or town... you will hear stirrings, rumours, threats of insurrection.... An Indian revolution? No, sir. It won't happen. People in this country are still waiting for the war of their freedom to come from somewhere else... That will never happen. Every man must make his own Benares." (303-04)

Dalits are not waiting for *Ramrajya*, because in Ramrajya Dalits were not in good position and lived at the bottom of India's social pyramid. We find an episode in *Ramayana* about the untouchable woman '*Sabury*' who offered Rama partial eaten plums. From Ramrajya to present time casteism is a social stigma of the forehead of India.

Dr. B. R. Ambedkar called them '*broken People*' and Mahatma Gandhi gave them a new name 'Harijans' the man of God and made so many efforts for upheaval of the Dalits. The freedom, got on 15th August 1947, is meaningless for them until the attainment of the social as well as financial freedom of Dalits. Now the Dalits literature has taken the shape of agitates on injustice and exposes the evil and hypocrisy of the upper caste. Literature always plays a vital role in the revolution and Dalits literature is revolution against the social unjust. Dalit literature reveals untouchables' quest for dignity, identity and the recognition of their human worth rather than to points out those unnoticed shades of a social problem which generally escape the eyes of social scientist. The novel,

The White Tiger truly exposes contemporary Indian political system, social evils including caste system, prostitution, poverty, caste and culture conflict, economic disparity, feudal system, superstitions and rigged social thinking in today life.

Works Cited

Adiga, Arvind. *The White Tiger.* New Delhi: Harper Collins Publishers, 2008. Print.

Ambedkar, Bhim Rao. *Annihilation of Caste: With a Reply to Mahatma Gandhi. Vol. 1. Writings and Speeches*. Ed. Vasant Moon. Bombay: Dept. of Education, 1989. Print.

——. (2008). "Arvind Adiga: You ask the Questions". *The Independent.* November 10.

Anand, Mulk Raj. *Untouchable.* Penguin Books India: New Delhi, 1993. Print.

Bhattacharya, Bhabani. *So Many Hungers.* Orient Paperbacks: Delhi, 1978. Print.

Deaton, Angus and Jean Dreze. Poverty and Inequality in India: A Reexamination. 2005. Print.

Di Martino, Nick. "Interview with Arvind Adiga." October 6, 2008. http://universitybookstore.blogspot.com/2008/10/nick-interviews-aravindadiga.html

Drèze, Jean and Amartya Sen. (2002). "Democratic Practice and Social Inequality in India." *Journal of Asian and African Studies,* Vol. 37, No. 2, 6-37.

Ghosh, Jayati. (2004). "Income Inequality in India". *People's Democracy.* February 17.

http://www.independent.co.uk/arts-entertainment/books/features/aravind-adiga-youask-the-questions-1006643.html.

Jogdand, P.G. *Dalit Women: Issues and Perspectives.* New Delhi: Gyan, 1995. Print.

Keer, Dhananjay. *Dr. Ambedker: Life and Mission.* Popular Publication: Bombay, 1971. Print.

Naik, M. K. *A History of Indian English Literature.* Sahitya Academy, New Delhi, 1982. Print.

Rao, Raja. *Kanthapura.* Oxford University Press: Madras, 1938. Print.

The Sunday Times of India, New Delhi: Oct. 19, 2008.

4

Marginalization in Laxman Bapu Mane's *Upara: An Outsider*

Dr. Himanginee Kaushik

Autobiography is the story of a person written by himself or herself. Laxman Bapu Mane's autobiography *Upara: An Outsider* is a successful effort to highlight all the sorrows and sufferings of a community or a person due to his/her caste in the deep darkness of oppression, marginalization, exploitation, suppression and alienation. He is a Marathi writer and a social activist also from Maharashtra. Through his autobiography he has made an excellent effort to express the sufferings of the marginalized people. After publishing his autobiography *Upara (An Outsider)* in 1980, he suddenly shot into fame. His autobiography is considered as a milestone in Marathi Dalit Literature and Laxman Bapu Mane received Sahitya Academy Award in 1981 and Padam Shree in 2009 for this wonderful work. It was written in Marathi language and later it was translated into English by A. K. Kamat and titled *Upara: An Outsider*. Laxman Mane describes he never wishes to become a writer but he is inspired to write his autobiography because of circumstances. He says:

> If the readers succeed in understanding the sufferings of the nomadic tribals, who have been moving from one place to the other for generations leading their hearth and home on the back of donkeys, I would feel happy that Upara has achieved its goal (5).

It can't be said that Mane's goal of writing this autobiography is fulfilled but autobiography gets success in underscoring the problems of Kaikadi community. The writer Mane who is also from Kaikadi community—a nomadic tribe, gets education in an unfavorable condition, struggles hard, fights for his rights, comes forward and achieves liberty, dignity, name and fame in a sophisticated society in which he is not allowed for his basic rights of human being and treated like a beast. In the words of Arjun Dangle: "Dalit is not a caste but a realization and is related to the experiences, joys and sorrows, and struggles of those in the lowest stratum of society." (Dangle 264)

Upara: An Outsider narrates how a Kaikadi has to suffer and struggle in his life. The story in the present autobiography speaks for the whole Kaikadi community. 'Upara' means 'An Outsider' in English and according to *Oxford Learner's Dictionary* 'An Outsider' means 'a person who is not a member of or not accepted by a group of people'. *An Outsider* is a worldwide celebrated Dalit autobiography. It highlights the culture of Kaikadi community. Laxman Bapu Mane doesn't raise his voice only for himself but he raises his voice for the whole community. He discusses about the question of identity, injustice, misbehaviour and exploitation of these people. These people don't have work, opportunities, support, help, facilities, shelter and protection. These people are forced to live from hand to mouth and some of them even do not have two meals a day to eat. These people don't have fix income sources and a fine place to live. Even after independence the condition of these people is same and the basic need of food, cloth and shelter are a dream for them. These people don't cook daily and they arrange their food by begging in villages. Their children also help them in this process. They are treated like dogs and pigs and pick the food from dung hill. They are not allowed to live in villages. They are considered inauspicious by high caste people. They don't have their own houses, land and farm. They are forced to live outside the villages by the higher caste people. Laxman recalls: "*In Khopoli, our huts erected on a plain by the side of a road……our hut was in the open. At night, a Kerosene lamp without a glass cover was lit……I grew in this hut like a small plant growing on the dunghill.*" (71-72) Laxman Bapu Mane is also forced to live in such circumstances. So, he turns towards Buddhism and tries hard to enlighten the life of his people.

Laxman Mane memorizes about his childhood days. His mother and father travel village to village to sell the handmade baskets and other articles. Laxman and his sister have to wait for them sitting hungry in their hut as they have nothing to eat. Their mother gets stale food from the village people and it is her daily practice. Laxman says:

> Three of these were given by the village chief's wife. She had also given by the village chief's wife. She had also given the left overs of the night before. In addition, the women whose baskets mother had mended had given her something or the other which she had packed in the loose end of her sari. Mother had borrowed some butter milk from somewhere. She had also brought some flat leaves, drum sticks, curry, sauce, pickle all stale and of course collected as alms. Mother would sell some baskets in the village, mend the old ones and in exchange acquire all this food. We ate all it. This was our everyday meal (3).

These people don't get proper food, clothes and even place to live. These people have to spend their life on stale food which they get in exchange of cane baskets. The writer, Laxman Bapu Mane, also has to face all these problems and because of that so many questions rise in Laxman's mind like, why he is not able to eat good food and sweets, why his parents do not have a good house and why he is not allowed to go school and get education like the children of high caste people. Later because of all these unsolved questions he is inspired to gain education and gets a reputed place like high class people. His fight is not fight for himself only but it is for the whole community. It is the fight of their rights.

Jat Panchayat also has an important role in Kaikadi community in Maharashtra. Four types of Panchayat are mentioned by Laxman—Jamat Panchayat, Thal Panchayat, Village Panchayat and Maddhi Panchayat. The main work of Jat Panchayat is to solve the problems and quarrels of people living in their community. Laxman's father wants to send him school so that he may get education but this is not allowed for this community. It is a revolutionary step because it is the violation of the rules made by Jat Panchayat. But his father gets success to convince Jat Panchayat and he also promises them that education will not spoil him but in the school children of high caste do not like him and they hate him. None talks to him and everybody makes fun of him. Laxman says: *'From our Panchayat's point of view, the very writing of this book is crime and I am aware of the provision of the punishment or such wrong doing. I am prepared to face the consequences"* (6). No one in the village has the courage to disobey the judgement of the Panchayat. If anyone tries to do then his complete family is excommunicated from the society. That means now no one would touch them and they are given food and water from a distance and these people are also not permitted to take part in any ceremony, ritual or marriages and no one is allowed to marry with the members of such excommunicated family.

The exploitation of Kaikadi community does not end here. Laxman again mentions that these people are also not allowed to live in clean place. His maternal aunt Paru is fond of cleanliness which is treated as an offence. It is supposed by his caste people that people living on dirt need not to follow cleanliness. Kaikadi ladies are not allowed to look beautiful because it is thought an invitation to molestation. Paru's case is the worst example of it. As she is young and beautiful, she is raped by four and five men. After this incident no one in the village has sympathy and soft corner for her and she is also divorced by her husband as she is raped by someone and culprit is not punished.

Kaikadi community is also treated as untouchables. If anyone touches them unknowingly he has to take bath. People of high class give them food and water by keeping a proper distance. They are not allowed to attend any festival, auspicious ceremony, marriage and other ritual also. High class people think that if Kaikadies would touch the water it would get poisoned. Once Mane goes in a marriage ceremony and falls in a water tank unexpectedly, when bridegroom's father comes to know about this incident and also caste of Mane, he empties the water tank. They cannot have any relation with high caste people and they are not allowed to sit and speak with them. A girl who loves Mane when comes to know about his caste, abandons him. Mane also remembers about a marriage ceremony when he is forced to leave half-eaten meal along with his friends again because of his caste only, there is no any other reason behind this inhuman attitude. Laxman recalls:

> The row was full of Maratha children. Then there came a bearer who happened to be from our village and an invitee to the wedding. As he approached me, he opened his eyes wide, bent down and thundered—Son of Kaikadi low caste! Have you taken leave of your senses? Get up and get out! (161)

Later when this incident comes into the knowledge of Laxman's father, he beats Laxman very badly because he also thinks the like high class people. He considers himself and his community untouchable and he also believes that they have no right to participate in the marriages and any other function of high class people. This is self exploitation nothing else.

After a lot of efforts of Laxman's father he is allowed to attend school. His father dreams of him becoming a master. During his school days, the high class children tease him and teachers also teach him without any reason. He regularly goes to school but he never gives attention towards teasing and mocking. He has no knowledge about books, notebook, pen and pencil because his parents are not educated. Even they are not allowed to enter in school campus. So they hardly know about the needs of a student and study material. Other children of high caste never try to communicate with Laxman because of their ego and because of their attitude Laxman also does not like to speak them. About this he says:

> I am going to school regularly, when we made a halt in a village. I had to go to school of that village. Now I was used to it. I don't mix with the other students. They too were not prepared to approach me (69).

The life of Kaikadi people is already hard because they have no sources of regular income, good food to eat and a proper and clean place to live but after all this they have to bear the tortures of other people without any complain. Before their arrival in any village, they have to inform the chief of the village and also tell about their belongings. They are also not allowed to live inside the villages. Mane recalls:

> Jaisingea and Father had gone to the village to inform the village chief of our arrival. It was obligatory for the nomadic tribes to inform the village chief on their arrival. Also they had to give him the details of the numbers of people, donkeys, fowls, dogs and so on (32).

They are not considered as human-beings and treated like beasts. Mane's parents are given punishment for pilfering canes is not beyond justice.

> Father was being pushed ahead by a small crowd. Mother was behind him. She had no blouse on. She was wearing father's shirt. Her sari was torn. Father had only his dhoti on. One could see black and blue lashes

> over his body. He was followed by four or five rough fellows. Mother was wailing loudly and father was consoling her (61).

Narrator memorizes about a day when he goes to Sascal with his mother to sell wares as usual. It is the tradition among Kaikadi community to sell their wares in a particular village. During harvest days, Kaikadies visit fields and work in those fields and in return they get green-chillies, groundnuts etc. and they accept gratefully whatever the farmer gives. Mane says: "As mother begged the village women to buy her wares, she had to sell them very cheap. She would free distress. She had to take whatever was given to her. Then she would tie the bhakri and the rest of the things in a bundle" (60). So after a lot of hard work these people get only left overs. This is the real and also harsh picture of Indian society. Here man is not recognized by his deeds but he is recognized by his birth and name of the family. Laxman again memorizes:

> ...caught red handed cutting down the canes, she would be cursed and abused held by the hair and even mercilessly beaten up by the peasants. Even father would be beaten up in such a situation. They call themselves lucky if they were allowed to go home after being beaten. For, at times, they were taken to the village chief and then to the police station and then before a magistrate. (60-61)

This type of humiliation they have to bear in their daily routine life. Regarding this Girish Kausadikar says:

> ...they have to live on the mercy of landlords and religious authorities. They earn only by weaving baskets brought of cane. Being unskilled and notorious image no one is interested to employ them for farming. (Kausadikar 105)

They have become habitual of it. They live totally on the mercy of villagers and land-lords. But the problems of Mane do not end here. Mane falls in love with Shashi who belongs to Marata community. When his friends come to know about his relationship with a girl of high caste, they try to convince him that he cannot marry her as the society will not allow this and this will create problems to him and his family members. But he is not ready to listen all of them. He does not want to end his relationship with Shashi at any cost and he is ready to fight with the society and its fake rules. Due to that his friends—Ramdas, Narayan, Maruti, Kalokhe, Bankar and Kumbhar leave the room and break their friendship with Laxman. After this he has a little pain in his heart because those who shared the meal in one plate; they left him just on the caste issue. Only Narayan talks to him. But life does not end with any relationship, it has to move on. When one relationship dies, another relationship takes birth. Same thing happens with Laxman. He gets new friends. Finally with the help of Prof. Patangaokar, Prof. Dhoble, Suresh, Bapusaheb and Prof. Deshpande, Laxman gets success to marry Shashi.

The people of Kaikadi community belong to a nomadic tribe. These people have to move from one place to other, loading their hearth and home on the back of donkeys, selling baskets made of cane, doing seasonal jobs like cattle-tending and working in farms during harvesting. These people even do not have records of their death as per seasons. Laxman's father remembers about Laxman's date of birth as he is born on the day when Mahatma Gandhi was died. Bijender Singh also contends about another Dalit autobiography where the life of Dalit tribal community is so moving and heart-touching:

> Lakshaman Gaikwad's autobiography *The Branded* tells the horrendous pictures of tribal life in rural landscape. The tribal life depiction in this book is so strong and touching that it can easily move the readers. The people of this criminal tribe are slaves of their senses and they do nothing except slavery, pick-pocketing, bribery, murder or robbery. (Singh 49)

Upara: An Outsider depicts the problems of people of the same caste as a writer. Although Laxman has to face too much struggle, pain and exploitation in his life, yet he does not feel depressed. On every step high-caste people impose difficulties on him, insult him and degrade him. In spite of all this, he never feels defeated and these things and injustice inspire him to fight for his rights. One by one he gets success on every step of life and society fails to bind him in its rules. He gains education and gets knowledge. This education enlightens both his mind and soul. Now he knows that a person cannot be judged on the behalf of his birth and caste, he can be judged on the behalf of his moral and spiritual values. He also encourages other oppressed people. He fights for others and asks people to raise their voice against injustice. So, as per above discussion it is clear that the present work is not only an autobiography or the journey of a single person but it is the true reflection of the society that is full superstition and fake beliefs.

Works Cited

Dangle, Arjun. *Poison Bread: Translations from Modern Marathi Dalit Literature*. Mumbai: Orient BlackSwan Publication, 1922. Print.

Kausadias, Girish. *Dalit Autobiography: Narration of Pain*. Aurangabad: New Voices Publications, 2013. Print.

Mane, Laxman. *Upara: An Outsider*. Translated from Marathi by A. K. Kamat. New Delhi: Sahitya Academy, 1997. Print.

Singh, Bijender. Dalit Resurrection in Laxman Gaikwad's *The Branded. Indian Scholar: An International Multidisciplinary Research E-Journal.* Vol. 1, Issue 1. Sept. 2014. pp. 49-55.

5

Pain, Anger and Agitation in Sharankumar Limbale's *The Outcaste: Akkarmashi*

IMRUL KAYES ALAM SARKAR

The reflection of traumas, anguish and wounded psyche of the marginalized or the downtrodden people has been depicted in Dalit literature. The Indian constitution has proclaimed liberty, equality and fraternity for the people of India but here the identity of Dalit people is always ignored and they are struggling for the quest of their identity. As a result, the prime concern of Dalit Literature is to protest against the established system which is based on inequality and injustice and it tries to reveal the illogical and hypocritical nature of high caste society. Through this literature, the writers present the struggling life of the exploited Dalits. The theme of poverty and untouchability has been depicted several times in Maratha literature but Dalit literature, at first, highlights it as a social issue—a result of caste discrimination.

As African-American literature speaks for the identity of Black people, Dalit literature talks about the condition of Dalit people and seeks an end to all discriminations against them. In Dalit Literature, the writers feel that discrimination prevails in every field of life. In main stream literature, they are often pictured as crooked, ugly, brainless and above all, foolish. Their voice is concealed by the hegemonic power of high caste writers. So the Dalit writers begin to write their autobiographies so that they can express their own experience—sorrows, sufferings, anger and agitation. Arjun Dangle points out: "In this autobiography we see varying facets of Dalit movement: the struggling of the survival; the emotional universe of a Dalit's life; the man woman relationship; an existence crushed under the wheels of village life; the experiencing of humiliation and atrocities, at times abject submission, at other times, rebellion." (Dangle 16) Limbale's *The Outcaste* is considered a landmark in the history of Dalit Literature and here he has shown his own real life experience. It is quite apt to say that *The Outcaste* is the painful story of Limbale's life and an expression of anger and agitation of his whole community.

The Outcaste has represented the tortured, harassed and painful life of Sharankumar Limbale. He does not belong to any caste or religion. As his mother Masamai is Mahar and his father Hanmanta Limbale belongs to Lingayat caste. Society considers him illegitimate offspring and his birth is considered inauspicious. So, he realizes that he is like the great pathetic character of *Mahabharata*—Karna. He painfully utters: "Which family could claim me as its descendant? Whose son am I really?" (Limbale 36) Being a casteless and fatherless, he faces oppression and exploitation of conservative, superstitious higher caste Hindu society and he cannot meet the basic needs of life. As a result, he has to lead his life like an animal. He faces the society which does not recognize him as in *Invisible Man*, Ralph Ellison expresses the similar identity crisis: "I am invisible, understand, simply because people refuse to see me." (Ellison 3)

The theme of poverty or starvation is a dominant theme in all the autobiographies of Dalit literature. In *The Outcaste* Limbale gives a very heart-breaking picture of starvation. He thinks that starvation is written in their lot from the moment of their birth. They often go sleep without eating anything as there is nothing to eat. In school, they often take the left-over foods of the high caste boys and girls. Once Limbale's sister Vani eats the banana skin and he snatches the skin and throws it away from her. But at once he changes his mind and starts eating them. Daya Pawar narrates similar condition in *Baluta* where he says: "Sometimes I used to feel that I have lost all my self-respect just for a morsel of food." (Pawar 72) They want to establish another significant fact that starvation forces a man to do wrong things. Limbale claims: "A woman becomes a whore and a man thief. The stomach makes you clean shit; it even makes you eat shit." (Limbale 8)

In *Upara: An Outsider*, Laxman Mane points out: "They (Dalit) have neither work nor opportunities, neither facilities nor support, neither shelter nor protection" (Mane 09) Limbale painfully records that Dalits live in a very dirty and secluded place which is away from the main part of the village. Everywhere there is heaps of garbage, human shit, cow dung around their huts. Dogs and pigs are their only companions. In monsoon, rain drenches them and makes their life more painful. At night they are threatened with the sound of collapsing of walls. The children are brought up in an unhygienic atmosphere. Limbale narrates: "Our houses were in the places that other villagers used as latrines" (Limbale 76)

Like food and shelter, Dalits are also deprived of proper education and there are so many hindrances behind it. The first problem that they face is the economic crisis. Their economic condition is so bad that they compel their children to earn money for their living and engage them in farms, hotels, tea-shops etc. At the very beginning of *The Outcaste*, it is easy to observe that the economic condition of Harya's parents is terrible. Everyone of that house is half-fed and they do not have proper clothes to wear. When he gets first class in final school examination, there is no money for his admission and it is not only his problem but the whole Dalit community: "We had entered the college… utter poverty behind us." (Limbale 83)

When the children of high caste Hindu are going to school, the Dalit boys are washing and cleaning liquor bottles and gather twigs, rags and bits of paper for fuel. Their poverty did not allow them to enjoy the school life and to them education is nothing more than luxury. In case if they are admitted in school, they face another problem that is casteism. The teacher who should be above all the caste, creed and religion, treats them like animals. They are "Shape without form, shade without colour" (Eliot 56). In *The Bluest Eye*, Toni Morrison speaks that the central character Pecola Breedlove does not receive any recognition in the class and is humiliated by the white boys and girls for her black complexion. Similarly, Limbale also suffers same problem and so everything that he faces makes his disgust for the society. He tells: "The humiliation I had faced was intolerable." (Limbale 59)

In *Akkarmashi*, Limbale draws a vivid picture of the wretched condition of Dalit women and this wretched condition makes him pathetic towards those women. Limbale informs that Dalit women survive by pleasing the Patils sexually and he records: "Dalit women were badly insulted. They were beaten as if they were slaves." (Limbale 79) According to him, poverty compels them to perform various odd jobs so that they can carry on the wheels of their family. His mother has so many children and she has to sell liquor while his grandmother begs for alms and works as a midwife. Dalit girls are married in their childhood and they often become widow at their teenage and then they have to sell their bodies in order to keep their existence.

As Dalits belong to the lower caste, they only get sympathies and ill-treatment from society but not pure love. Limbale gives a very painful love story of Harya who loves Shobhi—a high caste girl. Once he is carrying a carcass on his shoulder and at that time Shobhi is approaching and she holds her nose to avoid the stinks of the carcass. He feels deeply embarrassed in this event and he does not dare to express his feeling for her. In her marriage ceremony, he sweeps the wedding tent and carries a gas lamp on his shoulder and does other trivial activities. When Shobhi goes off with her husband, Harya is hanging restlessly around the bus stand as a bitch searches for a right place.

Limbale's *The Outcaste* delineates the dark aspect of Indian society which permits the practice of untouchability. For it, the Dalit men and women are maltreated and extremely humiliated by the upper class society. Even in school, they are asked to sit separately from the boys of Wani, Brahmin, and Marwari. As they are low-caste, they cannot play together and they just keep them watching. They are ordered to give side and keep some distance while any man or woman confronts them. Once Limbale and his friend Parshya are on the way, Shobhi ordered them to let her pass and arrogantly says: "Can't you see I am carrying Drinking water? Your touch will make it impure." (Limbale 70) He feels humiliated and it gives him intolerable pain in his heart.

In an interview with S. N. Bolledu, Sharankumar Limbale points out: "I want [to] write about my pains and pangs. I want [to] write about the suffering of my community… I am writing for a social cause. My autobiography is a statement of my war against injustice." (Limbale 2) The stigma of untouchability increases his anger from his infancy. The blind casteism disapproves his arrival in Shivapa Teli's mansion. When he enters and a servant slaps him, he is angered and burning within and without. He feels that they are garbage that the village throws out and considers: "To be… Dalit is a curse." (Limbale 37) He is also angered with the fact that the Mahars dug the wall and build it but the same Mahars are not allowed to draw drinking water from it. Anger limits no bounds when Limbale is not capable to find a room in Latur. Though he finds out a place in Bhimnagar where corpses are burnt, women use to shit openly, the surroundings of this place does not allow him to live peacefully. He says: "Someone's body is burning on a pyre, but I am burning within." (Limbale 108)

Limbale is terribly angry at the customs, conventions of the high caste society and ashamed of this rotten culture. The idea of marriage is intolerable to him. As he is an illegitimate child and belongs to Dalit community, nobody agrees to give his daughter to him for his impure blood. Janabai wildly shouts at him: "We have not yet lost our self respect. Our family is of pure blood so we also expect the same of a bridegroom." (Limbale 88) All these make his tremendous disgust for society. He angrily says: "A bastard always be matched with another bastard. No one else will marry their daughter to a bastard like me." (Limbale 98) So he compels to marry the daughter of a drunkard father-Maraappa Kamble.

Limbale always thinks that Kaka and his mother are husband and wife. Kaka always visits their house and behaves as if he is their father. Once Limbale visits his mansion, expects to be invited and wanders around his mansion. But when he notices his appearance, he shuts the door, Limbale at first does not understand his strange behavior but later he realizes reason and he becomes discontent and angry with him. The humiliation or insult that kaka has shown to him makes him livid with rage.

Limbale lives in a caste-ridden society and the problem of casteism follows him as a shadow follows a man. Even after getting job in Ahamedpur, he has to conceal his caste. There he greets people with a Namaskar instead of Jai Bhim and he is always haunted by the feeling of terror and anxiety if anyone would really recognize his caste. He feels: "If they came to know my caste they would drive me out of the house

...I would be beaten badly. They would torture my wife." (Limbale 104) After sometimes, he is transferred to Latur where he feels that his caste follows him like an enemy. Though Latur is a place full of huge buildings, houses and bungalows, he cannot get a single room as the city dweller does not agree to give him a room: "We don't want to rent out our house to Muslims and Mahars." (Limbale 106)

The wretched condition and the humiliation of the high caste Hindus over the Dalits agitate his mental equilibrium. He cannot put up with the hypocritical nature of the society. He becomes fierce when people forbid them to enter the temple or refuse to give them room or touch water for their untouchability. He feels Rousseau's famous quote: "Man is born free but every where he is in the chains." (Rousseau 2) All the maltreatment of society agitates him and as a result he wants to shake all the pillars of casteism through his writing. He asks the practitioners of casteism: "Is the premise of religion greater then mans? Is religion made for man or man made for religion? Cant man exists without religion and cast?" (Limbale 40) As a consequence, he and his friend Parshya insult Shobhi and want to rape her. To them, she stands as a symbol of the high caste and their insulting suggests that they insult and rape the practices of casteism and untouchablity. "Her feet, her thighs, everything was a part of the system she belongs to." (Limbale 71)

Extreme agitation arises in Limbale's mind as all the higher castes—Patil, Wani and Marwari use their power, position and pelf as a medium to torture the poverty stricken Dalit people. Through this strategy, they compel the Dalits to work hard on their farm and Dalit women to live the life of a whore. When Santamai go to a money lender to demand some money for Sharan's admission in college, he stares at the breast of Santamai. At this incident, he is angered, agitated and burned within and wants to rebel against such humiliation. Harya works hard in Girmallya's farm and he receives very small amount. Similarly Masamai's former husband Ithal Kamble works hard, day and night on the field as well as in the house of Hanmanta but fails to carry on his family. Limbale says: 'He was one of the beasts that toiled on the farm' (Limbale 35)

Limbale is agitated with fact that God himself has discriminated between high caste and lower caste man. He sarcastically says: "We don't approve this God, nor his religion, nor his country because they ostracize us." (Limbale 62) Limbale is also agitated with the fact men are imprisoned by the blind conventions of hypocritical society and there is also bloody carnage, riots and crusades and untouchability. He points out: "I used clean clothes, bathed everyday and washed myself clean with shop... and brushed my teeth with toothpaste... Then in what sense was I untouchable. A high caste who is dirty was still considered touchable!" (Limbale 107) As they are confined by the caste and religion, he is agitated for their future life. He asks: "Who will undertake Dada's funeral after his death? Who has created such values of right and wrong and what for? If they considered my birth illegitimate what values am I to follow." (Limbale 113)

Sharankumar Limbale has hated the idea of untouchability throughout his life and he is not regulated by the inflexible rules of religion. He considers that religion is secondary thing while love for every human being without judging caste and creed is very appreciative and acceptable. Though his grandfather belongs to Muslim community, it never influences their relationship and there is not even a sign of casteism. He feels extremely happy for the love and affection that he has gained from his grandfather. So he realizes: "Neither his religion nor my caste was hindrance to us." (Limbale 39) and he further adds: "I felt that somehow we were of the same flesh and blood. Dada's affection did not smell of his religion." (Limbale 58)

A revolutionary change has taken place in Limbale's life when he has joined Dalit Movement. Babasaheb Ambedkar becomes the source of his inspiration and his mind is burned with various thoughts. He is angered and agitated whenever he has heard the news of the atrocities against Dalit and it makes him impatient. While studying in college, he becomes mentally aflame and there is growing a conflagration within his mind. He realizes that Dalit writers ought to keep their pen against the injustice and they should not suffer this for a long time and they have to reject all this. He feels that they are awakening under a new consciousness: "We were becoming aware of a great struggle ahead and felt the need for an organization to meet the challenge." (Limbale 91)

Sharankumar Limbale's engagement with the Dalit Movement has changed his vision of his life and inspired him to rebel against the discrimination. He always dreams of a new world where human relations are controlled and guided by liberty, equality and fraternity. He is very eager to see the regeneration of the Dalit community and break the age old customs, conventions and spiritual inertness. His *The Outcaste* serves as a mouthpiece for the whole Dalit Community and it projects the painful account of his life from childhood to adulthood to give a transparent picture of the contemporary social, cultural and economic condition. Here he protests against the atrocities inflicted on the Dalits and at the same time he seeks to discuss his rights for them and demands the facilities which have been neglected for thousands of years. Being a Dalit activist, he confidently points out in his poem *White Paper*:

> I'll uproot the scriptures like railway tracks.
> Burn like a city bus your lawless laws
> My friends!
> My rights are rising like the sun.
> Will you deny this sunrise? (29-33)

Works Cited

Dangle, Arjun. *Poisoned Bread.* Mumbai: Orient Longman Ltd, 1982. Print.

Eliot, T. S. *The Complete Poems and Plays*. New York: Harcourt Brace Jovanovich, 1971. Print.

Ellison, Ralph. *The Invisible Man*. United Kingdom: Penguin Books Ltd, 2014. Print.

Limbale, Sharankumar. *Interview* by Siva Nagaiah Bolledu. The Criterion. II.I (2009):2. Web. 15 July. 2014.

____. *No Entry for the New Sun*. Ed. Dangle, Arjun. Hyderabad: Disha Books, 1992. Print.

____. *The Outcaste: Akkarmashi*. Trans. Santosh Bhomkar. New Delhi: OUP, 2003. Print.

Mane, Laxman. *Upara: An Outsider*. Trans. A.K. Kamat. New Delhi: Sahitya Academy, 1997. Print.

Morrison, Tony. *The Bluest Eye*. New York: Vintage Publication, 2007. Print.

Pawar, Daya. *Baluta*. Mumbai: Granthali Prakashan, 1982. Print.

Rousseau, Jean Jacques. *The Social Contract*. Cosimo Inc. 2008. Print.

6

Excruciating Pangs of Untouchability in Om Prakash Valmiki's *Joothan: A Dalit's Life*

DR. NARENDRA KUMAR

Dalit literature, more or less, is an authentic record of the pains, pangs and anguishes in which different writers have portrayed the saga of sufferings of the socio-economically backward people generally called Dalits in India. Dalits are called by different names in different parts of India and the name Dalit is associated with those upper caste people also who live under the suppression of dominant people as Ratnakar contends:

> Dalits literature deals with not only about Harijans, Mangs, Mallas, Chambhars, Pulayas but also the upper caste people who are suppressed by the domineering people. The writers say the emergence of low-caste literature has taken place alongside a broader growth of consciousness and activism, particularly in urban India. (Ratnaker 5761)

Dalit literature is written primarily in the form of autobiographies; though much work has been done in the other genres also. Biographies, short-stories, poetry etc. are such illustrations. There are some writers also who have written novels and autobiographies on Dalit themes but they neither belong to Dalit community nor personally have such soul-numbing experiences of the so-called Dalit people. They have written their books either on the basis of their intellectual imagination or by the bad experiences of other people. Omprakash Valmiki's autobiography *Joothan: A Dalit's Life* is one of the best autobiographies in which the theme of casteism is very dominant.

Omprakash Valmiki is a famous Hindi Dalit writer who was born in 1950 at Barla, Mujaffarnagar, Western Uttar Pradesh. He was born in a Chuhra family. He has done his M. A. in Hindi and he has written many stories, articles and poems. His works are *Sadiyon Ka Santap*, *Bas! Bahut Ho Chuka*, *Salaam* and *Dalit Sahitya Ka Saundarya Shashtra*. His creativity can be acclaimed after reading his article entitled "Ek Dalit Ki Atmkatha" which is published in a book *Harijan Se Dalit*. He has got Dr. Ambedkar National Award (1993) and Parivesh Samman (1995). *Joothan: A Dalit's Life* is an acclaimed autobiographical work by Omprakash Valmiki. It was published in Hindi in 1997 and it was translated into English in 2003 by Arun Prabha Mukherjee who is a professor of English at York University in Canada. He died of liver cancer on November 17, 2013 at the age of 63 and left behind a rich literary legacy.

Omprakash Valmiki was born into the Chuhra or Valmiki caste. The people of this caste generally do some inferior kinds of job like cleaning the sewers, sweeping the roads, disposing off dead animals, cleaning the cattle barns, working in the fields and doing the other jobs ordained to them. According to Moon Dalits can be defined as *"Downtrodden, oppressed. Used first by Jotiba Phule in the mid-nineteenth century. The word gained currency as a self-chosen, proud name with the early 1970s development of the Dalit Panthers and Dalit literature. Today it has replaced most other names in the vocabulary of the politically aware ex-Untouchables and the press"* (Moon 181).

Valmiki describes some harsh realities of his life and especially his childhood experiences in *Joothan*. The life of the Dalits or Chuhras has been projected in the novel. There was no social status of these Dalit people in the society and they had to live aloof and segregated from the other people of the village. The word 'Joothan' literally means scraps of food left in the plate for stray animals or dustbin after eating. The people of low caste have to eat this left-over food just to satisfy their hunger.

Omprakash Valmiki opens his autobiography in a pictorial way in which he describes incidences of his life since his childhood. There is a description of Chuhra community in which he was born; it was situated at some distance from Tagas' locality. The village described in this autobiography is located in Gaya District in Bihar, India. The Chuhras of this village had to live segregate from the other society just because they were considered impious and untouchables. Even the very opening lines describe the graphic description of castes:

> Our house was adjacent to Chandrabhan Taga's gher or cowshed. Next to it lived the families of Muslim weavers. Right in front of Chandrabhan Taga's gher was a little johri, a pond which was created as a partition of between the Chuhra's dwellings and the Village (Valmiki 1).

There were no provisions for cleanliness for these people and they lived in unhygienic conditions. Cleanliness—the main problem of Dalits—more or less, persists these days also in their life. The condition of Dalit people was not good and they were forced to live unhygienic life. Girls and women as portrayed in *Joothan* were forced to sit in open to relieve them:

> All the women of the village, young girls, older women, even the newly married brides would sit in the open space behind these homes at the edge of the pond to take a shit. Not just under the cover of darkness but even in daylight. The purdah observing Tyagi women, their faces covered with their saris, shawls around their shoulders, found relief in this open air latrine. They sat on Dabbowali's shores without worrying about decency exposing their private parts. (Valmiki 1)

This is not the problem of one particular community or caste. This is the problem of many people in other castes also. The people who are economically poor have to resort the open land to relieve them. In another autobiography *Uchalya: The Branded* the problem of the latrines has been projected where especially women has to face a lot of problem:

> Even while we were roasting the pig, women from the village sat in front of us and sat as if that was the only spot available. In the morning heaps of human-dung could be seen all over the place. Often as we moved about, we steeped on these heaps. It is in such a shit-yard that we roasted and ate the pigs. (Gaikwad 13)

There was no any source of income for these people except some low-paid occupations. They were scavengers, washer-men, barbers, water-carriers or leather-workers. Their life was not much better than animals and their position was like slaves. They had no any right to ask for their wages even after working throughout the day. They had no identity of their own except their caste and they were called not by the names but caste: *"Oh Chuhre". If the person was young or of the same age, then 'Abe Chuhre' was called."* (Valmiki 2) untouchablity was so rampant that the people of this *bhangi basti* were considered untouchables and they were not allowed to involve in any socio-economical or cultural activities. Even their touch pollutes the high caste people and they had to take bath again to purify them. They were considered at lower level than animals: *"Untouchability was so rampant that while it was considered all right to touch the dogs and cats or cows or buffaloes if one happened to touch a Chuhra, one got contaminated or pollution. The Chuhras were not seen as humans".* (Valmiki 2) Gayatri Spivak says in her controversial essay *Can Subaltern Speak?* that the Dalits or subalterns, especially females, do speak but they are not properly attended by other people: She argues that *"Subalterns speak but their speech is not properly heard and interpreted."* (Spivak 272)

There was no provision of education of the children of these Dalit people. There was a Christian priest named Sewak Ram Munshi who used to teach these children. Omprakash's father Chhotan Lal was an illiterate person but wanted to see his son as an educated person. One day Omprakash's father, along with the priest, went to the school to admit his son and pleaded: *"Masterji, I will be forever in your debt if you teach this child of mine a letter or two"* (Valmiki 2) but the headmaster made one or the other excuses for a couple of days but ultimately he admitted Omprakash in his school. Even the people of his caste were against sending him to school: *"What is the point of sending him to school? When has a crow became a swan?"* (Valmiki 6)

The problems of caste did not spare Omprakash in the school also. Actually, it was the place where he had to face many problems. One day headmaster says to Omprakash in a harsh voice: *"Go climb that tree. Break some twigs and make a broom. And sweep the whole school clean as mirror. It is often all, your family occupation"* (Valmiki 4). Next day also he does not allow him to sit in the class and orders him to clean the school verandah and playground. There was no any sign of a teacher in his language and he abused him badly: *"Abey Chuhre ke, motherfucker, where are you hiding… your mother… Go sweep the whole playground… otherwise I will shove chilies up your arse (anus) and throw you out of the school"* (Valmiki 5). Three days pass in this process and it is the third day when Omprakash's father coincidently passes from that way and loses his temper to see his son in this position. When his father criticizes the headmaster for his mean act; he says: *"The*

Chuhra wants him educated... Go, go... Otherwise I will have your bones broken." (Valmiki 6) the Dalit students were not allowed to drink water from the glass; they had to wait for the peon to pour water on their cups of hands.

Another dominating theme in the book neither is that of Joothan nor left-over. The people of Chuhra or Bhangi caste had to depend on the left-over thrown in pattals or plates in the marriages. They ate it with relish:

> After the baratis has eaten, the dirty pattals or leaf-plates were put in the Chuhras' basket, which they took home to save the Joothan, sticking to them. The little pieces of pooris, bits of sweetmeats and a little bit of vegetable were enough to make them happy. The joothan was eaten with a relish. The bridegroom's guests who didn't leave enough scraps on the pattals were denounced as gluttons. (Valmiki 6)

The people of this Chuhra community had to face many problems at the name of caste. At the occasion of weeding of Sukhdev Tyagi's daughter, Om's mother was badly humiliated by Sukhdev Tyagi just because she had begged for some sweets for her children. Omprakash was the eye-witness of this incidence and his injured soul could not forget this insult throughout his life when Sukhdev Singh insulted his mother by saying: *"You are having a basketful of Joothan. And on the top of that you want food for your children. Don't forget your place Chuhri. Pick up your basket and get going."* (Valmiki 10-11) There were no any health facilities for Dalits that's why Omprakash's elder brother died due to lack of proper medication. Sound health was one of the biggest problems for these people because they have no any clean and pure water to drink; they had dirty houses; their job was always to clean the human and animal excreta; their houses oozed in rainy seasons etc. the rainy season aggravated their problems when they developed some skin diseases: *"The feet became mangy. The space between the toes filled up with reddish sores started itch. Once they started to itch, they would itch nonstop."* (Valmiki 19)

The worm of the caste did not eat the upper caste people even the other low caste people did not co-operate one another. One day Omprakash goes to the dhobi shop to get some of his clothes ironed but he refused to iron his clothes on the pretext that he irons clothes only of the high caste people: *"We don't wash the clothes of Chubra-Chamars.*

Nor do we iron them. If we iron your clothes, then the Tagas won't get their clothes washed by us. We will lose our roti.'" (Valmiki 17) Omprakash's teacher beats him when he says that there are instances of Dronacharya in Hindu epic when he had to give floured mixed water to Asvatthama in poverty but why their names are not written in books they have to drink mar (rice-water): *"Darkest Kaliyug has descended upon us so that an untouchable is daring to talk back... Chuhre ke, you dare compare yourself with Dronacharya... Here take this, I will write an epic on your back." (Valmiki 23)* When Omprakash gets Science education in his school his chemistry teacher, Brijpal not only dislikes him but disallow him to attend the lab classes also. He makes one or the other pretexts to keep him out of his class: *"I felt that whenever I went to the lab for practical. Brijpal would keep me out on some pretext or the other" (Valmiki 65)* and not only this he gets failed owing to the cold behavior of his chemistry teacher.

The people of Dalit castes had to eat in separate dishes and if they hid their identity and later it was revealed they got very harsh punishment. The Chuhras and Muslims had to eat in separate dishes. One day a girl named Savita invites Valmiki at her home for a cup of tea. He comes to know that SCs are given tea in separate pot. When Omprakash asks about it she says that they cannot give same cups to SCs:

> 'Oh... why, are you mad? How can we feed them in the same dishes?'
>
> 'Why not? In the hotel... in the mess, everyone eats together. Then what is wrong in eating together in your home as well?' I tried to reason with her.
>
> Savita defended the discrimination as right and justified by tradition. Her arguments were infuriating me. However, I remained calm. According to her, SCs were uncultured. Dirty.' (57)

Omprakash gets a job as an apprentice in an ordinance factory. When he tells his father about it, his father becomes very happy and he thinks that now his son has come out from the cruel clutches of casteism: *'At last, You have escaped "caste".' (78)* But he knows it better that the caste follows a Dalit person from his birth until he dies. After one year training Valmiki passes a competitive exam and he goes to Jabalpur for further training. He finds a new environment there. He finds the roots of casteism everywhere in Jabalpur, Dehradun, Mumbai and Uttar Pradesh equally. He is aggrieved to see this: *"I felt a fountain of hot lava erupting within me". (95)* Omprakash says through his autobiography that caste remains an indistinguishable part of Dalits' life wherever they go. He accepts: *"This surname is now an indispensable part of my name. (132)* and he further says:

> 'Caste' is a very important element of Indian society. As soon as a person is born, 'caste' determines his or her destiny. Being born is not in the control of a person. If it were in one's control, then why would I have been born in a Bhangi household? (134)

Conclusively, caste is a social evil at the face of Indian society and this evil must be uprooted. The people of India are still not free after many years of Indian Independence; they are slaves of casteism, traditionalism and orthodoxy. Though Government is working through its many plans and policies still cannot be uprooted until public co-operates fully in this campaign with the Government as Singh says:

> Caste system, despite of many efforts of the government and other organizations has become a stigma on India. Though India has got independence but the mentality of the people in India is still distorted and narrow-minded that needs new liberated thoughts based on *vasudhaivkutubkam* (all the world is a family). (Singh 96)

Works Cited

Moon, Vasant. *Growing Up Untouchable in India: A Dalit Autobiography*. Trans. Gail Omvedt. New York: Rowman and Little field, 2000. Print.

Ratnakar, Om Prakash. "Resistance and Assertion in Om Prakash Valmiki's *Joothan.*" *European Academic Research*. Vol. I, Issue 12/ March 2014. pp. 5761-5769.

Singh, Bijender. "Mapping Caste-Subjugation in Omprakash Valmiki's *Joothan: A Dalit's Life.*" *Sangharsh/Struggle: E-Journal Of Dalit Literary Studies*. Vol. 2, Issue 03, July to Sept., 2013. pp. 90-97.

____.Dalit Resurrection in Laxman Gaikwad's *The Branded. Indian Scholar: An International Multidisciplinary Research E-Journal.* Vol. 1, Issue I. September, 2014. pp. 49-55.

Spivak, Gayatri. *Can Subaltern Speak? Marxism and Interpretations of Culture*, Eds. Cary and Nekon & Lawrence, Grossberg, Urbama, Uni & Illiois. 1988. Print.

Valmiki, Omprakash. *Joothan: A Dalit's Life*. Kolkata: Samya, 2003. Print.

7

A Quest for Identity in Bama's *Karukku: An Unconventional Autobiography*

PATIL SANGITA SHARNAPPA

I'm the sea, I soar, I surge,
I move out to build your Tomb's
The wind, storms, sky, earth
Now all are mine
In every inch of the rising struggle
I stand erect.
(Prasad & Gajjan, I Have Become the Tide, 76)

The above quoted poetic lines aptly convey the strong determination of Dalit to break the long endured silence and leave the footprints on the sand of time by self-assertive writings, which have attempted to go beyond the age old stereotypical framework and to establish their own identity. The undercurrent theme is resistance move in the form of autobiography. The autobiographies exhibit the historical, social and cultural milieu of the particular time. This holds good to Dalit autobiographies that have emerged as the strong voice of resistance in a society flooded with caste biases and unequal opportunities. Such autobiographies also offer a glimpse into the life of a community as the entire community battles against deprivation and discrimination, exploitation and humiliation and thereby struggle to enter the mainstream. Thus Dalit autobiographies have become one of the strong medium to win back the dignity and honor denied to them since long time. In this context, one can witness autobiographical works by Dalit writers, like Omprakash Valmiki's *Joothan* and in Hindi Tiraskrit (Vol. 1, 2002) by Suraj Paul Chauhan and *Meri Safar aur Meri Manzil* (2000) by

B. R. Jatav. These books shocked the readers of mainstream literature into the realization of the inhuman and morally repugnant ways in which Indian people continued to treat segments of society (Omprakash 2008).

The present paper is an attempt to study Bama's the epoch-making autobiographical novel *Karakku.* It is one rare Dalit autobiography that describes various dimensions of Dalit identity, lodged in the world literature and represents a whole class of people who have been kept out of mainstream literary and social venues for many centuries. Bama gives us a picture of the caste oppression meted out to Dalit Christians not only by the upper caste society but more so within the Catholic church itself. She has fervent inner urge to alleviate the suffering of the oppressed. *Karakku,* is an unusual autobiography, exhibiting personal crisis and in the author's life. The events in the novel are not arranged according to chronological order, as in most of the autobiographies, but in such a manner to reflect different perspectives, grouped under different themes as religion, recreation, work, education, double oppression of women, etc. It is a compelling saga of trauma, self-identity and strategies of survival.

In this context, this paper is a plausible attempt to study Bama's *Karukku* as a journey in search of oneself. Bama is the pen-name of a Tamil Dalit woman Faustina Mary Fathima, from a Roman Catholic family, who was born at Puthupatty near Madurai in 1958. She became a renowned writer in Dalit literature after the publication of *Karukku,* an unconventional autobiographical novel, which was first published in 1992 in Tamil and won the Crossword Award in 2000. Later it was translated into English by Lakshmi Holmstrom. The seminal works of Bama's are *Sangati* (1994) a novel, *Kismbukka* (1996) a collection of short stories, and *Vanman* (2003). The works of Bama in Tamil exemplify the forerunner of Dalit writings. She is one of the leading lights and crusader of Dalit women writers in India. *Karukku* is an estimation of uneven, unanswered, unfinished, ambitious, frustrated, yet quite astonishingly painful journey of a Dalit woman's quest for identity, integrity and equality. The general tenor of Bama's *Karukku* is marked by a subtle sense of paradox, suppression, humiliation and deep pathos emanating from a life haunted by personal tragedies.

Karukku means Palmyra leaves, which, with their serrated edges on both sides, are like double-edged swords. By a felicitous pun, the Tamil word karukku, containing the word Karu, embryo or seed, also means freshness, newness. In her foreword, Bama draws attention to the symbol and refer to the words in Hebrews (New Testament) *"For the word of God is living and active, sharper than any two-edged sword piercing to the division of soul and spirit, of joints and marrow, and discerning the thoughts and intentions of the heart"* (Hebrews 4:10) (Bama 1).

The saw edged Palmyra Karakku plays very significant role in Bama's life. She not only picked up the scattered Palmyra Karakku as firewood, which scratches and tears her skin but also became the embryo and symbol into the book. The social exploitation and oppression, caste inequalities, prejudices of upper caste and Christianity cut her like Karukku and make her bleed, which later became a driving force to throw away and destroy the chains of Dalit. Dalits, who silenced for centuries and remained voiceless with a passionate drive to create a new society made up of justice, equality and love and wants to be double edged sword to challenge the oppressor.

Similarly, Arvind Malagatti's "Government Brahman", the English translation of Kannada autobiography underlines the parallel theme: a painful, disturbing and thought provoking memoir in the form of series of episodes from the author's childhood and youth, which projects the cruelty practiced by upper caste on Dalit. Dalits encounter many problems as isolation in school, where even drinking water is an ordeal, in the village, where Dalits perform the filthiest tasks and are denied access to common wells; they cut their own hair because no barber would touch them and even consume dead animals as meal. (Malagatti 2007)

Karukku is an endeavor to understand its multiple meanings expressed and meditated through different identities such as caste, class, ethnicity, religion, focusing different perspectives, grouped under different themes for example works games, recreation and belief, etc. Through these perspectives, Bama portrays clear picture of the caste oppression meted out to the Dalit Christians by upper caste society. Bama has never heard or experienced untouchability until her third standard in school. The first time she comes to know her community's pathetic plight, is paradoxically humorous. One day when Bama was returning from school, she saw an elder man carrying a small packet of eatable, holding out the packet by its string, without touching it and giving it to Naicker in the village. She burst with laughter at the sight of such a big man carrying small packet in that strange fashion. The truth is unfolded by her brother; Annan that the man wasn't being funny when he carried the packet like that. He said everybody believed that Naickers were upper caste and therefore must not touch Paraiyar. This incident wounded her soul and the quest for identity has begun with fervent appeal, so she writes:

> What did it mean when they called "Paraiyar"? Had the name become that obscene? But we too are human beings. Our people should never run these petty errands for these fellows. We should work in their fields, take home our wages, and leave it at that (Bama 13).

Bama's grandmother works for Naicker families. Being a servant she sweeps cowshed, collects dung and dirt, and brings home the leftover of the previous day, when she works in the fields, even small children of that family call her by her name because they belong to upper caste, but Bama's grandmother calls them Ayya, which is another name for master, and runs on their beck and call. Bama further depicts incessant hard labour of Paraiyar from very childhood. Everyone has to work in order to earn their living by laboring either for the Naickers or in the fields. In spite of this, they work as construction labour: digging wells, carrying loads of earth, gravel and stone. Sometimes when this work is not available then they go to hilltop to gather firewood, or work with palm-leaves, or at kilns making bricks because three quarters of these parts is in the hands of the Naickers. Many children work at match-box and firecracker factories, sticking on match-box labels and making firecrackers by using chemicals. They are shut up in the factories from early dawn to late dusk instead of going school. So Bama comments: *"But these little ones' fate is the smell of match-box solution, not the smell of knowledge or learning. How can they afford to study, when it is such a struggle even to fill their bellies?"* (Bama 47)

Bama then takes us to the world of such underprivileged children of Dalit community. No sooner the children grew twelve years old, the boys had to find some way of making or else graze the cattle, the girls had to carry their younger siblings on their hips up to the age of ten or twelve and after that they had to look after the domestic work such as to gather twigs and sticks, learn to boil gruel and entire day to do other household jobs. During the harvest time these young children used to do winnowing, thrashing and collecting the grain to take home. Whatever grain they got after their hard work, they used to sell them in the shop to buy their basic amenities, where they were exploited utmost. So how can they expect any progress in their community where they were not able to fulfill their basic needs in spite their day's hard work. Bama tries to show the pathetic plight of the young children. As the Dalit men and women start their struggle of survival from early morning by balancing the domestic work and field work by consuming a little bit gruel if possible. In this busy schedule, it was very difficult for them to look after their children and send them to the schools. Moreover they were assisting them in the earing and to meet the both ends. Bama says:

> If you look at our streets, they are full of small children, their noses streaming, without even a scrap of clothing, rolling about and playing in the mud and mire, indistinguishable from puppies and piglets (Bama 68).

Bama's autobiography is a detailed description of how she struggled and strived to get education and be a teacher and nun. She is crystal clear that being nun would give her space and freedom for prospective future to uplift the caste instead of traditional marriage. Her elder brother's counsel makes a deep impression on Bama. With this strong inspiration and determination she wants to prove herself by studying very hard. She always tries to stand first in the class. Bama writes: *"In fact, because of that, many people become my friends, even though I am a Parachi"* (Bama 15). The caste in the form of untouchability became a painful reminder for Bama throughout her education. Even the government's financial grants and special tuitions to the Harijans is a curse for her because it signals out her caste identity and the value systems that are prevalent in their communities. As Kancha Ilaiah's *Why I am not a Hindu* shows a parallel theme that there is the wide gulf that exists between Dalit and upper caste children in terms of their life at school, their ability to identify with that

(Ilaiah 2005). She completed her primary schooling in her village with torment and contempt from upper-class and for high school she went to neighboring town, where she faced same humiliation and embarrassing situation in the different form. When the warden of the hostel comments, it is more than death for her: *"Look at the Cheri children! When they stay here, they eat their fill and look as round as potatoes. But look at the state in which they come back from home—just skin and bone"* (Bama 17-18).

In spite of many hurdles, she got through all these ordeals and stood first in SSLC examination, continued her education by pawning her earrings and completed under graduation and B. Ed. Bama later joined the convent school as teacher and worked for five years continuously battling and standing against other nuns and higher authorities for Dalit children's exploitation with some skill and success. On seeing the oppression at convent; it is Bama, who is suddenly struck with the idea of becoming a nun. She decides to sacrifice her life, help the downtrodden and Dalit children: "I wanted to be like her, living only for the poor and down trodden, so I entered that particular order" (Bama 21). In spite of knowing the response of family and friends on her decision of resigning the teaching position and becoming a nun, she took firm decision to be a nun and liberate the caste from the shackles and form a utopian society or casteless society. But Bama faced many crucial circumstances and situations she continued to stay in convent because of her determination and perseverance towards the poor and the Dalit children. When Bama was taking training with others to become nuns, they are very curious to find out to which caste Bama belongs. Whoever asks Bama about her caste, she answers honestly without any hesitation. The religious order itself has its own reservation about the Harijan women to become nuns in one context.

In the Christian religious order Tamil Paraiyar nuns are considered lowest. She notices the casteism and politics inside the convent. The nuns and the higher authorities marginalized and degraded all Dalits by insulting and abusing them and making them do all menial work. There is a constant fear for Dalits that if they protest the oppression then they may lose the convent. Bama feels a harsher and more unjust suppression and violent oppression unleashed on Dalit. Bama writes: *"I was dying several deaths with in". In this connection Stella writes, "She was disturbed and shocked to find that the convent and church are completely deviated from the doctrines they preached"* (Rao and Ambhore 250). She always imagines that the convent is a place where everyone is equal and the fundamental objective of convent is to serve the society especially the needy and poor. But she saw that the focus was more on the luxuries for nuns such as they used to feast throughout the day, the good accommodation which made Bama to recall the Naicker house and the most important thing was everyone had their own strategic plan and to achieve that they had jealousies, arrogance and cunning nature. Bama's dream was shattered of being a nun and serving the caste:

> Before I entered it, though, I read about the woman who founded the order. When I learnt how this woman had loved the poor and lowly, with steadfastness she had educated the children of the poor and helped them to go forward, I was greatly drawn towards her. I entered the convent with a deeply felt desire that I too should do my utmost to live my life usefully and meaningfully" (Bama 95). Bama is disillusioned and frustrated by the system of convent and she left the convent. Laxmi Holmestrom writes Bama thus leaves one community of religious woman in order to join another community a Dalit woman (Bama 2000).

Bama highlights institutionalized religion with caste hegemony which discriminates Dalits. The significant aspect of Karukku is her indictment of Christianity and the low status of Dalit Christian in the Roman Catholic Church. She wants to show how Dalit Christians are forced to sit separately, away from the upper caste, even made to use different graveyard beyond the outskirts of the village. The Paraiyar, who are converted to Christianity in order to escape upper caste exploitation, are greatly disillusioned because they are not able to get respectable position in Christianity. The attitude of looking down on the Dalits is not only among the common people in the society but also within their own church. The upper caste as entrepreneur and capitalist set up their own big business to extract as much profit as possible from Dalits, whereas in the churches, Dalit though more in numbers are the least involved in decision making. It is only the upper caste Christians, who enjoy the benefits and comforts of the church. Even among the priests and nuns, it is the upper castes that hold all high positions, and show off their authority. And if Dalits become priests or nuns, they are pushed aside and marginalized at the basic level. It is because of this that even though Dalits wish to take the path of renunciation, they find there is no place for them. In this connection Ajay Kumar remarks "The condition of a Paraiyar under Catholic Church is not different from the ill treatment that he or she within Hindu Society. Irrespective of their religious affiliation or even financial position the lower caste people suffered humiliation from the dominant sections of the society." (Kumar 131)

Thus, Bama's *Karukku* represents the most traumatic and suffocating lives of Dalits. It is not an armchair reading, but transits mind and heart and makes the reader to introspect and brood over it. It is also a spiritual journey and quest for identity and integrity. The autobiography can be taken up for Cultural Studies and also for Marxist reading.

Works Cited

An Article: *A palmyra leaf that sears us*, from The Hindu, date: 16 September, 2001.

Bama. *Karukku.* Trans. Lakshmi Holmstrom. Chennai: Macmillan India, 2000. Print.

Caren, Kaplan, "Resisting Autobiography: Outlaw Genres and Transnational Feminist Subjects," in *De/Colonising the Subject: The Politics of Gender in Women's Autobiography.* U. Minn. Press, 1992. Print.

Dalit studies/ scholars without boarders: the website for Academic Publication from India.

Dangle, Arjun. ed. *Poisoned Bread: Translations from Modern Marathi Dalit Literature* (New Edition). New Delhi: Orient BlackSwan, 2009. Print.

Geetha, K. A. & Srilata, K. "From subjugation to celebration: a study of Bama's Karukku and Sangati". *Language Forum* 33: 1 (Jan-June 2003).

Ilaiah, Kancha. *Why I Am Not A Hindu: A Sudra Critique of Hindutva Philosophy, Culture and Political Economy.* Calcutta: Samya, 2005. Print.

Kumar, Ajay. "Karukku: Essentialism, Difference and the Politics of Dalit Identity". *Littcritt.* (June 2007): 126-134.

Malagatti, Aravind. *Government Brahmana.* Trans. Dharani Devi Malagatti, Jane Vucinich and N. Subramanya. Chennai: Orient Longman. Pvt. Ltd. 2007. Print.

Nayar, Promad K. "Bama's *Karukku*: Dalit Autobiography as Testimonio". *The Journal of Commonwealth Literature.* 49:3 (2014). Print.

Prasad, Amar Nath and Gajjan M.B. Ed. *Dalit Literature: A Critical Exploration.* New Delhi: Sarup and Sons, 2007. Print.

Rao, M. Koteswar and Ambhore, Uttam Bhagavan. "Quest for Integrity a Reading of Bama's Karukku". Shodh, Samikshaaur Mulyankan. *International Research Journal* 2:7 (August 2009): 245-250.

Spivak, Gayatri. Selections from *In Other Worlds*. London: Routledge, 1988. Print.

Tamil Dalit literature: An Overview. Round Table India for an Informed Ambedkar Age. The Free Library.

Valmiki, Omprakash. *Joothan: A Dalit's Life* Trans. by Arun Prabha Mukherjee Columbia University Press, 2008. Print.

8

Exploring Dalit Aesthetics in Rohinton Mistry's *A Fine Balance*

DR. SUMITRA SINGH

In Rohinton Mistry's works, there is a flavour of Dalit aesthetics combined with the enigma of class consciousness and of getting ahead in life. Rohinton Mistry's characters sometimes don't understand the purpose of their lives. He projects the pictures of Dalit exploitation and suppression in his novels. Politics also is one of the dominant themes in his novels. This preoccupation moves increasingly closer to contemporary times as politics also emerges as a sub-texts. in *Such a Long Journey*, there is a mention of Bangladeshi war with Pakistan and in *A Fine Balance* there is an instance of Indira Gandhi's declaration of a State of Emergency and finally, in *Family Matters* Hindu fundamentalist agitation and the post-Babri Masjid riots.

A Fine Balance is Rohinton Mistry's second novel, set in Bombay between 1975 and 1984 during the time of Emergency. Rohinton Mistry's *A Fine Balance* novel revolves around four characters—Dina Dalal, a Parsi widow, Maneck Kohlah who grapples with his problems and two Chamars-turned tailors Ishvar Darji, his nephew Omprakash Darji and a young student Maneck Kohlah. All these are from different backgrounds but come together and develop a strong bond. The book is a depiction of these four unfortunate characters. To Dr. Jaydipsinh Dodhiya: "*A Fine Balance,* Rohinton Mistry's one novel is set in mid 1970s India. Mistry's novel beautifully narrates the story of four unlucky people whose lives come together during a time of political turmoil." (Dodhiya 15)

The real Dalit story of the novel starts from the village of Om and Ishvar Darji. The story of the village is about Dukhi Mochi and his descendents. He is a cobbler by profession and lives his life under the suppression. He dislike this life of humiliation and wants to get rid of such life but that was impossible for him so he and his wife Roopa want that his sons may not face such problems and the tyranny by the upper class people. They send their two sons Narayan and Ishvar at the age of ten and twelve respectively to learn tailoring. Dukhi mochi's close Muslim friend Ashraf Chacha lived in Bombay. He takes such a bold step against the wishes of the upper-caste in his village. In such circumstances, "Dukhi Mochi's decision to turn to his sons to tailors was indeed courageous" (Mistry 109). The news spreads like fire in his community and village. Dodhiya says: "They say that Dukhi dares to break the timeless chain of caste, which high caste people would not like at all" (Dodhiya 15).

Ashraf Chacha and his wife Mumtaj take a good care of these two brothers and Ashraf makes them expert in tailoring. Ishvar starts living with Ashraf Chacha so that he may help him in his work but Narayan returns his village again and starts sewing the clothes for the low-caste people. His business flourishes and he makes a house instead of a hut and marries a girl, Radha. Thus, Narayan has a son and two daughters from Radha. Narayan does not work for the upper caste people and refuses to sew their clothes. At the time of parliamentary elections, he refuses to vote for the upper-class. He wants to vote for his favourite leader. Prakash's father asks for his own election ballot, instead of just giving his fingerprint and not allowing the landlord to vote for him. This action is considered as a revolt by him and the incensed landlord sends his henchmen to punish Narayan and his two other compliances to his flat. He behaves very badly with them. He hangs them on the twigs of a banyan tree with their ankles tied to a rope. Their clothes are put off and they are flogged mercilessly and in the evening when election is over, burning coals are thrashed in their genitals and then stuffed to their mouths. All of them cry loudly and their screams are heard in the village but there comes none to rescue them due to fear from Thakur Dharamdasi. They keep crying like a slaughtering animal and their tongues and lips melt away due to burning coal. When they all become silent then their bodies are taken down from the tree. There is little movement in their bodies till then but they are killed by the ropes tightly wrapped around their necks so that they may die due to suffocation. Thus, Dalits have to pay the price of their lives on being asked their rights. Such kind of inhuman and heinous acts are condemnable and punishable as Bama writes: "Are we not human beings? Do they not have common sense? Do they not have such attributes as a sense of honour and self-respect? Are they without any wisdom, banality, dignity? What do we lack?" (Bama 24)

Om flees to a nearby city and gets shelter in the house of a Muslim friend from the village. He finds more similarities with the Muslims than with the people of his own religion. But soon there is a Hindus-Muslim riot. Mistry points out that a liquor-baron called Thorkay decides who gets burned and who survives during the riots (163). Through his agent Nawaz, the baron extracts money from the poor slum-dwellers. Then this extracted money is distributed among the corrupt government officials: "These fellows bribe the municipality, police, water inspector, and electricity officer. And they rent to people like you." (163) Nawaz is, at times, a hypocrite and he makes innocent people like Om and Ishvar his victims.

> On this last night, Nawaz's relief spurred him to greater generosity. If you prefer, you can sleep indoors. The thing is that where I was going to put you anyway, when you first arrived. But I thought to myself, the house is so cramped and crowded, better outside in the fresh air. Miriam brought the food to the table and left. Even obscured by the burkha, Ishvar and Omprakash had been able to see her eyes cloud with embarrassment at her husband's hypocrisy. (163)

The unique feature of the Indian caste-system, projected by Mistry, is that there is no chance for any development for Dalits and backward people and if any attempt is made by the lower-caste people, they have to face dire consequences which Mistry vividly portrays in his novel *A Fine Balance*. Om and Ishvar break the unwritten rule by breaking out of their caste. These baseborn leather-workers drop their shoe-making profession and become tailors with the help of a Muslim friend who has apprenticed them in his tailoring business. As tailors they are employable and have opportunities and they have resources to re-shape their destinies, but there was something else in their storehouse. To see the sufferings of Om and Ishvar the reader discovers that cruelty has no bounds. The corruption among the officials has been put on focus. The emergency called by Prime Minister Indira Gandhi is considered good: "The Emergency is a good medicine for the nation" (583). These words echo in the years: "The Prime Minister's message is that she is your servant, and wants to help you; she wants to hear things from your own lips". (583)

These are many programs by the government for the betterment of Dalits and economically backward people but only a few are successful and much money is distributed among the corrupt officials. City beautification programs are run to clear slums and make thousands of slum-dwellers homeless. All these programs take their toll on Om and Ishvar's lives. However, they get shelter in Dina Dalal's house and thus start living with Dina Dalal and Maneck Kohlah who are kind to them. Dina Dalal also had a life full of struggle. Her bad days start when she loses her father, a doctor who volunteers for a hazardous job, falls sick and dies. Dina is forced to leave school at the age of fourteen and she is denied a university education that would have been her right. When she grows adult, she is harassed by her elder brother to marry rich but unappealing suitors. She wants to get rid of her brother that's why she is in the search of her own livelihood. At the very starting she provides shelter to Ishvar and Om, the two tailors, to start a garment manufacturing business in her flat and develops intimacy with them and she takes in a student boarder, Maneck. They live like members of a family when circumstances throw them all together. This is a perfect example of humanity. These four strangers now come closer to one another and initially start sharing their stories and then they share their meals and living space also. In this one shabby little apartment, they spend their happiest moments together:

> The four of them cooked together and ate together, shared the cleaning and washing and shopping and laughing and worrying? That they cared about her and gave her more respect than she had received from some of her own relatives? That she had, during these last few months, known what a family was (Mistry 550).

Thus, all the four people of divergent caste and culture integrate in Dina's small apartment. Mistry ruthlessly criticizes the existing social pattern of India who claims to have attained new heights at the name of progress but first of all the nation must uproot its caste system to achieve real progress for the citizens.

> Burdened down with the complexities of bringing up children in this sophisticated and complicated society, she remains an object of sexual fulfillment for the white man, and an 'invisible' woman to her white female contemporaries, especially, the 'establishment' of women's liberationists who chatter on about sexual oppression and the competitive orgasm, and who spare not a thought for the true object of sexual oppression in this country today" (Bobbi Sykes 313-21).

Major writers differ from minor ones, even great minor ones, in their ability to handle the big questions: death, family, the passing of time, the inevitability of loss, God or the corresponding God-shaped hole. Mistry handles all of them in an accomplished style entirely his own. He also manages, with gentle insistence, to focus our attention on what we have and what we are constantly in the process of losing. Children leave; families disintegrate; love slips away; moments of happiness, too often unrecognized at the time, vanish into the past. Mistry's work illustrates the comment only too effectively; and yet this essence, seen through his eyes, is still beautiful.

On the other hand, his brother Omprakash Darji lives with Ashraf Chacha after that he is hired by Dina Dalal for tailoring. Dina Shroff, later known in the novel as Dina Dalal when married to Rustom Dalal, is from a traditionally wealthy family. Her father was a doctor but he died when she was only twelve years old. Her mother was withdrawn and unable to take care of Dina after her father's death. Now her brother Nussawan is at home for him. But Nussawan does not behave well with Dina and abuses her also. He forces her to do household work, cooking, cleaning and all. He bans her school-going and hits her also when she misbehaves. He is, once, on the verge of molesting her just because she gets her hair cut without his permission. Dina rebels against Nussawan, his brother and his brother's prospective suitors for her when she grows young. She finds her own husband, Rustom Dalal herself at a theatre.

Nussawan and his wife Ruby were happy to get rid of Dina when she marries with Rustom so that now she will move to his flat. Dina and Rustom are also happy after marriage but their happiness is short-lived and only after three years of her marriage, one day Rustom dies accidentally after hitting by a bus. Now Dina in her early forties and has no way to live her life. She does not want remarry or return to her brother's house again. To make both ends meet, she becomes a tailor under the guidance of Rustom's surrogate parents. But her eyesight gives out from complicated embroidery work and she has to quit this work. She is once again jobless. By a lady's advice she starts working in a company called Au Revoir Exports, who bought ready-made dresses in Au Revoir patterns. Then she prepares dressed for this company and the company pays her for it. As she has poor eyesight, she has to hire tailors for this work. Dina hires, Maneck Kohlah, the paying boarder; the son of a Parsi school chum, and these two Chamaar tailors, Ishvar and Omprakash Darji, to sew dresses for her. At first she does not socialize with them but gradually she allows them to sleep on the terrace of her flat. On the first day of their work Ishvar asks, "Dinabai, what is this Emergency we hear about?" "Government problems—games played by people in power. It doesn't affect ordinary people like us", replied Dinabai. "That is what I said", murmured Omprakash. "My uncle was simply worrying" (Mistry 88).

In this novel Thakur Dharamsi is a symbol of injustice, tyranny and corrupt politics prevalent in Indian society. Such people spread terror in the society and they snatch their powers by their power and positions and dalits always keep grinding in utter poverty. Thus, Dalit and poor people have been kept under the critical camera in this novel. The life of these Dalit people is not so easy in the caste-ridden society and they have to strive a lot in their life. In *A Fine Balance*, Mistry depicts how the upper-caste ruling class mocks at the democratic rights to be enjoyed by the Dalits and other down-trodden classes in India. An impression of this stark reality is conveyed in the novel through a pitiable tale of Om and his grandson, Prakash. These both are born in a Chamar or leather-workers' family in a small village in India. After independence, the caste distinctions were abolished officially but the respite from humiliation was hardly ensured. The landlords in the village exerted inhuman torture to subdue the Dalits. Power is the issue in the politics of literature, as it is in the politics of anything else. To be excluded from a literature that claims to define one's identity is to experience a peculiar form of powerlessness (Fetterley 492).

Works Cited

Bobbi, Sykes. 'Black Women in Australia: A History' in Jan Mercer ed. *The Other Half Women in Australian Society*. Penguin: Ringwood, 1975. Print.

Fetterley, Judith. "Introduction: On the Politics of Literature." *The Resisting Reader*, rpt. in Feminism, 1977. Print.

Mistry, Rohinton. *A Fine Balance*. London: Faber and Faber Limited, 1996. Print.

Bama. *Karukku*. Trans. from Tamil Lakshmi Holmstrom. Chennai: Macmillan India Ltd, 2000. Print.

Dodhiya, Jaydipsinh. *Novels of Rohinton Mistry: Critical Study*. New Delhi: Sarup & Sons, 2004. Print.

____. *Perspectives on the Novels of Rohinton Mistry*. New Delhi: Sarup & Sons, 2006. Print.

Luhrmann, T.M. The Good Parsi: *The Fate of a Colonial Elite in a Postcolonial Society*. Cambridge, Mass: Harvard University Press, 1996. Print.

K. Ratna and Shiela Mani. *Moral Dimension in Rohinton Mistry's A Fine Balance*. Parsi Fiction Edition. Novy Kapadia, New Delhi: Prestige Books, 2001. Print.

9

Sufferings under Suppression in Mulk Raj Anand's *Untouchable*

MD. NAZME FURKANUL HOQUE

Anand wrote his novels chiefly in the pre-independence days where the relationship between the Britishers and the Indians or the natives plays an important part in his novels. Anand, in his earlier novels triumphs over the cause of the underdogs—sweeper, coolie, labourers and points to their inhuman tortures and their dehumanization under the degraded conditions of cruelty, dirt and degradation. With his first novel *Untouchable*, he inaugurated the literature of the marginalized. He not only interpreted the soul of India, the real India of the villages to the West but also convincingly made known to the colonial rulers and by their influence the poor conditions of the marginalized and their living.

In the novel *Untouchable* we find Indian society that facing with the challenges of the crippling poverty, the paralysing slavery, the inhuman exploitation of the masses especially of the 'Dalits'. One of the major problems that make the Indian society more complicated is the caste system—that means the four castes—Brahmana, Kshatriya, Vaisya and Shudra. From the very past the caste system had a racial origin but it had also its base on the economic condition of the society and its people of the labour class. According to the Vedas, the Priest or the Brahmana possesses the authority to become a spiritual mentor and the highest order in the Hindu sociological-pyramid. The Shudras remained at the bottom of the pyramid. In such a caste system the priests stood as middlemen between the worshipper and the worshipped. It is the priests who create a gap between God and the worshipper and this gap paves the way for exploitation towards any particular class of society.

Anand depicted the untouchables in his novels very minutely and almost all the characters have been taken from his real life experience. Very often we too, come across the similar experience of the poor, insulted and the discriminated. But we never feel or make the experience a history as Anand does in his novels and all of that was possible due to Anand's sense of kind humanity. His first novel *Untouchable* claimed the attention of the sophisticated readers for its humanistic theme as well as for its compact structure and stream of consciousness technique. It depicts a day in the life of Bakha, a sweeper boy and the central character of the novel. *Coolie* is the second novel of Anand which published in 1936 and depicts the life of an orphan who works as a coolie in different places in the short span of two years only. Both the novels are episodic novels giving a panorama of the social and political conditions of India under British Raj and in the pre-independence India. It has the loose structure of a picaresque novel but there is a chronological narration of various phases of Bakha and Munnoo's life. For Bakha it also reflects the other events and characters from his point of view—a view that has experienced the sufferings under suppression in the name of caste and his untouchability.

Bakha is the central attraction of the novel *Untouchable* and there is the human centrality in it. Human relationships in various aspects are delineated against the social and political background of India. Bakha is an eighteen years old boy, son of Lakha, the Jamedar of all the sweepers. Bakha helps his aged father to clean the latrines. He and his family live in twelve feet by five dark, dingy one-room house. The only furniture of the room is the two string cots, one of which is broken, and a cane chair also broken and lying outside. Apart from that few other things are also there like two quilts, the carpet on which Bakha sleeps on the floor, his second hand army blanket, an earthen water pot and cooking pot and the tools of the latrine cleaner's trade that means a shovel, a basket, and brushes which sometimes decorates the outside of the front wall. The novelist does it just by narrating the life of Bakha—an untouchable boy during one day. He gets up early in the morning and goes to work at the dawn. The boy cleans three rows of latrines several times single handedly. He does his work efficiently and the hard-toil makes him very strong both physically and mentally. Each muscle of his body, hard as rock when it came to play, seemed to shine forth like glass, 'what a dexterous workman!' the onlooker would have said and though his job was dirty, he remained comparatively clean. Same as a doctor who devoted himself for the society, he prevents several infectious diseases from attacking the caste—Hindus by cleaning their latrines and sweeping their roads but the people who enjoy his services never treat him with a little compassion. The point to be noted here is Bakha, the untouchable only 'enjoys' the insult and humiliations of the caste-Hindus.

In this novel Anand depicts the events of a day of the protagonist of the novel Bakha. He starts his day with the call of his father *"get up ohe, you Bakya, ohe you son of a pig!"* (15) and Bakha starts to begin his work of cleaning the public latrines without even having a glass of hot water to warm his throat. He returns home with the hope that he may have a cup of warm tea but there is no tea and not even water. Due to that Sohini, his beloved sister takes an earthen pot to fetch water:

> The outcastes were not allowed to mount the platform surrounding the well, because if they were ever to draw water from it, the Hindus of the three upper castes would consider the water polluted. Nor were they allowed access to the nearby brook as their use of it would contaminate the stream ...So the outcastes had to wait for chance to bring some caste Hindu to the well, for luck to decide that he was kind, for Fate to ordain that he had time—to get their pitchers filled with water." (26)

The outcastes are at the centre of vehement sufferings and deprivation in this novel. Anand portrays very poignantly how society treats with them—that means they are at the 'kind' mercy of the caste Hindus both for food and water. For them, no matter how hard they work, they—the untouchables have no rights even to the most basic necessities of life and living. Take for example, the water fetching case of Sohini that shows how the untouchables have been deprived by the caste Hindus. Anand depicts this incident as:

> They crowded round the well, congested the space below its high brick platform, morning noon and night, joining their hands in servile humility to every passerby; cursing their fate, and bemoaning their lot, if they were refused the help they wanted; praying, beseeching and blessing, if some generous soul condescended to listen to them or to help them. (26)

It shows the suppression under the case of the very fundamental rights of a human being especially the untouchables. The sufferings of Sohini in the case of her physical molestation is also brings our conscience back to the undemocratic barbaric medieval tortures and inhuman conditions of women, especially those who belong to the family of the untouchables. Anand gives the description of Sohini as:

> She had a sylph-like form, not thin but full-bodied within the limits of her graceful frame, well-rounded on the hips, with an arched narrow waist from which descended the folds of her *salwars* and above which were full, round, globular breasts, jerking slightly, for lack of bodice, under her transparent muslin shirt". (26)

Now the point to be noted that how Sohini became the victim of her beautiful figure by none but a priest—Kalinath who agrees to get water from the well for the low caste people who assembled to fetch water from the well like Sohini. He sees Sohini and feels enchanted by her appealing youthful beauty. What he did then is a hint of an omen. He drives others away and pours the water into the pot of Sohini and orders her to come to his house to clean the courtyard and when she goes to his house he seeks erotic pleasure from her. The Hindu upper caste priest now hardly finds out any discrimination in the case of sexual pleasure from an untouchable. His sense of being superior in the society leads him to seek sexual pleasure from an outcast and for that reason he has no guilty. For him the outcast Sohini has no self dignity or respect. To him she is only an untouchable and so she can be treated according to his wishes and only for that reason he throws the proposal of having erotic pleasure to Sohini.

For that, he hardly hesitates to commit such an abhorrent act. Having such frightening proposal from the priest she shouts in high pitch. Bakha arrives there and urges her repeatedly to tell him the actual incident. She intimates his brother Bakha on his continuous request: "That man, that man!... that man made suggestions to me when I was cleaning the lavatory of his house there. And when I screamed, he came out shouting that he had been defiled… He-e-e-e teased me… When I was bending down to work, he came and held me by my breast" (69). Realizing that he is on the back-foot, he plays the trick of his priesthood and scolds her, and not only that he also accuses Sohini of polluting his holy house—a house of the Brahmana, the superior amongst the Hindus. As a result, a crowd of angry caste—Hindus gathers there to defend the priest and to blame Sohini, and they successfully defend the priest and rebuked the poor innocent untouchable Sohini. The original crime and malpractices of the caste-Hindus remain concealed, and in spite of being innocent and fair, Sohini becomes the victim of harsh marginality in society.

Bakha is the mouthpiece of Anand in this novel. Through him the author represents his observation of the sufferings of the untouchables. In this novel, Bakha knows well about his place in society as an untouchable. The events of the sweet shop show us the suppression of the outcastes in the society. Bakha expresses his own intension as:

> Eight annas in my pocket... Dare I buy some sweets. If my father comes to know that I spend all the money on sweets ...but come I have only one life to live ...let me taste of the sweets: who knows, tomorrow I may be no more. (51)

Bakha is attracted to a sweet shop and he orders *Jalebis* in a low voice as he was ashamed at being seen buying sweets despite his identity as an untouchable. The shop keeper throws the packet of the sweets and Bakha catches it and opens it. He started enjoying the sweets then. In the mean time he accidentally brushes against another man and the man convicted Bakha for polluting him and his fresh dress. Not only that, for that reason he hears: "Ohe low caste vermin !...why don't you call, you swine, and announce your approach ! Do you know you have touched me and defiled me, cock eyed son of a bow-legged scorpion! Now I will have to go and take a bath to purify myself. And it was new dhoti and shirt I put on this morning." (52) It shows how vicious attack has been experienced by Bakha—and all due to his untouchability:

> Bakha stood amazed, embarrassed. He was deaf and dumb. His senses were paralyzed. Only fear gripped his soul, fear and humility and servility. He was used to being spoken to roughly. But he had seldom been taken so unawares. The curious smile of humility which always hovered on his lips in the presence of high caste men now became more pronounced. (53)

The author is concerned with the predicament of people especially the 'Dalits' or the untouchables or the marginalized in the society of the caste-Hindus sensitively exploring the possibilities of personal salvation in a world which is nightmarish and inhuman. Actually he is appalled by the seemingly inexorable march of social juggernaut stamping out the possibilities of love, compassion, nobility and justice. In this novel he asserts with deep courage that the world devoid of tenderness is nothing but a grim reality of hollowness and Bakha is the epitome of a large chunk of humanity which has been the subject to age-old social discrimination. This social discrimination he wants to fight out is not limited to the sin of untouchability only, but it also involves the problems of just wages among the male and female day workers, the dignity of labourer and other basic fundamental issues are also there and that's the reason the problem of untouchability is still in its different forms in the post-independence Indian society.

Bakha is a good athlete and he likes to play hockey and plays well as he has good command over his hockey stick and physical fitness as well. He makes a goal in the evening match and due to that the rival group feels jealous about it and this leads to a quarrel among the players. While fighting, a caste-Hindu boy falls down. The pity in Bakha leads him to lift the boy up and this particular event is observed by the mother of that boy. As a result Bakha is rebuked by the caste-Hindu mother because he has polluted his son. Imagine, here we find the reward of a good and noble deed of an untouchable meets with castigation, rebuke and humiliation. One may ask why society holds its position with this double standard of acknowledging a noble action which, if done by a caste-Hindu, would have been rewarded as smiling 'thank you' or a polite 'thanks'? The answer is very simple which the title of this novel *Untouchable* bears with. One can easily imagine the unspeakable poor condition of the untouchables and the strong undercurrent of their sufferings in everyday life in a society which firmly believes in its caste discrimination.

Unlike Dickens' philanthropic novels, Anand's novel *Untouchable* too, portrays the picture of the struggle of the individual to release himself from the communal and racial customs and beliefs. There is a social conflict that results in the isolation of the individual from the society. The same problems which Bakha faces in the *Untouchable,* are not only his own ; in fact it is one of the glaring forms of deprivation in the West among the society which discriminates people on the basis of their faith, caste, colour, gender and economic status. Bakha's struggle against his untouchability reminds us of the American Negroes during the sixties and the South African Blacks who had been the victims of racial discrimination. American Negroes' struggle resulted as Harlem Renaissance and Bakha's struggle in the novel *Untouchable* should be resulted into a new road of freedom and should become a universal gesture of protest against casteism, discrimination and social disintegrity as the novel shows the various vehement aspects of sufferings under suppression of the untouchables in the Indian society.

Work Cited

Anand, M. K. *Untouchable.* New Delhi: Arnold-Heinemann, 1984. Print.

Cowasjee, Saros. *So Many Freedoms: A Study of the Major Fiction of Mulk Raj Anand.* New Delhi: OUP. 1977. Print.

George, C. J. *Mulk Raj Anand: His Art and Concerns.* New Delhi: Atlantic Publishers and Distributors, 2000. Print.

Naik, M. K. *Mulk Raj Anand.* New Delhi: Arnold Heinemann, 1973. Print.

Paul, Premila. *The Novels of Mulk Raj Anand: A Thematic Study.* New Delhi: Sterling Publishers Pvt. Ltd, 1983. Print.

Vivekananda, Swami. *Caste, Culture and Socialism.* Calcutta: Ashutosh Lithographic, 1983. Print.

10

Poignant Narratives of Tribal People in Laxman Gaikwad's *Uchalaya: The Branded*

DR. ARCHANA BHATTACHARJEE

Literature is a mirror of its time of creation and the characters depicted in the literature are the sample pieces of real human beings of its time. To get the unique feature and common manners of a society at a particular time, going through the characters and society depicted by the literature of the times is enough. The character and theme for the literature are taken from the real life characters and society of its time. Writers of all ages have been conscious of their assignments and pious mission, and their role is guardians of society. Gauri Shankar Jha rightly opines:

> The writers gives a voice to what is voiceless, a name to what is yet nameless. Literature imposes patterns of language, vision, reflection and imagination and creates a model of value that is ethical and aesthetic at the same time. It is not a confirmation of values and acceptance of authority, but a criticism of the world and our way of looking at the world" (Jha 90).

Literature of Marginality is the literature that deals with the marginalized sections of the world who are deprived of their fundamental rights to participate in the social, religions, cultural, political, educational and economic spheres of their lives and are kept aloof, alienated or segregated physically from the general public called the sophisticated Hindu or the elite classes of the world. Literature of the marginality unravels the strands how the marginalized classes live a miserable life and how even the develop and developing countries are unable to solve the issue of caste and untouchability in an era where every country is claiming to solve the economical, sex and caste-based discrimination; and a large amount of money is being consumed on these socio-economical backward classes. These people deprived of their fundamental rights and live a half lived life because these people have nothing and it is very difficult to keep their body and soul together. If somebody peeps into their private lives, one can easily discover that sometimes these people live hand to mouth and sometimes it is very difficult to manage three squares meal for their family and children. The literature of marginality in brief, tries to highlight the hardship of the marginalized people so that the marginality may be uprooted from the world and the government can take adequate steps to resolve this burning problem of marginality. (http://www.boloji.com, 25-June-2013)

This paper attempts to examine a few 'Dalit' issues through a study of the English translation of the Marathi autobiographical novel *Uchalya: The Branded* written by Laxman Gaikwad. The researcher also examines the socio-cultural life of the tribe and their revolt against all forms of social injustices clammed upon them as members of a backward community. Dalit (oppressed or broken) is not a new word. Apparently it was used in the 1930's as a Hindu and Marathi translation of 'depressed classes', a term the British used for what are now called the Scheduled Castes. In 1970's the 'Dalit Panthas' revived the term and expanded its references to include scheduled tribes, poor peasants, women and all those being exploited politically, economically in the name of religion. So Dalit is not a caste. It is a symbol of change and revolution against the sub-human status imposed on them by the Hindu social order.

Arjun Dangle gives a harrowing picture of their wretchedness in a poem entitled "Chhavni Hilti Ha" (The Cantonment Has Begun to Shake). He observes:

> We fought with crows,
> Never even giving them the snot from our noses.
> As we shared the meat among ourselves,
> They use to love us then.
> We warned with jackals-dogs-vulture... kites
> Because we ate their share." (Amar Nath Prasad 79)

Dalit literature is one of the most important literary movements to emerge in post-independence India. In an era when issues relating to human rights have been under critical focus, literary depictions of the experiences of the marginalized groups have acquired great significance. The recent spurt in Dalit literature in India is an attempt to bring to the forefront the experiences of discrimination, violence and poverty of the Dalit. Expression of these experiences have long been silenced, often with religious and social sanction and relegated to the margins as non-literary. But the growing corpus of Dalit texts, poems, novels and autobiographies however, seek to rectify this phenomenon by examining the nuances of Dalit culture. The transformation of the stigmatized identity of these so called 'untouchables' to a self-chosen identity as Dalit is a story of collective struggle waged over centuries. Mahatma Jyotirao Phule and Dr. B. R. Ambedkar, two towering figures in the pantheon of Dalit history were the first to appropriate the word 'Dalit' as a noun and an adjective in the early decades of the 20th century to describe the extreme oppression of untouchables.

Dalit literature, whether oral or written has been an integral and enlivening part of Indian literary traditions for centuries. Eminent writer, academician, and Jnanpith Laureate U. R. Ananthamurthy said, *'For the depressed classes like tribal and those destined to live in the lower rungs of the social hierarchy literature had always been a means to achieve 'self-respect'.*" (*The Hindustan Times*, September 13, 2010) When Dalits themselves write about their situation, it imparts to the literature a new strength and idiom. "*Often a spark was conveyed through the rejection of the generally accepted 'respectful' language to express their 'disrespectful situation'.*" (*The Hindu*, September 13, 2013) To Vandana Pathak:

> Marathi literature witnessed a mushrooming growth of Dalit autobiographies (known as 'swakathan' or 'Atmakathan') in the last three decades of the twentieth century. These autobiographies were written by writers belonging to the grassroots of the Indian society. Some of these have been translated into English. Laxman Gaikwad a member of the Uchalya/Pathrut community based on his life experiences wrote his swakathan 'Uchalya' and it was translated into English as 'The Branded' in 1998. He employed the language of his community to share his stigmatized experiences of discrimination, exploitation injustice harassment, violence and atrocities and marginalization in the text. His autobiography is a socio-cultural ethnographic document." (Pathak 150)

Shedding light on his text Gaikwad confesses: *'I had little opportunity to acquire education and sophisticated culture. These are the reflections of a non-Matric social worker... It is an attempt of a sensitive mind to pen what it has felt and experienced. These writings have been inspired by the stimulating encouragement of Laxman Mane of Upara fame and Sri Balkrishna Renke, the Secretary of the Nomadic and Vimukta Tribes Association*". (IX) Laxman Gaikwad's literary career started in 1977 when he wrote a ballad expounding the innumerable agonies of the exploited people in the society. The Sahitya Akademi award winning work by Gaikwad gained him wider leadership after P. A. Kohlharkar's work of translating this into English. Gaikwad through his work describes his life and the society around him to convey that there resides a section of Indian society, which lives in sub-human circumstances and still a lot is desired to be done for the denotified tribe. Gaikwad does not write like a canonical author; he simply tries to dispel the myths and misconception about his people. He presents his life story in such a way that the readers get a comprehensive view of the problem and its causes. The members of this community have been deprived of equal social status by the peculiar socio-political religious structure of India which forced them to lead a sub-human life. Any attempt on the part of these communities to raise their voice against such humiliating treatment was vehemently suppressed by the upper castes. Consequently the members of these oppressed communities were deprived of all the necessities like food, clothing, housing and education that were indispensable for leading a respectable human life. Being a member of such a community Laxman Gaikwad was forced to go through the first hand experienced of ill-treatment at the hand of upper caste Hindus. Therefore, his autobiography faithfully unveils a factual and microscopic account of his sufferings not only as an individual but also as an unfortunate member of Uchalya community and focuses upon his relentless efforts to construct his self in the adverse circumstances. (3) The opening page, which reflects gross realism, gives us an idea of some of the harsh and brutal facts of Gaikwad's life:

> My name is Laxman Gaikwad... I was born in a vagabond family with no home, no land to plough, not even a caste to call our own. I told folks that I am from Ghanegao as I was born there and grew up during my early years. My childhood was spent in a bird-nest-like hut. To enter

> it, one had to bend their knees. My grandmother Narasobai ran the household. Her husband, my grandfather Lingappa had no job and had to report to the local police station twice a day. He once had a flourishing practice. He would go to far away towns, pick-pockets, steal shopping bags and come home by night. He was a famous thief of his time in this part of the country. His name was well known even in Nizaam's kingdom." (1)

The indoctrination into the thieving profession is carefully described by Gaikwad. There are categories, classifications and techniques in stealing, which seems to reach the form of an art if one can use the word. Thievery was one of the primary occupations of the tribal community in which Laxman Gaikwad lived. With the help of blades the pick-pockets stole money. But one day Gaikwad's grandfather committed an error while stealing: *"One day while picking the money with a blade, he mistakenly gave a deep cut in the stranger's body from buttocks to the waist. The man bawled in the pain as the blood gushed from wound"* (1). He was arrested for this. He was handcuffed and badly beaten for it. Police tortured him badly and inquired: "*Tell us where you have hidden the stolen money and gold. Show or we'll smash your bones.* (2) Their negotiation goes: *"Grandfather wailed piteous: See saab, see for yourself, there is nothing in the hut. Your whore will know.* THEY *grabbed our grandmother by the hair and thrashed her all over."* (2) Gaikwad reminisces his childhood days as well as his wanderings from one place to another while fighting poverty, starvation and exploitation. He presents a stark picture of the abdominally unhygienic living condition of the tribes. *"When law denied the Uchalyas all other vocations, they beat their children to teach them thieving skills."* (10) Gaikwad laments their animal like existence and questions:

> We are forced to take to thieving because we are denied work. Why is it that the whole community is branded as thieves? Why are we denied opportunities to live a decent life? Why is my mother forced to borrow from money lenders to pay the police? When the burden of loans piles up? Why are my all brothers forced to resort to thieving to pay off the debt? Are we to be proud of this varied heritage because we have been inured to these conditions for ages? I began to understand as I began to read. And when I read the pledge on the first page of the text book Marathi I realised how false it was and felt sad. (63)

Using a metaphor Gaikwad again highlight the plight of the young innocent boys of his community who are compelled to turn into hardened criminals. Dr. Vandana Pathak opines, *"As a tender sapling is plucked and thrown in the garbage the sub-inspector of Latur uprooted these boys from the decent life they were trying to lead and threw them into the hell of criminal world."* (201)

Gaikwad's voice rose in protest against many oppressive structures that forced, the Uchalyas to lead a pathetic miserable life. Gaikwad describes a world where people survive on just water for three consecutive days, and where poverty compels them to consume food comprising of cats, rats, roots and leaves and life is very unhygienic. Bijender Singh brings the pitiable condition of the Uchalya tribe through the following observation:

> When the people resorted to acts of criminality for survival they were arrested and the police demanded a huge amount for their bail. Having no other alternative they borrow money from money lenders at exorbitant rates. Consequently they resorted to stealing again to pay off debts incurred. Their education was also unique. From childhood they were taught the skill of thievery. The first lesson of young trainee both for boys and girls began with their beating. They were trained to withstand physical tortures so that they may not disclose the names of their colleagues. A person is permitted to join the profession only after this training. If anybody failed to clear this level they were severely dealt with. One day Manikdada was caught up by police at Renapur market while trying to steal. He was severely tortured by the police and had to reveal all the names. If this was not enough, he was doubly punished by his community for being a traitor. (Singh, 52)

Another illustration is: *"Santaren and Tiaro cursed and abused Manikdada. Monika, you bastard, f…k your mother, you cower in fear like vanes (merchants) and bammans (Brahmins). When caught red-handed you disclosed the names of the entire gang. You have brought shame upon and be-smirched the names of the tribes of thieves."* (6) We get to see another facet of torture and humiliation the womenfolk of this community face through the voice of Laxman's grandmother who ran the family. She was old, senile and physically bereft of energy to put up with any form of torture. But even she was not spared by the police: *"She told us, when the police catch me, they hang me upside down by the legs and lash the soles of my feet with a whip, thrush burning cigarette-buts into my anus. If I do not confess to the theft, they bring shit near my mouth and force me to eat it and keep on beating me."* (8) Unable to put up with such inhuman torture she fell ill and died shortly. The people of the tribe also had no sense of hygiene and had to survive in environment which was totally unhealthy. Except for the annual bath on Dushera day they never took bath, washed their clothes or changed their attire: *"I did not take a bath for months. Nobody from the household ever told me to take a bath. Washing clothes was not even thought off."* (12) Due to lack of latrine facilities even the women of the tribe had to defecate in the open: *"Even while we were roasting the pig, women from the village, sat in front of us and sat as if that was the only spot available. In the morning heaps of human dung could be seen all over the place. Often as we moved about, we stepped on these heaps. It is such a skit-yard that we roasted and ate the pigs."* (13)

Another very deplorable and ugly facet of women's life was also brought to light by Gaikwad. One day as he and his sister-in-law were sleeping in the yard, somebody came and brazenly lay on his sister-in-law. She tried to oppose but he pressed her mouth by his hand and had sexual intercourse with her. After that he ran away. She began to cry loudly but by then the intruder had disappeared into the darkness. On being asked she simply said that he did nothing but was just trying to molest her: *"The bastard was trying to lie on me and had put his palm on my mouth", she said. She knew full well what exactly the truth was."* (86)

Gaikwad's father was a bit different from other members of his community in his views regarding education. He got his son admitted in school with the hope of uplifting his life. However, this was not approved by other members of his community. Therefore, they threatened Gaikwad's father with dire consequences if he failed to remove him from school. Their superstitious beliefs led them to think that the disease of cholera, of which many children of the community were suffering, all this was due to Laxman's schooling. They said that it had infuriated Goddess Yellamma. Referring to this incident Gaikwad writes:

> Three-four weeks after I started going to school children living nearby our hut were affected by loose motions and vomiting. Our neighbours began to quarrel with my parents. Martanda, since your bastard of a son has started going to school, diseases are visiting us. Has anybody from our forefathers ever gone to school? If our children started going to school, our race would be doomed. Goddess Yellama will be furious.

> Look Martand, if your son continues to go to school we shall call the Panchayat and ostracize you. (16-17)

As Professor S. D. Sargar so rightly points out, *"Such kinds of incidents expose the quality of familial and community relations among the members of Uchalya community. However, it has to be taken into consideration that this inhuman behaviour amongst these people was definitely a result of the devlish treatment they received at the hands of the oppressor."* (Sargar 224)

Even in religious matters, the Uchalyas were subjected to various callous customs. Although they were Hindus, they were not allowed to practices their religion on equal footings. Their illiteracy was another reason behind their subjection. Even Gaikwad feared to raise his voice against the customs and beliefs imposed on their community:

> I could not hurt the feelings of my relatives and the people at home by displaying my atheistic thoughts. All the things that Anna liked, habituated to, were taken. They were: Bhajjas, Paan Supari, tobacco, Bombil. Even liquor was taken in a bottle. It filled me with deep sorrow to see these proceedings. The liquor that killed Anna was being carried as on offering to propitiate and release his soul. They wanted to ply him with liquor even after his death. Anna's soul would rest in peace only if I floured his habits diligently (218-219).

Incidents like this reflect the attitude of the members of the Uchalaya community towards Hindus rites and rituals which they have been following blindly over the ages and which is the root cause of all their sufferings. All throughout the book we have references to the traumatizing experiences of life of this backward community. It helps the readers to understand better the inhuman conditions these people have had to put up with as members of the most disadvantaged section of Indian society. Laxman Gaikwad was able to portray the life story of this community very realistically because it was a pen picture of his own life. For him, telling his story was important as he considered his work to be a social rather than a literary work. His aim was not to entertainment the readers but to create awareness to check such social evils prevailing in our society.

In conclusion, it may be said that what writers like Flaubert, Balzac and Dickens did in the 19th century with their novels and as a result brought about social transformation in England and France, Gaikwad sought to do the same in his country. The novel expresses his disillusionment with social conditions governed by traditions imposed upon these backward Dalit communities by hostile upper class people. His work reflects the changing attitude of the downtrodden people, seeking a sense of identity in a totally averse society. It also triggers off the great process of self-examination and imprints upon the minds of the readers the notion that things need to be changed, and that they can be changed and must be changed.

Works Cited

Prasad, Amar Nath, (ed.) *"Dalit Literature: A Critical Exploration"*, New Delhi: Sarup & Sons, 2007. Print.

Gaikwad, Laxman. *The Branded.* New Delhi: Sahitya Akademi, 1998. Print.

Kuortti, Joel. *Joothan: A Dalit's Life.* Mumbai: Popular Prakashan, 2003. Print.

Jha, Gauri Shankar. "*Current Perspectives in Indian English Literature*", New Delhi: Atlantic Publishers & Distributors (P) Ltd., 2006. Print.

Pathak, Vandana, *"The Branded: A Literary Ethnographic Oeuvre"*, Published in Research Scholar, Vol. 2, Issue. III, August, 2014.

Paswan, Sanjay; Jaideva, Pramanshi, (ed.) *Encyclopaedia of Dalits in India: Literature*, New Delhi: Gyan Publishing House, 2002. Print.

Sagar, S. D., "*Dalits and the Literature of Protest: An Overview*", Published in Electronic International Interdisciplinary Research Journal (EIIRJ), Vol. I, Issue. II. April, 2012.

Singh, Bijender. "Dalit Resurrection in Laxman Gaikwad's *The Branded.*" Indian Scholar: An International Multidisciplinary Research E-Journal. Vol. I, Issue I. September, 2014.

www.boloji.com/index.cfmpmd.content&sd=Articles&ArticleD=146000-BijenderSingh

www.hindustantimes.com/india-news/dalit-literature-an-integral-part-of-indian

www.rasnet.lu.se/EASASpapers/4JugalKishorepdf

11

Self Ignorance to Self Knowledge: A Journey of Prakriti in Rabindranath Tagore's *Chandalika*

ANITA GEHLOT

"*A religion that insults is a false religion.*" (Tagore 154)

The statement itself is showing us the real path towards spirituality. A religion, never allows human beings to hurt or insult any other people regarding their casts, status or anything else; a religion teaches us the lesson of equality. At the first time the suffering of Dalit people tormented by the great soul of Lord Gautam Buddha. He introduced the concept of equality to the society. During the Buddha's lifetime, the caste system was one source of discrimination in society. Under such circumstances, the Buddha preached against the caste system and advocated equality of all people. In India caste has always defined the socio-political scenario of the country. Whether it is the debate on the reservation policy for government jobs and education to aid the socially and economically backward classes or political gimmickry, everything has an undertone of caste and religion. The mention of Caste, Community, and Religion on admission forms to school and colleges is one such example. Just being an Indian is rather insufficient to get one's basic rights. Untouchability is an ancient malady of Indian society, religion, and culture. In Rigvedic times there were four classes in society—Brahmin (knowledge), Kshatriya (power), Vaishya (money), and Sudra (waste). In a broad context Untouchable may be subsumed in the category of the fourth class. Chandals are considered to be of devilish origin. From the ancient times they have been the victims of untouchability. They did not have the right of proper living according to the classification of karmas.

In the realm of Indian dramatic writing Rabindranath Tagore carves a specific niche for his plays. For the insertion of universal motifs in his works he is often regarded as a writer of world literature. He draws upon mythology, philosophy, scriptures and ancient history for the execution of his themes and represents some complex metaphors of spiritual enigma. He strives to question the stagnant power structures which construct the metaphors of 'high' and 'low' (Singh 32). Based on an ancient Buddhist legend, the play, Chandalika Rabindranath Tagore is the tale of an untouchable girl who forced to live on the fringe of the society as chandalika. Prakriti, a poor Chandal girl, who, so far never realized her self-worth. What all she knows is that she is an untouchable and she should stay away from the people of higher casts as her touch can impure them.

This play is the journey of Prakriti from ignorance to self realization. A journey which leads you to the path of equality; a journey which takes you to the pavement of humanity; a journey which shows you the realm of spirituality is a journey of self-knowledge. It is, indeed, ironic to see how a girl named Prakriti meaning 'nature' can be enmeshed in a web of class, caste and gender distinctions. The story of *Chandalika* centres round Prakriti (Chandalika), a self-ignorant and a low caste girl, who for that reason is thoroughly despised by her neighbours so much that even hawkers in the street would not sell their goods to her. She broods over her destiny and curses her mother for bringing her into the world.

At the very onset of the play we find Prakriti completely lost in wonder. Wonder which is out of the world for her; wonder which she calls a new birth of her, as being a chandalika she can never think of such wonders in her life. And this wonder was when she saw a Buddhist monk standing before her in yellow robes and asking her for water from the untouchable's well in spite of her warning him of her low birth. His words, *"don't humiliate yourself, self-humiliation is a sin, worse than self-murder"* (Tagore 148) ring in her ears. *"As I am a human being, so are you, and all water is clean and holy that cools our heart and satisfies our thirst."* (Tagore 149)

This is the moment of awakening for the daughter of Chandal when the monk tells her she is not 'impure' but the child of the same almighty like others. All this while when Prakriti had internalized herself as a victim of social stigma and negated her selfhood suddenly elevates to a moment of recognition. Till now Prakriti was told that she is untouchable and the water from their well was declared as polluted by high caste people. But after listening to monk's words she realized her self-existence and this was the great revolution for her, which she felt like a new birth of her, free from all social obligations and free from all inequalities she was facing since her birth. *"Such a little water, yet that water grew to a fathomless, boundless sea. In it, flowed all the seven seas in one, and my caste was drowned, and my birth washed clean."* (Tagore 149)

The water which she offered to the monk, Ananda, for her, it becomes the symbol of life, of the recognition and respect which is the rightful due of every human being regardless of his or her birth. And by this she feels like she is no more untouchable and all her impurities being a low caste girl is cleanly washed as Ananda himself accepted her service.

Prakriti is enlightened after meeting the monk and her sense of identity begins to bloom. All her effusive gratitude turns into desire for the monk and she falls in love with him. Her existence has lost all significance as she waits in agony for the return of the monk. Without him she feels as dead and unproductive as a 'waterless waste' (Tagore 150).

Prakriti tells about her meeting with monk and her new birth afterwards to her mother and persuades her mother to cast a spell over him and bring him to her bed. The mother is a fatalist and she argues that there is no redemption for the low born. She says: *"You are unclean; beware of tainting the outside world with your unclean presence. See that you keep to your own place, narrow as it is. To stray anywhere beyond its limits is to trespass"* (Tagore 150).

But she further argues with her mother not to humiliate herself by these old age concepts. For self-humiliation is a sin. Prakriti who had all along felt humiliated among the higher caste people finds it beyond belief that even a flower from a 'poisoned-plant' can be offered for service. *"O words of great wonder! That I may serve, I, a flower sprung from the poison plant! Let him raise that truth, that flower from the dust, and take it to his bosom."* (Tagore 150)

Here Prakriti is feeling an immense change in her thoughts that till now she has felt like a flower bloomed from a poisoned plant and there is no value of her life but now she has realized her value and according to her she is no longer poisonous because of her untouchability, she is like beautiful flowers that can be offered at worship. Again her mother compelled her to forget about the monk as she is slave by birth: *"You were born a slave. It's the writ of destiny, who can undo it."* (Tagore 152) But Prakriti replied: "*Will he not mingle his longings with mine, as the Ganges mingles with the black waters of the Jumna?*" (Tagore 152)

Here we can clearly understand that Prakriti's adoration of the monk's desire is changed into an erotic desire of him. Here the river Ganges symbolizes higher caste people like the monk and the low caste people like Prakriti can be considered as the black water of the river Jumna. And she was dreaming of the conjugation of these two edges which is impossible according to her mother.

Though her mother warned her against her drastic desire and reminds her about the king's proposal who was mad in her beauty but her desire for the monk has become so strong that she discards her mother's words and says that the king had never recognized her as a human being because of her caste, she had been to him like a beast only whom he wanted to bind in a gold chain. But Ananda, as according to Chandalika recognized in her the real beauty of a human being.

Here we come to know that Prakriti is not a wicked girl roused to lust by the physical beauty of the monk, but a very sensitive girl, condemned by her birth to a despised caste, who is suddenly awakened to a consciousness of her full rights as a woman by the humanity of a monk, who accepts water from her hand and teaches her to judge herself not by the artificial values that society attaches to birth, but by her capacity for love and service. She is a rebel who questions societal norms that relegated her to an existence of a lesser being, an untouchable.

Prakriti's mother wanted to bring her in the real world as according to her she was lost in the world which doesn't has its own existence; which is not made for the low caste people like them so she recalls old age religious dogmas in front of her daughter and asks her if she doesn't scare of religion. And Prakriti replied that she doesn't respect the religion that insults others and for her it is a 'false religion'. The pain of longing for the handsome monk becomes even more intense when, later in the play during Ananda's second visit to the same place, he immersed in his inner spiritual self totally ignores Prakriti's presence and moves on chanting the hymn of lord Buddha. It is a great shock to her sensitive mind. Her female ego gets crashed and the newly awakened woman feels deeply hurt.

> O wretched woman, who raised you to bloom for a moment in the light? Fallen in the end into this same dust, you must mingle for all time with this same dust, trampled underfoot by all who travel the road. (Tagore 155)

She was raising the question upon her reawakening that why to crave for self liberation when falling in the same dust is the destiny of an untouchable woman; when meshed under the foot of the higher caste people is in her fate. Prakriti's mother tries to convince her to leave the thought of mingling with the monk as it was just a momentary dream and nothing else so better to let the monk go to his own way. Her mother says that it is a crime to attract a monk with the magic spells. But Prakriti was not ready to understand. She replies very boldly: "...... *and if there is a crime, then I will commit the crime. I care nothing for a code which holds only punishment, and no comfort.*"(Tagore 154)

Prakriti denied letting him go as she was so much hurt that she was feeling like a *'prisoned bird that beats its wings unto death'* (Tagore 155). Here Tagore presented Prakriti as a newly re-awakened woman who is craving for real liberation and the love for a man of her choice. She was bursting in anger so she pleads her mother to cast the magic spells to bring him to her. Further with a great anger she tells her mother to chant the magic spell. *"Chant your spells, bring the bhikshu to the side of the chandalini. I myself shall do him honour—no one else can honour him so well.*" (Tagore 153)

Her mother couldn't see her daughter crying and burning in the fire of her pathetic love with the monk so she decided to chant the spells over monk to bring him back to her dear daughter's bosom. She gives her daughter a magic mirror to follow the progress of the agonized monk drawn helplessly by the power of the old woman's spells.

The tension between her mother's will and the monk's resistance makes Prakriti nervous. She feels that she will not be able to survive the possibility of his being beyond her reach for ever. Her desperation drives her to express herself in violent images of destruction:

> Something far greater than fear. I beheld the God of Creation, more terrible far than the God of Destruction, lashing the flames to work His purposes, while they writhed and roared in anger. What lay at his feet in the casket of the seven elements—Life or Death?" (Tagore 159)

She has lost all religious scruple or fear, for she owed nothing to religion save her humiliation. For her the monk has become the God; according to her she is his creation as he is the only one who recognized her as human being and not as an untouchable. So she wants to serve him with her whole being. Because of monk's humanity Prakrati gets self-knowledge; a feeling of self-respect; she gets the knowledge of the worth of her own life; she gets the knowledge of her power as a woman and more than a woman as a human being. This self-knowledge is necessary up to a point for self-development but it is difficult to control and if not tamed timely it can create a chaos in one's life. This is what exactly happened with Prakriti in the play. Blindfolded by the awakened consciousness of liberty and overpowered by the freshly sprung need of equality and spiritual union, Prakriti oversteps this morality and ethical boundaries. That results in her spiritual tragedy in the end.

As mother's magic spells bind the monk's thoughts and drag him against his will through long agonizing distances towards her hut, she saw Ananda at her door having a distorted face with agony and shame; completely transformed and degraded by lust because of the effect of magic mantra; she feels horrified and guilty at the selfish and destructive nature of her desire. The hero whom she yearned to devote herself was not like this. He was a handsome monk with a divine glow on his face. But because of the effect of the magic spells he is no more that radiant monk now. She curses herself and destroy the magic paraphernalia and falls at his feet begging her forgiveness:

> O Lord, you have come to give me deliverance, therefore have you known this torment. Forgive me, forgive me. Let your feet spurn afar the endless reproach of my birth. I have dragged you down to earth, how else could you raise me to your heaven? (Tagore 162)

Here Prakriti had undergone a greater cleansing than the mere self-realization. She realizes that though she is an untouchable but she can be as pure as Ananda by getting rid of all the impure thoughts and developing a spiritual self. Her mother died at monk's feet. Ananda returns to his spiritual way with his shining purity and divine glow. He has also given us a new idea altogether and if it is followed honestly; can change our perspective towards love and life. The idea is, never ever 'Fall' in love. If you truly love someone then always 'Rise' in love. 'Come...Rise in Love.'

It is evident that *Chandalika* is a drama for social change. It supports elevating the consciousness of the Dalits and the women and leads to social change in India. By addressing the theme of untouchability through this dance drama Tagore was making an extremely bold socio-political statement against the discrimination of untouchables. (Singh 33) Chandalika awakens the Dalits to new consciousness of their rights as human beings. Prakriti's mother represents the old suppressed Dalit consciousness while Prakriti represents the new awakened Dalit consciousness. In nut-shell *Chandalika* is Prakriti's journey from self-ignorance to self-knowledge; from marginality to spirituality; form impurities to a complete pure soul as a modern woman who is craving for real liberation and equality.

Works Cited

Singh, Arun. "Contradicting the Discourse of Untouchability in Tagore's *Chandalika*". RJELAL. Vol. 1. Issue 2. 2013. pp. 32-35.

Tagore, Rabindranath. 1950. *Three Plays.* Trans. Marjorie Sykes. O.U.P., 1969. pp. 148-168. Print.

12

The Burden of Surname in Omprakash Valmiki's *Joothan*

UDAYAN GAUTAM

"What's in a name"—asked Juliet in Shakespeare's *Romeo and Juliet* (II. II. 43, 1017). In Indian caste based context she might have asked "What's in a surname" and the answer would have been a resolute 'yes'; there exists a lot in a surname in India. This tradition dates back to the Vedic age and its societal divisions. The hierarchical society was made of divisions, though with a view to constructing communities based on labour and duty, yet it later turned out to be based on birth and familial living standards. The four-fold 'Varna System' lost its purpose and became merely a tool for exploiting the lowest caste by every means possible. Once a baby is born, whatever congenital quality it might have, is identified only by the caste in which it takes birth. He/she might possess outstanding capabilities, but had to remain under suppression carried out by the other three higher castes. This custom, naturally, was backed by culture—the Sanskrit Smritis and other compositions manipulated solely by the Hindu higher castes. These were devised so arbitrarily, the ideas of caste-division according to birth were injected so deep in our thoughts, the social malpractices were so artfully wrapped up with religion that the caste system has become integral to the Hindu ideology. We don't have to be social analysts, but a simple reference to the incident where Ekalavya had to sever his thumb for being a Sudra in spite of attaining excellence in archery. This is a symbolic of how the lowest caste was denied the dividend of its capabilities. A thumb is the most important finger that makes the other four do what a man wants them to do. Parting with it implies cutting off a man's ability by making him subtly impaired. The potentiality of so many Ekalavyas was fervently slaughtered in the guise of religious conventions. The blatant dicta of the Manusriti enabled the higher castes to make the most of the Sudras—socially and economically. They were put in menial jobs, dirty as they were considered to be, with no wages at all. The Sudras were always at the mercy of the ruling, powerful castes as if they were allowed to live on by the latter's magnanimity. A mere touch or even a shadow of a Sudra was as polluting as a pile of garbage. Though there were provisions in the Vedic prescription as found in the Gita for a Sudra to become uplifted to the other three castes [the Gita also advises not to change means of livelihood in any circumstance—*Swadharme nidhanang shreya, parodharama bhayavaha* (*Shrimadbhagabadgita* 3.35, 170) on the basis of quality of work, but these ideas, in the hands of the opportunistic priests, became extinct. The caste in which a man was born lasts till death, making way for a huge waste of human resources.

Studies have been carried out to seek the reason for caste discrimination in India and several issues have come to the surface. Considering them entirely, a major issue must not be overlooked—the economic one. The Vedic socio-economic system was agricultural. The influential people were land owners, thereby possessing the means of agricultural production. India's diverse and semi-bourgeois system, though differed in many aspects from its European counterpart, was greatly alike in one point—power and exploitation. French king Louis XIV is well remembered in history as a self-proclaimed controller of his subjects' fate by exercising authority over them and making himself richer in the garb of divine mandate. In India religious shibboleths exhibited more alacrity in serving the purpose of land owners. The Sudras were frequently used in farming, their congregated labour power was greatly taken benefit of, leaving them squeezed till mere bodily existence. So, what was behind such division was nothing but exploitative inclinations. Dalit literature, with its agitational purport, highlights such loopholes and at the same time speaks for the lowest segment of the society whose voices remain unheard. Though sometimes repetitive, yet, pieces from Dalit writings focus on individuals languishing in a caste-based society. Keeping this in view, *Joothan* may be considered as a case study where the plight of a Dalit is the central thematic concern. Before moving further into the text, it'd be worthwhile to speak a few words with regard to the titular proposition of this paper. Let's study the following lines:

> One sees merely the whole effort of a body straining to raise the huge stone, to roll it and push it up a slope a hundred times over; one sees the face screwed up, the cheek tight against the stone, the shoulder bracing the clay-covered mass, the foot wedging it, the fresh start with arms outstretched, the wholly human security of two earth-clotted hands.... One always finds one's burden again. (Camus 108)

What is the greatest burden in a man's life, has been argued by thinkers and philosophers through ages. Metaphysical and epistemological thoughts have been churned across the world. To arrive at a stoic conclusion like living in this earth is the most burdensome for all, we don't require any sage. Young Rosalind in *As You Like It* has summed it up beautifully, "O, how full of briers is this working day world" (*As You Like It,* Shakespeare, I.III. 11-12, 167) in a slight different context. Now, let's come to the Indian perspective. Here, even before being born, perhaps the foetus has to bear a burden, not of life, but of its surname defining its caste:

> When I knew nothing, I knew
> My caste was low (Lines 1-2, Anand & Zelliot 123)

Gruesome it may seem, but it is true till date. Surname determines a man's social status, his wealth (intellectual also), his daily life and behaviour. It is the 'cross' that every Sudra has to bear since birth, without visibility but having weight enough to make him socially collapsed, economically crippled.

This suffering gets its expression in the works of Dalit writers. It is more eloquent in Omprakash Valmiki's autobiographical bildungsroman *Joothan*. 'Joothan' is a Hindi word which means 'slop', something that is left over after use. The seven-lettered title at once frames the predicament of the Dalits. They are the hated, cast away social left-overs. *Joothan* is a representative novel on the predicaments of dalits assuming a centrifugal mode of narration; experiences are subjective but their expanse is far more widespread. Let's take an assistance of facts and figures of that period as presented by Ram Ahuja in *Social Problems in India:*

> The total population of the SCs (called today as Dalits) according to the 1991 census was 138.33 million. The SCs comprised 16.3 per cent of the country's total population […] About 84 per cent of the SC people live in rural areas and are working as agricultural labourers, sharecroppers, tenants and marginal farmers. Almost all persons engaged in jobs like sweeping scavenging and tanning are from SCs. (168)

Joothan candidly depicts the life of Dalits through almost verbatim details of everything a man has to undertake as challenge for being a Dalit, how many impediments a man has to come across in his way of life. Being Dalit is the impetus of the novel, being Dalit is the cause for recalling the events, being Dalit is the reason for a number of unanswered questions made in the novel and finally, being Dalit generates the fundamental interrogation from the entire Dalit population—*Jati hi meri pehchan kyun* [Why should caste be my identity?]. Below is a paradigmatic excerpt from the novel which would evidently prove how much load a Dalit has to carry: *Abe Chuhre Ka* (13)

Not only identity, caste to a Dalit is an entity, an inseparable tag, a pre-determined axiom that comes into action when a woman conceives, after birth a child is addressed as being a child of a Dalit mother. His/her nomenclature does not require anything more than this. He/she is marked with an everlasting stamp which will bear his existence in the society. This derogatory term is frequently used by the higher caste people not only to remind them of their menial profile, but also to instigate in the higher castes a spirit of superciliousness.

> *Arre! Chuhre ke jakat ku jharu lagane ku keh dia toh kaun sa julm ho gaya* (17)

The literal meaning of the line may be "What is the crime in commanding a low-caste to sweep?" But, the question contains the answer in it. A Dalit is destined for sweeping. He can't help doing that, as per the social norms. So, if a teacher orders a Dalit pupil to sweep instead of studying, if a teacher makes him stand outside the class for being a Dalit, he is only carrying out his role in terms of castes, not with regard to whatever nobility his profession entails. And he gains support from the big guns of the society!

Phir kisi bhi mahakavya mein hamara zikre kyun nehi aya? (34)

In *The German Ideology* we find Marx commenting on the role of the ruling class in controlling the intellectual forces. The economically stronger class always moulded culture, literature and art by their own ideas. Epics always record the deeds of those in power or struggling to come to power—always belonging to the higher levels of society. Aristotle recommended the misfortune of a person of 'high birth' to be considered for a well versed tragedy. Hence, Valmiki urges for a proletarian voice to be heard through epics since they were devoted to the bourgeoisie. No epic hitherto has been composed on the oppressed; rather they are busy delineating the rulers—those who oppress. The great epics, irrespective of nation or culture, always overlooked the epic struggles of the downtrodden.

Apne shram ka mulya mangna apradh kyun hain? (52)

Joothan registers many instances of unpaid labour performed by the dalits. And they are *always* unpaid. They are utilized whenever the wealthy men desired, they are made to toil without objection, their labour is considered as one's private property, they have to work for free and the little they earn is an outcome of the higher caste's condescension. Lack of class consciousness made them divided and vulnerable.

Atithi ki jati hi use adar dilate hain (66)

This statement makes the line of the Upanishada blur—'*atithi devo bhava*', which stands in sharp contrast to what Valmiki has expressed. So long as he kept his caste in secrecy, he was taken care of warmly in his teacher's rural habitat. The moment his identity (caste being the only one) is divulged he was hurled into the road. The above line is not only information; it is the author's bitter realization.

Bachchon ko ye sab gharon mein sikhaya jata ki SC se ghrina karo (116)

A blooming love gets immensely disrupted by caste-discrimination. Love may be blind, but not enough blind to miss the lover's caste. The infatuation of Savita for Valmiki became out of tune once he revealed his caste. He comes to know about the custom of children's parroting against the lower castes.

> *Naam ka uttarardha, jise upanaam ya surname kaha jata hain, mere naam ke sath jurkar kayin prakar ki bisham parithitiyan utpanna krnewala siddha hua hain, apni jatibodhkata ke karan* (148)

Valmikis are those in Uttar Pradesh, who belong to the lowest stratum of the Dalit communities. The caste division does not end in the four major denominations. The dalits were not only burdened with backwardness, they burden themselves further with a number of sub-castes, e.g. Mahar, Mang, Chamar, Mehtar and many more. This resulted in disintegration amongst the dalits which obstructs their unification and development of fundamental collective class consciousness. The burden of surname makes them not only an object of disdain to the upper castes, but the smaller sub-castes in the dalits possess disunity and difference between themselves. This fact often forced them to alter their surnames for assuming a somewhat respectable one to survive in the society; otherwise it would become intolerable for them.

In *Joothan* the stifling load of surname is all pervasive. It builds the atmosphere of the novel. If we keep the surname related matters apart, the novel would become a very simple, ordinary story of a mere struggler. But, the surname and its everlasting holocaust have imparted to the novel an altogether different setting.

Not only the rural illiterate people hold the casteist views, but the urban, educated, sophisticated, aristocratic families are sterner in keeping untouchability alive. It is well known that in remote villages the shadow of casteism looms large, but in semi-urban and urban regions situations are just alike. Things are the same in teachers also. Many dignified adjectives are used to bring out the importance of the teacher in a society. Our heritage teaches us to respect the teacher even more than we do God. But a few incidents in the novel make us think otherwise. The depth of darkness in the minds of the teachers is so much that some ornamental degrees cannot illuminate the whole. Teacher Mr. Narendrakumar Tyagi hesitated to swallow drinking water from the hands of a Dalit, and later drank water himself. The scar of such occurrence was clearly visible in the author's mind as he comments that in spite of obtaining a Masters Degree in mathematics, his teacher lacked the courage of drinking water touched by a low caste boy.

Joothan showcases lots of paradoxes which subvert and sometimes shatter our long preserved conception of a rich, glorious cultural tradition of our country. It strips our motherland off its skin-deep idea of social integration, pointing towards the omnipresent diversity in pseudo-unity. The author caters us many an example of the thread-bare texture of Indian society. Mr. Gupta of Ordinance Factory of Jabalpur, a transferred commandant, the Kulkarnis of Chandrapur, Mohandas Nemisharay of Delhi and surprisingly the author's close relatives and even his wife were too much concerned about the surname. Some drove him away, some humiliated him, some hid it in stark secrecy and some even thrust the author into sheer insult—only because of his birth, his caste, his surname. He feels the pain of being regularly stabbed with the knife of casteism. At the end of the novel Valmiki has presented his idea of the Indian society and does not seem at all hopeful of its future, as long as the country continues to impose burden on the dalits.

Works Cited

Ahuja, Ram. *Social Problems in India.* Jaipur: Rawat Publications, 2012. Print

Anand, Mulk Raj & Eleanor Zelliot. (Ed.) *An Anthology of Dalit Literature*, New Delhi: Gyan Publishing House, 1992. Print

Camus, Albert. *The Myth of Sisyphus.* Trans. Justin O'Brien, London: Penguin Books, 2000. Print

Shakespeare, William. *The Arden Shakespeare Complete Works* Eds. Richard Proudfoot et al. London: Methuen Drama, A&C Black Publishers Ltd. 2001. Print

Shrimadbhagabadgita. Ed. Sri Krishnananda Swami. Calcutta: Guptipara Sri krishnananda Harimandir Trust, 1969. Print

Valmiki, Omprakash. *Joothan.* New Delhi: Radhakrishna Prakashan Pvt. Ltd. 2012. Print.

13

Indian Dalit Writing in English: A Cry for Freedom

Dr. Anand Kumar

The emergence of Dalit as a political category and identity coincides with the emergence of Dalit literature. Dalits haven't been portrayed truthfully in religious literature to contemporary Indian literature. In the present scenario, Dalit writers focus on oppressions, sufferings and demands of their dignity as human beings. People may not believe such barriers of castes, creeds and breeds but in fact, it gets flow in the blood of Indian society.

Dalit literature occupies a prominent place in Indian literature. It is actually born out the heinous system of untouchability and caste discrimination that have been practiced in India from centuries. Dalit means broken, oppressed, untouchable, oppressed, exploited, ground-crushed, broken-down and reduced to pieces. They come from poor communities and are socio-politically backward that's why they are known as untouchables. It was the Manu Smriti which divided Hindu society in four varans or castes according to the occupations of the people.

Dalits haven't been portrayed truthfully right from the time of Hindu religious literature to contemporary Indian literature. Dalit literature is a response to the exploitation and the humiliation of the Dalits. Equality, freedom and social justice are the basis of Dalit literature. Dalits have been deprived of these. These people were silent and mute in the history. The first systematic exploration of anti-caste idea is included in Buddhist works. Later, the Bhakti poetry of the 14th century attempted an amalgamation of the castes and outcastes. The Bhakti poetry was anti-orthodox, mostly inclusive and highly racial.

Dalit literature emerged into the forefront and as a prominent voice after 1960, starting with the Marathi language and soon appeared in many other languages in India which stood out due to their stark portrayal of reality and the Dalit political scene. It was in the 20th century, in 1958, that the term "Dalit literature" was used for the first time, when the first conference of *Maharashtra Dalit Sahitya Sangha* (Maharashtra Dalit Literature Society) was held at Mumbai; a movement driven by thinkers like Jyotiba Phule and Bhimrao Ambedkar. Mahatma Phule was the first to use the word Dalit in connection with caste. Dalit literature blossomed with the revolutionary writing of Dr. Babasaheb Ambedkar.

Gradually, other writers like Namdeo Dhasal paved way for the strengthening of Dalit movement. Dalit literature grew out of the Dalit Panther movement which was established by two writers Namdeo Dhasal and Raja Dhale in April 1972. The emergence of the Dalit Panthers (a political organization formed in 1972 in Maharashtra) is a significant moment in the history of Dalit literature which was furthered by various political and literary movements across India. Like Black Literature, Dalit writing was characterized by a new level of pride, militancy, sophisticated creativity and above all sought to use writing as a weapon. The Dalit Panthers is a significant moment in the history of Dalit literature. Soon this movement was spread in the various fields across India. Like Black Literature, Dalit writing was characterized by a new level of pride, militancy, sophisticated creativity and above all sought to use writing as a weapon for their freedom. It was not a cry but a strong voice for their rights.

Dalit literature was disregarded and not taken seriously in the literary circles for a long time. In its initial stages Dalit literature was identified as specific protests directed against everyday humiliations. A beam of Dalit literature can be seen in a few glittering works of some very famous writers such as Munshi Prem Chand, Raja Rao, Om Prakash Valmiki, Laxman Gaikwad, Mulk Raj Anand and Arundhati Roy.

Most of the novels of Munshi Prem Chand deal with the social themes. Raja Rao's greatest classical novel *Kanthapura*, portrays radical social changes and marks a turning point in the history of Dalit literature. It presents a clear picture of deep-rooted orthodox caste-ridden society. Village was divided in different segments according to their castes. Moorthy, the protagonist of the novel, is from the upper caste and deeply influenced by Mahatma Gandhi. He preaches them Harikatha and doesn't keep any difference between touchables and the untouchables. But his mother is deeply orthodox and don't like all this. She warns him not to enter the house except he gets bath with Ganga water. Even Moorthy, when he comes back to home he too takes bath with sacred Ganga water and sits in the courtyard to eat. He can't forget that he is a Brahmin. He doesn't keep the barriers of casteism but he can't give up in which community he is born and what his social status is. Casteism is fixed in the mind of the people and it is discernible in the words of Achakka:

> Oh! To have a son excommunicated. Oh! To have gone to Benares and Rameshwaram and to Gaya and to Gokurna and to have a son excommunicated. I wish I had closed my eyes with your father instead of living to see you polluted. (Rao 46)

One another prominent Indian writer Mulkraj Anand also reflects the deeply rooted casteism in Indian society in his famous work *Untouchable.* The protagonist suffers due to his belonging to a low caste. It also highlights how an 'untouchable' leads the life meaner than the animals and how he has to tolerate inhumane insult and abuse. Bakha represents all those untouchables who have been oppressed and suffered for thousands of years. It is as Bakha says to his father: "*They think we are mere dirt because we clean their dirt*" (79). Bakha represents all the people who suffered lifelong. The anguish of his soul expresses through these lines: *"I am an Untouchable!" he said to himself, "an Untouchable!"*(52)

Noble prize winner, laureate Rabindranath Tagore, a non-dalit writer also expresses the same type of picture in *Gitanjali* (1913) and *Chandalika (1925)*. Prakiti wishes to transcend her socially-imposed status *"Don't humiliate yourself…self-humiliation is a sin, worse than self-murder (Three Plays 148)* She truly says: *"How can I? I respect him who respects me. A religion that insults is a false religion. Everyone united to make me conform to a creed that blinds and gags" (154)*. In the stories of Munshi Premchand we identify that untouchability is the worst evils of the existing Indian society. In 'Shudra' there is a tale of untouchable woman who is transported as a part of a racket involving trafficking in women.

In "The Thakur's Well" an untouchable woman, Gangi rebels against the caste laws: "*Why are we considered low and these so people high? Is it because these people wear a thread around their necks?*" (Orsini 85) In 'Kafan' (1935) Ghisu says: "*What kind of a custom is it when a living person does not get a rag to cover his body, the dead must have a new shroud.*"(Orsini 237) *It shows a real and pathetic picture of Indian society.*

In other story 'Mandir' there is a pathetic tale of a wretched Dalit mother who is desperate to take her sick child to the temple to pray for his recovery. But the priest by no means allows her to enter as her entering will defile the temple. The famous lines form the poem of well known Dalit writer Sharankumar Limbale, express this situation very aptly:

> The church bell rang
> Everyone entered in
> The ajan heard from mosque
> Everyone entered in
> The bell of temple rang
> Some entered in
> And some stood out.' (generallyaboutbooks)

Arundhati Roy's *The God of Small Things'*narrates the same shocking experience of inhuman treatment of the Dalits. She says that: *'Fifty years after independence, India is still struggling with the legacy of colonialism, still flinching from the cultural insult …. We are still caught up in the business of "disproving" the white world's definition of us"*(Roy 73-74).

Baburao Bagul is one of the most prominent Dalit writers in Marathi. His first collection of stories, *Jevha Mi Jat Chorali* (1963) created a strong stir in Marathi literature. Om Prakash Valmiki is an Indian Dalit writer who is well known for his autobiography *Joothan.* He considered a milestone in Dalit literature. In this autobiography he talked about the discrimination he had faced in the school at different points. He has expressed the agonies of Dalits in this book. In this concern we find one of the most breathing atmospheres in the works of Om Prakash Valmiki who has given the horrific picture of their wretchedness. Producing their own literature Dalit writers have created their specific corner in the literary revolution called 'Dalit Literature.'

Dalit Literature is like burning charcoal in present scenario. This could also be an opportunity to examine Dalit expression and literatures in a renewed way and from different perspectives. The position of Dalit literature can be fully understood in term of oppressed or oppressor, victimized or victimizer and ruler and the ruled. The indelible impact of Mahatma Phule and Ambedkar on this literature is clearly perceptible. Dalit literature can be seen as the post-colonial literature. Now Dalit literature is the solid voice in the literature which has been represented firmly by the writers with the exactness. Dalit literature is the outcome of the society in which the inequality of the human doesn't exist. In the end we can say Dalit writers do not have any readymade solution of such evils like social degradation, untouchability, casteism, classism, upper and lower. But they portray the social realities in such a way that we feel completely shaken out of complacency.

Works Cited

Anand, Mulkraj. *Untouchable*. New Delhi: Penguin, 1935. Print.

Deodhar, S. K. *Rigveda*. Trans. Pune: Prasad Prakashan, 1981. Print.

Limbale, Sharankumar. *The Outcaste: Akkarmashi*. Trans. Santosh Bhoomkar. New Delhi: Oxford University Press, 2005. Print.

Orsini, Francesca. *The Oxford India Premchand*. OUP: New Delhi. 2004. Print.

Rao, Raja. *Kanthapura*. Bombay: Oxford University Press: 1938. Print.

Roy, Arundhati. *The God of Small Things*. New Delhi: Penguin, 1997. Print.

Tagore, Rabindranath. *Three Plays* (1960). Trans. Marjorie Sykes. Madras: Oxford University Press, 1970. Print.

Valmiki, Omprakash. *Joothan* (1997). Trans. Arun Parbha Mukherjee. New York: Columbia University Press, 2003. Print.

www.generallyaboutbooks.com/2013/05/dalit_writer_html,accessed on Dec 10, 2013.

14

Location as a Burden in G. Kalyana Rao's *Untouchable Spring*

Dr. Zainul Abid Kotta

Dalit literatures usually project the socio-economic concerns and worries of Dalit life. They are the biographies or autobiographies of the underdogs who were compelled to live in the outskirts of normal human life. They sympathize and sometimes propose suggestions for improving the sad plight and the wretched life of the victimized. In other words, they are the manifesto of the 'wretched of the Earth' (Courtesy to Franz Fanon). Those writings are the principled and systematic down pouring of the emotional casualties faced by the Dalit minds. In Indian context, Dalits are really the majority community, but they face myriads of problems. Even after the self-rule of seven decades, those communities are still trailing behind, and they were exposed to inhuman exploitation on all levels: body, culture and nation. G. Kalyana Rao's *Untouchable Spring* raises strong questions about the devilish discrimination faced by the untouchables by the ruthless hands of caste Hindus.

Caste system is a particular social evil seen in India, as such. Caste system, as practiced in India, cannot be seen in other parts of the world. It is generally an Indian crisis. Hinduism speaks about 'varnas', and in this hierarchy, Dalits do not come to the picture. They were called 'avarnas', which meant devoid of caste. In Indian cultural hemisphere, religion is a potential tool that was used effectively and enthusiastically to exploit the 'wretched of the earth'. In a wider postcolonial perspective, those exploitations have different connotations. Dalits were colonized by the upper caste both physically and emotionally. The upper caste people even colonized their minds and imaginations.

The world Dalit is derived from the Sanskrit word 'dal' meaning 'oppressed'. Now the term is used to denote an identity. As we know, Dalits were denied basic human requirements for a standard life. They were misappropriated politically, socially and economically. This exploitation has many levels: they were uneducated or undereducated and were forced to believe that education was not meant for them. Secondly many of them accepted the state of being exploited as their destiny. Kalyana Rao was intellectually attuned to Dalit consciousness and his vision was illustrated in the novel *Untouchable Spring*. The opening of the novel in the form of the dedication sheds light to the sad plight of the Dalits. The book was unusually dedicated to four influential people in the life of Kalyana Rao. He bluntly opens the novel with a sympathetic but eye opening reference to the casualties faced by the Dalits.

> When I started writing 'Untouchable Spring', I thought of dedicating it to my mother and father. But by the time the novel was to be completed as a serial, Shyam, Mahesh, Murali and Lakshmirajam became martyrs along with them. That is why I dedicated it to the four of them along with my parents (Rao 5)

The quotation shows how insecure the life of an average Dalit in many parts of India. They are living in the perpetual danger of extinction and massacre. Absolute fear looms on them. In such a threatening atmosphere, how can those communities think and act freely? How can they strive for better education? How can their women be kept at home? These are the issues, Kalyana Rao brings up for discussion.

The Dalit communities in the novel of Kalyana Rao were colonized and kept away from higher literary discourses. They were fugitivized and were not able to articulate their emotions since they do not possess either a tongue or a voice. Later the Dalit intelligentsia began to seriously think about writing, and they had realized that writing had to be taken as a tool to express the inner turmoil. So they have taken writing a way of their self-expressions. Their writings are not the celebration of the luxuries of their lives, but the victimized emotion of their existence, as Sharankumar Limbale said once:

> I never have and never will write for entertainment. I am a writer of people. How can I forget problems of my people? How can I neglect

> the cry of my people? The unrest of my people charges me-to think and to write (www.generallyaboutbooks.com)

This is the reason; most of the Dalit writings are either autobiographical or confessional. Kalyana Rao's Untouchable Spring, is memory text furnished with wounded memories of a Dalit family. It deals with a family of Dalits for seven generations. The novel exposes indigenously rich and vibrant cultural traditions of Dalit community. Sambaiah and Sreekanth suggested:

> Probably it is the first Telugu novel which clearly formed Dalit identity. There is surge of an ideological war at every phrase of the novel. No doubt, it raises pity for all that is pitiable and rage at what a man has done to for their rights. (http://www.rjelal.com)

Kalyana Rao's *Untouchable Spring* showcases the major issues faced by the Dalit communities, Malas and Madigas in Andhra Pradesh. The original book was written in Telugu in the name *Antarani Vasantam*, which was later rendered to English by Alladi Uma and M. Sridhar. This article is based on the translated work. All the references go to the translated piece, not the original work. As Franz Fanon talked about postcolonial sensibility in his famous book the *Wretched of the Earth*, Kalyana Rao pinpoints the deplorable condition of Dalits in India. In another context Franz Fanon pointed out a condition that was equally applicable to Indian Dalit situation: "This cultural obliteration is made possible by the negation of national reality, by new legal relations introduced by the occupying power, by the banishment of the natives and their customs to outlying districts by colonial society, by expropriation, and by the systematic enslaving of men and women" (Fanon 1440). Fanon speaks these words to describe the predicament of a colonized society; but in Indian perspective all the terms are applicable to Dalit community. *Untouchable Spring* moves around all the burning issues faced by the two communities Malas and Madigas in Andhra Pradesh. The primary concerns are the questions of land, labour, poverty, education and untouchability. The novel depicts all the above said issues in a heart melting style and manner. The Malas and Madigas are exposed to abject poverty and they were treated like cattle class. They were not given the basic amenities of life like sanitation, nutritious food etc. They were the 'other' as the term used by Gayatri Spivak (2115).

All the major life concerns of Dalits were reflected in *Untouchable Spring.* Land, labour, segregation, untouchability, forced labour etc. were religiously practised in Yelena Halli, where the novel establishes its anchorage. In the first part of the novel, Rao gives a physical description of the village, where the Dalits were exposed to all forms of abuse. The secluded and racially segregated place was called 'palli', which means village in our phraseology. And there is a main village called 'ooru'. Rao's description was fantastic and pictorial.

> The place where those who belonged to the four castes lived was ooru. The place where Malas lived-malappalli, where the madigas lived-madigappalli. Amazingly, all those parts put together formed Yennela Dinni. (Rao 6)

Dalits were distanced from the mainstream both physically and metaphorically. In *Untouchable Spring,* Dalits were living in secluded areas called 'palli', away from 'touchables'. They were pushed to those sites from time immemorial. The upper caste received textual support for this inhuman slaughter against the Dalits. Yellanna's case is a master example for this push to the outskirts of the society.

> Yellanna's life was on this side of the horizontal line. One did not know when his ancestors were pushed on to this side of the line. Several hundreds may be born every second on this earth, may be thousands; or may be much more. (Rao 7)

This is a systemized brand of segregation, which is sarcastically unproductive in the modern sense. This locationalization helped the upper castes to plunder and abuse the underdogs, on the basis of their genetic composition. This apartheid offered the Dalit a bad luck, and they found it very difficult to live in such a hostile atmosphere. Even children were not permitted to enter the 'ooru', and if a child enters or moves to an upper caste abode out of his childish innocence, he will be beaten to near death by the high caste people. There is no room for mercy and fellow feeling. Yellanna in the novel was beaten once near to death by the upper castes for entering the 'ooru' once. Rao pathetically illustrates the underdog life throughout the novel. Even hygienic drinking water was a distant dream for the poor. They had to wait hours and hours to get water, until a soft hearted comes for water. The wretched underdogs were not permitted to pass through the 'ooru', because of their 'potentiality' to pollute the whole area. Rao provides a few example of mingling of the Dalit community with upper castes. One such incident occurred during a natural calamity, in which all the segments of the people assembled together. Very rarely the malas and madigas were given chances to watch movies and plays but there was no chance to sit together with caste Hindus. In the novel we can see an episode where malas and madigas were watching a play. While watching the play, the madigas and malas were supposed to sit far behind the rest of the village and they should take all precautions for not being visible to the karanams who usually occupied the front rows. The karanams did not allow the pedda mala and peddamadiga to stage their play, for the former were afraid of the respect the latter may receive. Interestingly for the modern ear, even the panchayats were organized outside the ooru.

The mind-set of the upper caste in the novel was that of the one advocated by *Manusmiriti.* Education and letters were not the tools in the hands of the Dalit community. They did not have access to education even at the primary level. Language was completely controlled by the upper caste. As Christians believed of logo centricity of languages, the Brahmins believed of Brahmin centricity. Higher form of articulation, be it verbal or pictorial, is meant and created for the Brahmins. The mainstream, foreign and the vernaculars are controlled by them. They strongly believed and propagated that they were the people chosen for higher cultural discourses. Even the languages used by the underdogs must accredited by the aristocracy.

> Even if it is utterly obscene, what the Brahmin speaks alone is the Veda. Whatever is spoken must be spoken by them alone. Only when *they* utter, Sanskrit becomes Sanskrit. Telugu becomes Telugu. Finally, even if English has to become English, it has to be spoken by them. If need be they can make a Brown of a Brahma and a Brahma of a Brown (98-99)

All chances of becoming modern in the Dalit community were minimal. The folk performance of Naganna and Yellanna were very powerful. But their songs were never scripted in to a book. In this context Rao says: *"An untouchable's song. That's why Yellanna's songs never got written as a book." (98)*

Location and the 'other' are the two stigmas attached to the Dalit sensibility. Kalyana Rao's writings are the metaphors by which he wanted to liberate the Dalits from their traditionally colonized mind-set. Education, literature, music etc. were widely used for creation and inculcation of awareness in the minds of both the upper caste and the down trodden.

Works Cited

Fanon, Franz "The Wretched of the Earth" in *The Norton Anthology of Theory and Criticism,* Second Edition General Editor. Leitch Vincent B Leitch 2010. Print.

Limbale, Sharan Kumar. Thursday May 9 2013 www.generallyaboutbooks.com. Web

Rao, Kalyana G. The Untouchable Spring. Trans. Maya Pandit. New Delhi: Orient Blackswan, 2009. Print

Spivak, Gayatri Chakravorty. "A Critique of Postcolonial Reason" in *The Norton Anthology of Theory and Criticism,* Second Edition General Editor. Leitch Vincent B Leitch 2010. Print.

Sambaiah, Dr. Medikonda et al "Untouchable Spring' Without Ambedkar's Touch: An Ambedkarian Criticism on Marginalized Propaganda of Left Wing Extremism on Dalit Liberation" *Research Journal of English Language and Literature (RJELAL) A Peer Reviewed International Journal,* http://www.rjelal.com Vol. 1. Issue. 4; 2013. 285-292. Web.

15

Social Atrocities and Exploitation: A Reading of Narendra Jadhav's *Outcaste: A Memoir*

DR. HIMANGINEE KAUSHIK

Dr. Narendra Jadhav's *Outcaste: A Memoir* represents the life of untouchable world. It is based on personal experiences and depicts the pain of isolation and humiliation. It is an expanded English version of Dr. Narendra Jadhav's best seller in Marathi *Amcha Baap Aan Amhi* that means 'Our Father and Us'. It was first translated into French named as *Untouchable* by Fayard and later it was also published in other European languages. But by chance Dr. Jadhav is not happy with English version named *Outcaste: A Memoir*, he admits this thing in an interview given to Anand, the editor of *Touchable Tales* and says: *"It does not convey anything. What the book is, is not conveyed in the title."* (S. Anand 38)

Outcaste: A Memoir is basically a work about Dalits. The word 'Dalit' comes from Purusukta of *Rig Veda* where caste system is discussed and it is the place where caste system is discussed very broadly and for first time also. According to that, Brahmnas are born from the mouth of Brahma, the Kshatriyas from his shoulders, the Vaisayas from his stomach and Sudras from his feet. So, Brahmnas are considered the most superior and Sudras are most inferior in our society. People think that this caste system is God made and not man-made. Hindu caste system is based on birth not on aptitude and also very rigid because of that Sudras are considered outcastes, down-trodden and inferiors. So, they have to face exploitation by the higher caste people. Dalit literature also shows the same condition of Sudras. Arjun Dangle writes:

> Dalit literature is not simply literature; it is associated with a movement to bring about change. It represents the hopes and ambitions of a new society and new people. (Dangle 266)

The literal meaning of the word 'Dalit' means a person who has been trampled under feet or who is humiliated, exploited, oppressed, insulted and also thrown outside the pale of civic society and called untouchable. Dalit literature is a revolutionary step with the aim to highlight the destruction of the caste system and to establish equality in social and political spheres. Arjun Dangle says:

> Dalit literature is one which acquaints people with the caste system and untouchability in India, its appalling nature and its system of exploitation. In other words, Dalit is not a caste but a realization and is related to the experiences, joys and sorrows, and struggles of those in the lowest stratum of society. It matures with a sociological point of view and is related to the principles of negativity, rebellion and loyalty to science, thus finally ending as revolutionary. (Dangle 265)

Narendra Jadhav's *Outcaste: A Memoir* describes how his parents struggle hard against the rigid and superstitious society and hostile surroundings while bringing up Narendra and his siblings. Damodar Runjaji Jadhav and his wife, Sonu are the main characters in the work *Outcaste: A Memoir.* Damu is the main protagonist of the story. He is against the word 'Harijan'. He thinks that if Harijans are the people of God, who are the other people, are they people of devils? He used to ask always this. When *Outcaste* starts, 20 years old Damu is addressed as 'Mahar'. Mahar is Damu's caste and stigma also. This word shows that he is the lowest in the Hindu chaaturyarna system, the system of four castes. He is an untouchable and people used to think if they will touch them they will also get polluted.

Narendra Jadhav's *Outcaste: A Memoir* highlights the story of three generations of a Dalit family. It's his dedication to the vision of the blind grandmother, his father and his mother who struggled a lot and killed her hunger to keep them alive and it is also a dedication for every man and woman in the world who stood up for human rights and against exploitation by higher caste people. Damu, the main protagonist of the novel (here autobiography) belongs to the first generation. The work is written in the first person narrative, from Damu's point of view. This is a heart touching story about the tradition of untouchable Mahar caste family. He struggles and fights against all odds of conventional caste codes followed by the society and religion. Damu lives in his ancestral village in western Maharashtra. He is an uneducated engine machine in Mumbai Railways.

This book is a wonderful narrative, which describes how his illiterate parents raise their six children and all of them become successful human beings. Later Narendra Jadhav is also chosen as the best international student of Indiana University, USA. From there he also completed his Ph.D in the early 1980s. In his interview with *Reader's Digest*, he shared his views about the unfortunate fellow beings.

> You know the Hans Christian Andersen story of the ugly duckling? Unfortunately, in our hierarchical society there are millions of swans who, because they don't get a chance, believe they are ugly duckling and waste their lives. (Mahadevan 115)

Dr. Narendra Jadhav is a good thinker also. He suggests that we should not deprive the children of opportunities at the higher education level due to high drop-outs at the school level. He asks to find a right way to decrease the drop-out rate. Narendra Jadhav's parents never went to school but they knew the importance of education and his father taught himself to read basic Marathi. Jadhav went to Chhabildal Boys' High School. There the medium of instruction was Marathi. He tells about his personal experience in school and says: *"I used to sit in a corner like a sacred rat. I studied Sanskrit because this was denied to all my forefathers."* (Mahadevan 116) Narendra Jadhav highlights the situation that he has to face due to his caste. His tone is loud but he expresses real situation. His way of thinking is different from other Dalit writers. His protest against exploitation is right.

Damoder Runjaji Jadhav and his wife Sonu are not so much literate but Damoder (Damu) protests against injustice. He is irritated by 'Harijan' word. He has so many questions in his mind regarding this word and he always used to ask these questions but he never gets satisfactory answers. One day Damu gets a chance to attend a meeting addressed by Dr. B. R. Ambedkar which inspired him a lot and he decides to spread the message of Dr. B. R. Ambedkar: *"Educate, unite and agitate."* Later when Dr. Ambedkar gives a call to join Buddhism then they convert to Buddhism in 1956. Buddha says to Look into our hearts and to follow our nature. Buddha never asks to follow any scripture or to follow him. Damu and his wife understand this thing fully. But Damu keeps a picture of Goddess Saraswati who is a symbol of wisdom and knowledge. He gives more value to knowledge than money. He knows that knowledge can be used to earn money but knowledge can't be purchased with the help of money. Knowledge is unlimited and priceless. Damu's children get good education and as they are highly qualified, they are well settled in their lives. This is the result of Damu's and his wife's dedication and hard work. Damu says to Sonu: *"Our engine is good and dependable no doubt.... But it makes a lot of noise."* (Jadhav 218)

Damu does not like polite language and he never uses ornamental and sophisticated language and he also does not expect the same from his children. He is not comfortable with decorative and ornamental language of daily use. He asks his children to call him 'Baap' instead of 'Baba' or any other decorative name. 'Baap' word is more comfortable for Damu than 'Baba'.

> Arre, call a spade a spade...... language when spoken should come alive with meaning; It should have flavor... your polite, bland language is as insipid as boiled potatoes. (Jadhav 216)

Although Damu is not highly qualified, yet he has all the qualities those an educated person should have. He knows the importance of knowledge and he also has full respect for his wife. He never underestimates his wife. Both of them follow spiritual path and also lead their children towards education for their bright future. Damu has to face a lot of bitter experiences, while bringing up the children. One day one villager calls Narendra 'Damu Mahar's son' while others use a dignified language. Dr. Amar Nath Prasad has rightly opines:

> Yes, even a Dalit or an untouchable can become an engineer or a doctor or a lawyer or a professor if he is given proper education and proper facilities. God never makes any difference between touchable and an untouchable; between the poor and the rich; between the rough and the sublime. The minds of all men are almost equal. (Prasad 199)

The present work is a dramatic piece of writing that depicts inhumanity and injustice in the society and tells how a low-caste person is treated like animals. Damu raises his voice against all these injustices. In the opening pages of novel *Outcaste*, Damu is doing his yeskar duties which are assigned to him due to his Mahar caste. Later he is also assigned the duty to guard the dead body of a woman found floating in the well. He is also not allowed to go home and inform his wife and to have his food. He is forced to stay near the well and the tragedy does not end here, he is also abused and insulted. On the very next morning Fauzdar (a police officer) comes and asks Damu to get into the well to draw the corpse out. Damu refuses to do this work because she is not allowed to touch the dead body of an upper caste woman. Narendra Jadhav says:

> The caste system is so deeply ingrained that change can, at best, be cosmetic. The caste system was disposed by God and not by mortals. It has such a powerful sanction behind it that no laws, no reform movements, and no revolutions will ever change it completely. (Jadhav 24)

For neglecting the order Damu is beaten up by the Fauzdar. But Damu never gives up and he says:

> In spite of these inhuman traditions, I am not going to abide by such traditions. I am a man of dignity and I will not go from house to house begging for Baluta. What are all of you going to do? Kill me? (Jadhav 10)

Damu decides to leave his village on that night and goes to Mumbai with his wife in search of freedom. Damu struggles hard in Mumbai and works in the Railways, the Port Trust and in Textile mills to earn his living in Mumbai. He also takes active participation in Dalit Movement at the call of Dr. B. R. Ambedkar. He also takes part in the Nasik Temple Entry Movement in 1930, in Mahad Satyagraha in 1927, in the Buddhist conversion movement in 1956, Ambedkar's funeral procession and a lot of other activities of the Dalits. Damu does not decide his path of life according to others wish and he is the master of his own will. He proves himself as a self made man in many ways. He never loses his heart by all the odds in his life. Damu is an ordinary man but he does a lot of extra ordinary things. He stands against the exploitation of the caste system. He struggles hard to live with dignity and self respect amidst casteism from 1920s till his death 1989. In spite of his low caste and status, he never sacrifices his individuality though he always takes decision according to situation. But finally he gets success in his efforts as he manages to save his children from the clutches of casteism, social stigma and economic backwardness through education. He does now want to live only for two times meal a day. He tries to convince Sonu and says:

> We must self respect. We must have dignified as human beings. How can I take to begging from door to door? Baluta is our right, they proudly claim! My food! Have you seen how they throw the food? I don't want rights as a dog. I want my human right...... If we just think about filling our stomach, how are we any better than animals? (Jadhav 19)

The main purpose of Narendra Jadhav by his work *Outcaste: A Memoir* is to raise the issue of discrimination based on caste system. Many debates on caste and Dalit rights at the universal level gave a new dimension to the fight against caste with the emergence of non-governmental organizations. Narendra Jadhav says:

> There is wide spread interest in Dalit writing now, all over the world. The upsurge is not because it is politically correct but because people want to know more about the underprivileged sections, about the lives of these whom they knew so little. I was amazed at the range of questions about the caste system that were raised during my public interactions in different parts of France. (Anand 31)

The Memoir tries to show that inter-personal relations between low-caste people and upper caste people. Dr. B. R. Ambedkar himself is a Mahar that's why he is the major source of inspiration for the millions of Dalits. Now they feel that they are not chasing a shadow only and a bright tomorrow is waiting for them. Due to the inspiration of Dr. Ambedkar Dalits are inspired to take the leadership of anti caste movements into their fold without telling either Hinduism or the congress party middle with their affairs. So, in this way the events those are narrated in the Memoir throw light on the lives of Dalits with the help of Damu and his family. It does not go deeply into the inter caste differences that existed among the Dalits but it highlights the situation of Ozar village. In that village there are so many untouchable castes like Mahar, Chamar, Dhor and Mang. But the castes differences are not so much rigid in the cities as in the villages. Damu also realizes the same thing when he goes to city. He thinks that city has brought touchability to his life. In his village people keeps him away while offering them food but in city Gora Sahib treats him like a human being. He also suspects that may be sahib is not aware about his caste and does not know that he is untouchable. All these incidents in Mumbai make him aware of his rights as human being and dignified person. After some time when he comes back to his village for a while, he finds that the condition of his life was miserable in the city but also dignified. Now he finds more difficult to digest the inhuman behaviour of the upper caste people. But he never loses his heart and educates his children to avoid all these injustice. Dr. Narendra Jadhav realizes that it is a bitter truth of the society that whatever heights a man might scale his caste is never cast off; it remains as inseparable part of his identity. His caste always remains a cause for contempt. People now also humiliate him but in a different manner.

Conclusively, Dr. Narendra Jadhav is successful in his effort to trace the histories of Dalits and also their bitter experiences in this cruel society. He tries to give voice to voiceless people and he also attacks on the social structure of Hindu society. He also highlights the life of Indian villages and Mumbai's slums. This work ends on a note of realization that some good changes are required in the society and appeal all the suppressed and exploited communities to come together to come forward and enable themselves through education and finally stand together as human beings.

Works Cited

Dangle, Arjun. Ed. *Poisoned Bread. Translations from Modern Marathi Dalit Literature.* Mumbai: Orient Longman, 1992. Print.

'High Flier' by Ashok Mahadevan RD, Face to Face, *An interview in Reader's Digest,* October 2006. Print.

Jadhav, Narendra. *Outcaste: A Memoir.* New Delhi: Viking, 2003. Print.

Prasad, Amar Nath. "Arundhati Roy: A Novelist of the Dalit and the Deserted." Ed. Dr. Amar Nath Prasad. *Indian Novelists in English: Critical Perspectives.* New Delhi: Sarup and Sons, 2000. Print.

S. Anand. Touchable *Tales: Publishing and Reading Dalit Literature.* Pondicherry: Navayana, 2003. Print.

16

The Genetics and Lineage of Dalit Literature: History and Prospects

SEEMA RANI

The phenomena of caste and untouchability evolved over time as a result of conflict over land resources and cultural practices between a people who began arriving in India. These conflicts produced the *chaturvarna* sociological configuration. Through the doctrine of the four varnas Dr. Ambedkar rejected caste as a God-made system. He studied the Vedic texts rationally and systematically; re-examined the foundational beliefs of the caste system. Ambedkar theorized that the practice of untouchability began after the fierce struggle for dominance between the Brahmins and Buddhists. Theories such as this were put forth: *'Dalit literature is not simply literature... it is associate with a movement to bring about change ...*" (Dangle 7-8).

The term 'Dalit Literature was first used in 1958, when the first conference of Maharashtra Dalit Shitya Sangh was held at Mumbai, a movement driven by thinkers like Jyotiba Phule and Bhimrao Ambedkar. Today it is seen by many critics as an epic that portrays lives of the Dalit. It has expended the horizon of Indian literature and criticism and transformed people's preferences. Dalit literature has given a new genre to the writings of various writers.

The term Dalit means oppressed or broken; Dalit study is a growing body of works foregrounding the experience of the caste-based oppression rife in Indian society. Dalit literature is a literature of pain, suffering, agony and protest. The origin of Dalit Literature can be traced in Marathi Literature. Dalit writing brings out the trauma and suffocation of untouchables in the hands of upper class society. For thousands of year Dalit sincerely served the upper class of the society. It was the belief that this was the way of their down-trodden life. In earlier days, Dalits did not have any kind of rights. They were humiliated and rejected by the people of high cast. They did not play their roles as human beings. They were just salves.

It is at this point that the term Dalit came to be used and widely accepted as a mark of identity. Prior to this, the Dalits had been the object of naming rather than its agency. Names such as Achhut, Panchamas, Atishudras, Avarnas, Antyajas, Asparshyas, Pariahs or government designated terms—Depressed Castes or the name with apparent emancipator intentions given by Gandhi were considered as deeply humiliating or patronizing. Ambedkar envisioned a democratic community of people based on liberty equality and fraternity. Equality he contended may be 'fiction' but nonetheless one must accept it as a governing principle. A person's power is dependent on (1) physical heredity (2) social inheritance or endowment in the term of parental care education accumulation of scientific knowledge everything that enables him to be more efficient than the savage and finally (3) on his own efforts. In all these three respects men are undoubtedly unequal. But the question is *"shall we treat them as unequal because they are unequal"?* (Ambedkar 26-27). Hence the development of Dalit literature is not just a literary event but a sociological phenomenon whose significance needs to be viewed against the desirability of social change.

The best example of untouchability is the movie 'Achhut Kannya' (Untouchable Maiden). The story of this movie is written by Niranjan Pal. The movie came in 1936. The film deals with the position of Dalit girls and considered a reformist period-piece. The central story is of the unhappy love affair between Kasturi, the Harijan daughter of the railway level crossing guard Dukhia, and Pratap, the Brahmin son of the grocer, Mohan. It is a solid love story between a Bramhin boy and an untouchable' girl within the backdrop of India's cast system which separated the couple. The story based on caste system where Pratap and Kasturi come from the two ends of the social spectrum and fall in love. Although the two are evidently in love, social conventions preclude any possibility of marriage. Both of them bow to social pressures and marry someone else. Not unexpectedly, the consequences are disastrous.

The oppressed, depressed and broken people are called Dalits in the Indian society. They are called Dalits because they live under the pressure of high-classes. They are mere puppets in the hands of the people of higher society. But because of the efforts of many social reformers like—B. R. Ambedkar, Jyotiba Phule, Mahatma Gandhi etc.; this community has also rise and been progressing day-by-day. Although Dalits have risen but still there are many problems related to their existence in the present scenario.

The novels like *Untouchable, The God of Small Things, Coolie* etc. are the sagas of suffering of the protagonists respectively Bhkha, Velutha and Munoo. These novels deal with the theme of untouchability, exploitation, poverty, hunger and suffering of the Indian masses. In *Untouchable,* Mulk Raj Anand described Bakha as a *'young man of eighteen, strong and able-bodied, who does his job of cleaning the public latrines promptly and satisfactorily.'* (Anand 1). As A. S. Dasan reveals that *'Anand shows that what the world of inhumanity denies, negates and repudiates is affirmed… That the poor have which the rich do not, and they have them in spite of the innumerable hardships and humiliating experiences they endure….'* (Dasan 14) Roy has successfully described the sufferings of an untouchable hero Velutha who not only becomes the victim of cruelty of an upper-caste family but have to pay the cost of his life. Like Roy, Anand has also presented a truthful portrayal of his untouchable hero Bakha.

There are many writers in Indian writing in English who have dealt with the theme of untouchability. But nobody is able to come nearer to Mulk Raj Anand. He has depicted the harsh reality and dark side of life. The theme of suffering caused by vicious circumstances in life has been realistically depicted and the heroic struggle of the central figures, against heavy odds, raises these novels to the lofty heights. Both the heroes—Bakha of *Untouchable* and Munno of *Coolie* may be rightly called the un-heroic heroes. Neither they belong to the upper caste nor they are kings or princes. They are just instruments in the hands of the fate. These protagonists are from dust and dirt. They are too meek to report against the evil forces which tend to suppress them and their likes. The portrayal of Bakha in the novel is so realistic and convincing that it imparts to the work a new meaning and depth. Bakha, it must be noted, is both an individual as well as a type. As the title of the novel *Untouchable* does not have a definite article 'the' before the novel, Bakha seems to be a representative untouchable exemplifying the predicament of not only a specific untouchable but also of dispossessed men everywhere.

Anand has a remarkable sympathy for his hero who symbolizes the predicament of a miserable victim pitted against the forces of orthodoxy. But Bakha has no tragic status other than his status as a scapegoat and a victim, tyrannized by a recalcitrant society. He is simultaneously a rebel and a victim. His anguish becomes our anguish, his sorrow becomes our sorrow. Thus Anand has successfully made him a hero which is not like actual filmy heroes. Alaster Niven comments that in the destiny of Bhaka, *"the novelist has dramatized the theme of social reality and theme of untouchability….."* (Niven 56).

Two textual representations of Dalits by non-non Dalit women writers represent ability of Dalit experience by those outside the social formation, but imaginatively, intellectually and empathetically are able to connect with it: Velutha in Arundhati Roy's *God of Small Things* and Shanta Rameshwar Rao's Kittu in *Children of God.*

Dalit literature must have been published earlier but it was really only in 1980-81 when the anti-reservation agitation took places that the production of Dalit literature gathered momentum. The literature assumed a rebellious tone and set the stage for the revolutionary Dalit literary movement. With the publication and circulation of Gujarati Dalit Varta, Gujarati mainstream literature (non-Dalit literature) negotiated a new turn which changed its course. A storm was created in the psyche of conservative and orthodox Gujarati mainstream writers, many eyebrows were raised. With aesthetically written stories becoming available, opponents of Dalit literature had no sheathe their blunt swords.

The genre of prose was enriched with interesting use of dialects judicious depiction of events as well as various innovative and subtle descriptive narrative styles. Similarly Dalit poetry was appreciated for its originality of themes. The short stories in Gujarati Dalit Varta preceded by the harvest of Dalit poetry were instrumental in providing impetus to evolutionary awareness in Gujarati Dalit literature. Credit duly goes to the founder of Rangdwar publishing house Shri Raguvur Chaudhary and the editors of the anthology and last but not the least to the short story writers. This may rightly be considered the first step in the direction of the evolutionary consciousness in Gujarati Dalit literature.

There are at present, about seventy to eighty writers actively engaged in Dalit Literature by writing poetry and prose. About twenty five of these not only create literature that is excellent even from the aesthetic point of view but that which is also better than non-Dalit literature also. A glance through Dalit short stories is enough to prove the point. Among Dalit writers in Gujarat Joseph Mackwan, Dalpat Chauhan, Pravin Gadhavi, Madhukant, Sahil Parmar, Raju Solanki, Shankar Painter, Dr. Pathik Parmar, Arvind Vegda, Kesharshivarn, Daksha Damodara, Dharmabhai Shrimali, Chandraben Shrimali, Ramanbhai Vankar, Balkrishana Anand, Prof. Mansukh Gajjan, Prof. Rupalee Burke, Harish Mangalam, Priyanka Kalpit, Mina Kamle, Prof. Ratilal Rohit, Dr. Vinod Gandhi, Kantilal Katil, Tikesh Makwana, Tushar Parmar, Dinu Bhadresariya are wholly committed to the Dalit cause. On the other hand Dashrath Parmar, Mavji Maheshwari, Jayant Parmar, Raman Vaghela, Manish Parmar, Shailesh Christie, Hari Par, Kisan Sosa, A. K. Dodia write both Dalit and non-Dalit literature.

In modern times, there is a mighty chasm between the majority casts and the Dalit population—often known in the west as "untouchables"—a strong group which is still considered to be unworthy, impure and unfit. Even today, its members are routinely excluded from temples and made to use separate eating utensils from other Hindus. In a bid to escape this humiliation, many are converting to Buddhism. In December 2006, under external pressure, Prime Minister Manmohan Singh admitted that "untouchability" remains a "blot on humanity." The subjugation of the Dalits forms an instinctive part of the rest of India's sense of superiority and self-worth.

Despite India's constitutional commitment to equality, the sufferings of the Dalit lower people, in India, are routinely ignored by the government and affluent classes. But time has got a change. One enterprising group of Dalits, based in Pune in the western state of

Maharashtra, has been turning to the internet for relief. It has set up help lines, created press kit and thrown resources into exploring underreported incidents, interviewing people on the spot, taking pictures, writing up their findings.

Later on the Feminist Movement gave some relief to the women's writings and rights and dared to bring them forward because they have been marginalized for so long. Hira Bansode is one of the famous writers of Dalit Literature at the present time. Her father was a worker in the Bombay municipality and her mother was a simple and illiterate housewife. Bansode has won recognition as a Dalit writer. She uses her poetry to portray the reality of women at the cross-section of class, caste and gender. Her poems also challenge the validity of the male dominated society. In 2002, she was given the Maharashtra Government's highest award, Keshvut. Her poems, originally written in Marathi have been translated in English and some other Indian Languages. The poem 'Woman' written by Hira Bansode is one of the greatest poems in which the poetess expresses the Idea that the relationship between man and woman must be on the principle of equality.

There is a long line of women writers, both of great quality and depth like Kamala Markandaya, Nayantara Sehgal, Ruth Parwar Jhabvala, Santha Rama Rao, Attia Hussain, Padmini Sen Gupta, Nargis Dalal, Marinalini Srabai, Anita Desai to mention a few. As Shashi Iyer comments *"The women novelists have made a defiant contribution in their intuitive and clear perception of a women's role in society and her problems.*" (Femina 2 Jan, 1976)

The fact that religion, class, race and colour do make the vital difference in the condition of women was proved soon. These women writers portrayed the characters of the women existing in the Indian society. Women in these societies are perceived to be warm gentle, decent, dependent and ready to accept anything imposed by man and able to adjust to any situation. In fact, these kinds of women are preferred, while women who are of an independent nature, bold, brave and dominating are not liked and accepted by these societies.

In spite of this, the increase of women writers writing in English in the India has also greatly contributed to the development of women. Many social reformers have emerged who have worked hard to raise the status of women and it is due to their efforts that women have started emerging in all the spheres of life like science, technology, politics, sports, cinema, media etc.

Dalit writers are in the true sense, whether they are male or female, sentinels of humanity who vehemently protest against injustice. A great responsibility of social concern lies on the shoulders of the Dalit writer compared to the mainstream writer. Hence, it is difficult to write Dalit Literature. More so because sustained effect need to be made to ensure that the edge of commitment is not blunted in striving to maintain aesthetic standards. God never make any difference between a touchable and an untouchable, between the rich and the poor, between the rough and the sublime. The poor and oppressed are also the significant component of the nation. In other words Dalit Literature is the mirror of the society.

Works Cited

Ambedkar, B. R. *Annihilation of Caste*; New Delhi: Critical Quest, 2007. Print.

Anand, Mulk Raj. *Untouchable.* New Delhi: Arnold Heinemann, 1981. Print.

Dangle Arjun. Ed. *Poisoned Bread: Translations from Modern Marathi Dalit Literature.* Bombay: Orient Longman. Print.

Dasan, A.S. "The Art of Being Human: Critical Realism in the Novels of Charles Dickens and Mulk Raj Anand." *The Journal of Indian Writing in English.* 32: 1 (January) 2004. Print.

Iyer, Shashi. *An Introduction to Indo English Fiction.* (Femina 2 Jan, 1976)

Niven, Alaster. *The York of Pity: A Study in the Fictional Writings of Mulk Raj Anand.* New Delhi: Arnold Heinemann, 1978. Print.

17

The Orchestrated Voice of the Marginalized in Raja Rao's *Kanthapura*

VISHALI SHARMA AND DR. RATAN BHATTACHARJEE

The portrayal of the marginalized class in *Kanthapura* of Raja Rao is unique. He creates the heroic character from the Brahminic society but through him the marginalized are united to involve themselves in a two-edged fight against exploitation and oppression. Moorthy throws his gauntlet against the staunch supporters of casteism of pre-independent Indian villages and motivates the marginalized to fight against the British unitedly.

The dearth of study of the marginalized voice in Indian English literature necessitates the portrayal of the oppressed people in the pre-independent era. A new understanding of the correlation between the fight for freedom on the one hand and against upper caste people on the other was required. The story of Raja Rao's *Kanthapura* is more suited to the needs and aspirations of the marginalized people of India although the backdrop is here the village of *Kanthapura.* The prevalent social and cultural norms needed a strong resistance when the society suffered stagnation. The jolt should come from within and an impetus for social regeneration was the need of the hour. While going to study the life and culture of the marginalized people we are to keep in mind that Raja Rao's views are imbued with implicit and explicit doctrinal assumptions. He shows a sensibility to the struggle of people in this society which is dominated by the rigorous Brahiminic rules and customs. In *Kanthapura* his depiction of Gandhian philosophy and political viewpoints is made relevant to the expressive competence of the marginalized people.

The novelist brings the causes and effects leading to the age-old existence of oppression and despair of the lives of marginalized class of nation's vast population under a scanner. Raja Rao's *Kanthapura* is not known as 'the novel for the Marginalised', but the marginalized classes of people who at first were locked in slumber and then roused to unite against the exploitation of the British rulers are given a loud voice. The fight of the marginalized in this novel was two-fold: first, the marginalized had to fight against the caste system which is responsible for their subjugation and secondly they had to fight against the British rulers. In the second fight the marginalized had to join the Brahminical society. However, before the rise of Moorthy as a leader, the Pariahs were separated from the Brahiminic society. But when Moorthy, following the Gandhian principles wanted the pariahs to join him, the fight was stronger against the British. Thus, *Kanthapura* emerges as a loud voice of the marginalized people and their fights against oppression and exploitation in both shorter and longer terms. Here the character depiction of Moorthy was very significant. He himself belongs to the Brahminic society. But he is no less a rebel against the age old caste system as a devoted follower of Gandhi.

The literature for the marginalized obviously focuses on the caste system and untouchability in India. It matures with a sociological point of view. Marginality was deeply rooted in inequality which causes insecurity, injustice and exploitation. Marginalized sections were always on the periphery and distanced from the power centers. The people whom Gandhi called 'harijans', they were on the marginalized 'other' side of the Indian society. So, when they started voicing after centuries of silence, about themselves, the assertion of human rights becomes most prominent. Self-pride, revolt against social injustice, chronicles of personal and collective suffering, and hopes and aspirations for a new society devoid of discrimination were encouraged. The British used the term 'Dalits' to mean people belonging to the Scheduled Castes and Tribes. Marginalized are the 'depressed classes', and it has similar connotation like that of Dalits Some of the important writers specialized in voicing the pangs of the marginalized in literature are: Mahasweta Devi, Namdeo Dhasal, Daya Pawar, Arjun Dangle, Sachi Rautray, Rabi Singh, Basudev Sunani, Bama, Abhimani, and Poomani, Imayam. They threoritised the struggle of the poor people along Marxist line of thinking. But R. K. Narayan's *Kanthapura* is amazingly and unexpectedly a celebration of Gandhism and without much theoritisation becomes a faithful portrayal of the tragic stories of the marginalized. It is a new chapter virtually started with the depiction of the caste ridden people of *Kanthapura.* The novel beautifully shows how these people are roused from their age old stupor and slumber and politicalised against the British exploiters in the wake of freedom movement under the leadership of Moorthy who is a rural replica of Gandhi in the novel.

A group is made marginal in the larger social mechanism and a vast section is relegated to a lower status simply on the ground of caste and creed. The unjust treatment of the minority or minorities and weaker individuals or groups by the majority or stronger group of the rest of the society for the supposed benefit of the concerned stronger group or groups initiates the primary basis for marginalization. This segment of population is segregated from the mainstream of society and sometimes obliged to stay on the fringes or outskirts. The blanket exclusion of these people from the mainstream of society or national life makes them more marginalized. They are victims of harassment and fabricated police case and sometimes their citizenship too is doubted. Thus along with material deprivation, marginalized individuals are also excluded from services plan-programs and policies of a nation. The negation of an entire race occurs and the oppressive story brings with it pain, sorrow, bloodshed and death.

The basic myth of marginalization is that some people simply because they belong to Brahminic society are 'more equal' enjoying a cultural superiority. They pose to be more intelligent and more virtuous than the marginalized. On psychological level, upper caste identity is automatically equated with cultural superiority. The process of assimilation is hampered by this marginalization and all these happened in Indian rural areas in the pre-Independent period. Gandhiji knew that unless the vast segment of the marginalized people is united, real fight against the Britishers cannot begin. So in *Kanthapura*, Moorthy encouraged the assimilation process first by going to the Pariah quarters. He wanted to bring them to the mainstream of the movement that he is going to start. He shows his sensitive awareness of the cumulative shame as well as anger of the marginalized.

In *Kanthapura*, Moorthy the Brahmin young man worked for building effective resistance to the Brahmanic hegemony. He also worked the mobilization of the marginalized masses for assertion, protest. There are characters like Waterfall Venkamma and others who raise their voices loud against the Brahminic society. Moorthy had to go to the Pariah houses and take food there to show oneness with the marginalized. The very terms 'marginalized' or 'Dalits' give a sub human status to the poor people who are always kept outside the Hindu social order. Now, the subaltern communities found a new name by coming together with the perspective of the Fourth World literature. The term 'Marginalized' rejects the sub-human status imposed on the poor people by the Hindu social order.

Raja Rao in *Kanthapura* questioned the mainstream literary theories and upper caste ideologies and explored the neglected aspects of life. A good story teller, Raja Rao appears to be totally without any theory to impose on his readers. But telling is doing. He makes use of the language of the out-castes and under-privileged in Indian society. Shame, anger, sorrow and indomitable hope are the stuff of subaltern literature. Because of the anger against the age-old oppression, the expression of the writer becomes sharp. This is done on the individual level and the community level. Dr. Jugal Kishore Mishra rightly points out in his article 'A Critical Study of Dalit Literature in India: Dalit literature questioned the mainstream literary theories and upper caste ideologies and explored the neglected aspects of life. Dalit literature is experience-based. This 'anubhava' (experience) takes precedence over 'anumana' (speculation). Thus to Dalit writers, history is not illusionary or unreal as Hindu metaphysical theory may make one to believe.

Moorthy like Gandhi believes that politics and religion are inevitably interlinked. Through the depiction of the political, social and the religious aspects Raja Rao gives a faithful record of a village community. Mohit Ray observes in Moorthy as "the confluence of the three strands of experience that make up the action of *Kanthapura*—the political, the social, and the religious" (285). Moorthy's *Kanthapura* illustrates the

Gandhian rejection of Hindu caste system. The inspiration given by Gandhi stirred even the remote villages which discarded the artificial and hierarchical distinction perpetrated in the name of caste system. The novel shows how the Kenchamma temple is opened to the paraiahs and this is absolutely a picturisation of the Gandhian principle of equality of human beings before God. Pariahs have the same access to the temple as the Brahimins and the upper class people. Thus, Gandhian ideals envelop also enlightens the Indian spirit, the equitable status of human beings in the society. Moorthy is Gandhian in many things. He encourages people to resist colonialism by discarding his city clothes and adopting kadhi clothing. He unites in his fight against the Britishers all classes of people. What Gandhiji did in India is done in *Kanthapura* by Moorthy and here India in macrocosm is found in microcosm of *Kanthapura.*

Many depict the pangs of marginalization but Raja Rao shows that empowerment which involves development of capacities is also needed. The empowerment of the marginalized is also suggested in *Kanthapura* through the political, social, economic or spiritual strength of individuals and communities. *Kanthapura*, the "dynamo" of the Gandhian ideals conveys the new message that propelled the freedom struggle against the British. But this is done through the orchestraion of the voices of the marginalized people of *Kanthapura.* Gandhi's 'harijan' myth in a broader sense is a moral support for the marginalized which we find in the efforts of Moorthy. Iyengar identifies, in *Kanthapura,* the "veritable grammar of the Gandhian myth." The novel demonstrates two faces of Gandhian vision: the social and the political. Moorthy's friends and followers made him aware about the consequences which he might encounter for going against the Brahmin statutes. Here in lies Moorthy's heroism and he cares the least about such warning. Human welfare over casteism is foremost in his mind. Man has made caste and it is not divine. Therefore, he works hard to empower the lives of harijans or the marginalized.. The villagers counter the Brahmin subjugation: "Why should not Pariah, Ranchamma and Sampanna learn to read and write? They shall, And Bade Khan can wave his beard and twist his moustache. What is a policeman before Gandhi's man? Does a boar stand before a lion or a jackal before an elephant?" (*Kanthapura* 37)

The portrayal of Moorthy's communication with the marginalized and his efforts to orchestrate them into the Freedom movement is fraught with an ironic meaning. The resistance comes from his own mother. Moorthy's mother, Narasaama feared a possible danger for her son's life. Swami Narasamma says: "He is mixing with the Pariahs as a veritable Mohammedan, and the Swami has sent word through Bhatta to say that the whole of *Kanthapura* will be excommunicated… he can go sleep with these Paraiah whores… but let him not call himself a Brahman" (*Kanthapura* 57-8). She is heartbroken and Moorthy's defiance of her brought her to the verge of death. Narasamma dies. But the fight continues Moorthy is a revolutionary in his challenge against the age old ideas. A Brahmin hero voices the cry of the marginalized people.

Another aspect is linked to Moorthy's charismatic struggle. Women who had that time been marginalized are also brought the forefront and they sacrificed their homely duties to join the movement. He convinces the women in *Kanthapura* to maintain the national cause by spinning their own clothes as advocated by Gandhi. We should do our duty. If not, it is no use belonging to the Gandhi-group.' Rangamma says, 'That is right, sister,' and we say, 'We shall not forget our children and our husbands.' But how can we be like we used to be? Now we hear this story and that story, and we say we too shall organize a—cloth boycott like at Sholapur, we too, shall go picketing cigarette shops and today ships, and we say our *Kanthapura*, too, shall fight for the Mother (*Kanthapura* 110). Moorthy's success is that he convinces the marginalized people of *Kanthapura* to follow Gandhi.

Works Cited

Augustine, Thomas. "The Village in Raja Rao's *Kanthapura.*" Encyclopaedia of Literature in English. Ed. K. Bhatnagar. New Delhi: Atlantic Publishers and Distributors, 2001. 1542-1553. Print.

Dayal, P. *Raja Rao: A Study of His Novels.* New Delhi: Atlantic Publishers & Distributors, 1991. Print.

Iyengar, Srinivasa K. R. *Indian Writing in English.* New Delhi: Sterling Publishers Pvt. Ltd., 1993. Print.

Mishra, Jugal Kishore Mishra 'A Critical Study of Dalit Literature in India' (http://www.sasnet.lu.se/EASASpapers/4JugalKishore.pdf)

Mondal, Anshuman. "The Ideology of Space in Raja Rao's *Kanthapura.*" *Journal Commonwealth Literature.* 34:1 (1999). 103-114. Print.

Mukherjee, Meenakshi. *The Twice Born Fiction: Themes and Techniques of the Indian Novel in English.* Delhi: Arnold Heinemann, 1974. Print.

Patil, Mallikarjun. "Kanthapura: A Potrait of Village Gandhi." *The Fiction of Raja Rao.* Eds. Rajeshwar Mittapalli & Pier Paolo Piciucco. New Delhi: Atlantic Publishers and Distributors, 2001. 112-117. Print.

Raja, Rao. *Kanthapura.* Oxford University Press: Delhi, 2005. Print.

Ray, Mohit K. Ed. *The Atlantic Companion to Literature in English.* New Delhi: Atlantic Publishers & Distributors, 2007. Print.

Sekhar, Ajay S. *Representing the Margin: Caste and Gender in Indian Fiction.* Delhi: Kalpaz Publications, 2008. Print.

Sharma, Kaushal. *Raja Rao: A Study of His Themes and Technique.* New Delhi: Sarup & Sons, 2005. Print.

18

State Apparatus, Repression and Resistance: A Critical Study of Bama's *Karukku*

DR. SOHEL AZIZ

Recent increasing interest in studying Dalit literature in India shows the concerns of academicians, theorists and critics to reposition and restructured the depressing social condition of Dalit class in every sphere of life for ages in the name of social class division. These academicians along with the writers belonging to Dalit community focus on the severe plight of oppressed people and critically analyse different issues like their class consciousness, identity formation, liberation and development in their much deeper academic discussions and writings. Many Dalit writers have questioned the validity of this social division, investigated in the patterns, apparatuses involved and functioning of oppression system, and sought a justified restructured society that may liberate them from the clutch of oppression.

Mostly Dalit writings are full of narrative accounts of author's first hand experiences of their lives and surroundings which emphasize on the collaboration of higher class and state agents that enable this perpetual oppression for the sake of selfish interest of higher class. Bama, pen name of Faustina Mary Fatima Rani, the first Tamil Dalit woman writer, has written her autobiography *Karukku* in which she poignantly depicts the lives and experiences of a Christian Dalit community, the Parayar community, their oppression in the hands of upper class people, and her personal journey from an identity less woman to self conscious entity that determines to raise the voices of oppressed people in a desperate effort to draw the attention of critics and thinkers—to expose the reality of the liaison of upper class people and state apparatus and how they jointly perpetuate the suppression of a Dalit community in the village.

Unlike other autobiographies, the main focus of Bama's *Karukku* is not her own life chronicles rather it is a vivid account of her community and village and their day to day life for which it has been considered one of the classics of Dalit autobiographies. Bama leaves the confessional tone of autobiography and positions herself in the "I" which is not the individual identity of Bama but it is the identity of the whole community in which she relocates her own self as a part of greater self. Thus from the very beginning Bama focuses on the formation of identity of a Dalit community through the eyes of a child.

The main hindrance in this identity formation is the predominant ideology of the society of which the community is a part and accepts its fate as it is. It is not a mere fact that Bama gives a detail account of the conflict between the Parayar community and the upper class; rather it is an instrument through which she focuses on the apparatuses through which the existing notion of ideology is presumably propagated in society for the benefits of higher class people and believed and accepted by the Dalit. Bama in her autobiography shows the various ways of propagating and formation of ideology and points out implicitly as well as directly to the various repressive state apparatuses and ideological state apparatuses that help the higher class people in this oppression of Dalit community. The function of literature is a true representation of society and Bama successfully presents the mirror of society in a well documented form.

Louis Althusser, a French Marxist philosopher, in his much anthologized essay "Ideology and Ideological State Apparatuses" has discussed the relation between means of production and reproduction of means of production in social formation and revised the concept of state and state apparatuses given by Karl Marx who has focused earlier only on the state apparatuses by which he means only repressive state apparatuses that help a capitalist or feudal society to continue its production and profit. But Althusser elaborates several state apparatuses and differentiates between the repressive state apparatuses and ideological state apparatuses.

For Althusser, ideology was not a passive relation between the economic base and superstructure, but a pervasive set of dynamic conditions suffusing the institutional apparatus of the state and shaping not just the idea of the person *as subject*, but more importantly for theorists to follow, clarifying in structural terms the idea of a *subject position*, wherein political and psychological forces converge to define possibilities of action and forces of constraint and repression. After distinguishing between 'use of the state apparatuses' and 'State power', he adds on further to classify different types of state apparatuses and says that there are two types of state apparatuses: Repressive State Apparatuses (RSA) and Ideological State Apparatuses (ISA). The former "function massively and predominately *by repression* (including physical repression)" (Althusser 145) while the latter "function massively and predominately *by ideology*" (Althusser 145). Althusser's particular interest here is in the functioning of the various ISAs which, although diverse (they are, he says, "multiple, distinct, 'relatively autonomous' and capable of providing an objective field to contradictions which express... the effects of the clashes between the capitalist class struggle and the proletarian class struggle" [Althusser 149]), are unified by their common function: subtending the dominant ideology and, thus, the interests of the ruling class. The RSAs function to secure the "political conditions of the reproduction of relations of production" (Althusser 149), which are "relations of exploitation" (Althusser 150), via media of repression that range from "the most brutal physical force, via mere administrative commands and interdictions, to open and tacit censorship" (Althusser 150). The ISAs function to secure the same goal (that is, the "reproduction of the relations of production, i.e. of capitalist relations of exploitation" [Althusser 154]) behind the "'shield'" (Althusser 150) provided by the RSAs by inculcating in all members of society and naturalizing the dominant ideology which is that of the ruling class. Each ISA accomplishes this function "in the way proper to it" (Althusser 154): the political ISA "by subjecting individuals to the political State ideology" (Althusser 154); the communications ISA "by cramming every 'citizen' with daily doses of nationalism, chauvinism, liberalism, moralism, etc. by means of the press, the radio and television" (Althusser 155); etc. "This concert is dominated by a single score...: the score of the Ideology of the current ruling class which integrates into its music the great themes of the Humanism of the Great Forefathers" (Althusser 154).

Further, Althusser mentions that ISAs inculcates the dominant ideology of the State in such a way that subject unconsciously and willingly accepts without questioning it. He says that the [i]ndividual is interpellated as a (free) subject in order that he shall submit freely to the commandments of the Subject, i.e in order that he shall (freely) accept his subjection, i.e. in order that he shall make the gestures and actions of his subjection 'all by himself.' There are no subjects except by and for their subjection. (Althusser 182)

Obviously, Althusser for the first time clearly defines the role of State in the oppression of subjects and if the subject is Dalit then all the machinery of State actively becomes functioning in the process of oppression as to reproduce the means of production as these Dalits are not only acquiescent in their ideology easily but also they consider it as their fate.

Bama, through the experiences and daily activities of her community, actually shows this process of 'interpellation' of the Dalit community and the functioning of State for making them 'subject' through different State apparatuses. Critics have focused on her treatment of women characters in feminist angle, social position of Dalit community, their formation of Dalit consciousness, identity, political consciousness, and issues of testimonials but little attraction has been drawn on the issue of the role of State apparatuses in the oppression of her community for the interest of the higher class.

When Bama was eleven years old, she narrated, there was a dispute between the Parayar community, the Dalit community, and the higher class people, the Chaaliyar community, regarding the ownership of cemetery in which the Parayar people bury their dead. This cemetery was situated beside the school of the higher class people and they wanted to encroach the cemetery for making it their playground. Since the Chaaliyars were more powerful and wealthy people, they easily took the police, the State agents, on their side by bribing and arranging feast for them. When the Parayar people retaliated after the incident of stabbing a Dalit man by the Chaaliyar, the higher class people fabricated a false story and used the police force to oppress the helpless and poor Parayar people. Bama has given a detail and tragic account of the torture police rendered on the Dalit people after trapping them near the field. Without investigating the real incident and truth, police force cracked on the Parayar people and the vicious torture forced them to flee from the village. Parayar men were rounded up and arrested and those who were hiding up in nearby villages or mountain were tracked down and tortured. The headman of the village was hiding in Bama's house but he was also arrested. Even the priest of the local church also informed about a man who was hiding in the church and got him arrested. The terror of vicious torture was such that nobody could sleep that night. Bama writes: "All through the night the police prowled and round our streets. There was no sound at all, except for the sound of policemen's boots and the barking of the dogs. The very sound of the boots was frightening. Each step felt as if the boot was treading on my chest and pressing down." (Bama 36-37) Even women were not spared from the torture. To make the situation worst, women were harassed by the police in the absence of their husbands. Bama says:

> It seems the police behaved deplorably towards the women as they went from house to house. They used obscene language and swore at them, told them that since their husbands were away they should be ready to entertain the police at night, winked at them, and shoved their guns their bodies. (Bama 40)

The purpose of all these torture is to crush their courage and audacity of fighting against a higher class people and break them from the inside so that the Dalit people will not be able to raise their voice in future. Since they were very poor they could not arrange their bail. The women share their money to get their husbands out in bail and fight for justice in court. The use of RSAs against the Dalit community is significant as the Dalits are supposed to follow the order of their 'masters' but instead of following it they unite and fight back against the higher class to save their graveyard. This act of revolt, though very little, is in actuality the resistance they have put after the generations of suppression and this revolt must be suppressed to make them acquiescent to the prevailing norms of casteism and social division. Despite the heavy cracking down by the police force, the Parayar community, in their pursuit of resistance and to acquire their right, arranges money to fight the case in court and finally their resistance has earned them the verdict of court in their favour. Bama declares:

> They treat us in whatever way they choose, as if we are slaves who don't even posses human dignity. And if ever a Dalit gets wise to this and wants to live with some honour and self-respect, they jump up and down as if something really outrageous is happening. They seem to conspire us in our place to think that we who have worked throughout history like beasts, should live and die like that; we should never move on or go forward. (Bama 27-28)

The RSAs are significant for the use of oppressive forces in their suppression but the use of ISAs by the State is more significant as the subject never becomes aware of the deplorable condition and thinks it as the natural rule. Bama focuses and criticizes these ISAs in her autobiography and raises pertinent questions against the prevailing ideology propagated by the State through its various agents. She points out:

> Because Dalits have been enslaved for generation upon generation, and been told again and again of their degradation, they have come to believe that they are degraded, lacking honour and self-worth, untouchable; they have reached a stage where they themselves, voluntarily, hold themselves apart. This is the worst injustice. This is what even little babies are told, how they are instructed. The consequence of all this is that there is no way for Dalits to find freedom or redemption. (Bama 28)

Though many theorists believe the Church as the main instrument in propagating the prevailing ideology in the society but Louis Althusser believes that it is not the Church rather the education system in the capitalist society is the most dominant form of instrument as it directly preaches to conform with the prevailing social codes and prepare them as the means of reproduction in the society. He argues that the "School-Family couple has replaced the Church-Family couple" (Althusser 154) of previous epochs:

> It takes children from every class at infant-school age, and then for years, the years in which the child is most 'vulnerable,' squeezed between the

> family State apparatus, it drums into them, whether it uses new or old methods, a certain amount of 'know-how' wrapped in the ruling ideology (French, arithmetic, natural history, the sciences, literature) or simply the ruling ideology in its pure state (ethics, civic instruction, philosophy). (Althusser 155)

And Bama in her autobiography has been very critical and invective against the role of education system as well as religion or the Church in the Dalit Community for the manipulation of information and teachings imparted among the students in order to keep them in the darkness and make them a proper 'subject' in terms of the ruling class.

Christianity, unlike Hinduism, is a casteless religion the principle of which is based upon love, equality, fraternity and justice for all as Jesus Christ did not recognize any division on the basis of caste, class or wealth. In spite of accepting Christianity, Parayar community is actually facing the same caste division and suppression in the name of religion and has been treated as Dalit even by the Priest. Their condition has not been improved because of this discriminatory treatment. Bama depicts that the Dalit Christians are not allowed to sing in the church choir; they are forced to sit separately to avoid any sort of physical touch with the upper caste Christians, and even they are not allowed to bury their dead in the same cemetery within the village rather they are forced to use a separate cemetery at the outskirts of the village. The Paraiyars who converted to Christianity in order to escape casteist oppression at the hands of orthodox Hinduism are shown to be greatly disillusioned as they are not able to escape caste oppression within the church fold.

Even later on when Bama enters the Church convent after being inspired by the Biblical tenets and with noble purpose to improve the condition of Dalit children, she experiences utterly different life as the none of the nuns from upper class are following the actual teachings of the Bible and all of them are leading their life lavishly. Even within the nunnery the same hierarchical system has been followed and nuns belonging to upper classes held the higher position within the Church whereas Bama and other nuns from Dalit community do the menial jobs. Disillusioned by the hypocrisy of the Church and its functioning in the society, Bama observes:

> [i]t is clear that they are all from upper castes. They are the ones who are in the positions of power.... These few assume power, control the dispossessed and the poor by thrusting a blind belief and devotion upon them, and by turning them into slaves in the name of God, while they themselves live in comfort. (Bama 108)

In her caustic criticism of the way of the Church she exposes how the Church robs the poor, and deliberately instils wrong teachings about religion so that the ruling class can control the Dalits. She says, "They teach them to shackle their arms together and to prostrate themselves in prayer at full length on the ground so that they should never stand tall... They make themselves into gods so that they can exploit others" (Bama 108).

But Bama, after experiencing all sorts of hypocrisies, discrepancies, and fraudulences inside the Church, realizes the ideology of the ruling class and raises her voice against such discrimination. She asserts that now Dalits have realized this deception and they "have learnt that these other have never respected them as human beings, but bent the religion to their benefit, to maintain their own falsehoods" (Bama 109). Education, as the most important and dominant instrument of shaping the ideology of Dalits, is also being used after altering the teachings and sayings of Jesus Christ. As most of the Dalit boys and girls cannot afford to go in the best schools of the town, they have to depend on the school run by the Church where besides education they also get meal which is used as a trick to allure the poor students to attend the school. The whole purpose of imparting knowledge has been, thus from the very beginning, politicized. The little education whatever they are getting is in reality the foundation process for appropriating the 'subject' to eligible and trained slaves. In school the nuns never tell them any cheerful stories but only stories of devil, demon and evil power to subdue them with fear.

Even good schools run by Catholic nuns and priests deny admission of Dalit students on the pretext that "if they take Dalit children, their standards will fall. They marginalize all of us as being of poor quality" (Bama 119). This denial of admission is actually denial of higher education to the Dalit students like the author herself and thus deny them any opportunity of enlightenment and liberty from oppression. Nuns in those schools have taken the vows of poverty, chastity and obedience before starting their lives as nuns but in reality, "the vows become a means of control and enslavement" (Bama 113). But Bama after being inspired by her father and elder brother continues her higher education despite discrimination and later on realizes the differences between what the Church and schools teach them and what is truth. After reading the Bible she has come to know about the deception and manipulation of teachings that she puts in very sensitive words:

> All those people who had taught us, had taught us only that God is loving, kind, gentle, one who forgives sinners, patient, tender, humble, obedient. Nobody had ever insisted that God is just, righteous, is angered by injustices, opposes falsehood, never countenances inequality. There is a great deal of difference between this Jesus and the Jesus who is made known through daily pieties. The oppressed are not taught about him, but rather, are taught in an empty and meaningless way about humility, obedience, patience, gentleness. (Bama 104)

Thus, she has decided that every Dalit should read the Bible to unmask the hypocrisy of the Church and the education system.

Karukku is a seminal work in the Dalit writings that traces the different means and apparatuses to propagate the ruling ideologies among the Dalits. Bama's self consciousness and eagerness to repositioning the Dalit identity compels her to wage war against these state apparatuses in very strong and rebellious words. She declares:

> We who are asleep must open our eyes and look about us. We must not accept the injustice of our enslavement by telling ourselves it is our fate, as if we have no true feelings; we must dare to stand up for change. We must crush all these institutions that use caste to bully us into submission, and demonstrate that among human beings there are none who are high or low. Those who have found their happiness by exploiting us are not going to let us go easily. It is we who have to place them where they belong and bring about a changed and just society where all are equal. (Bama 28)

Undoubtedly, Bama's voice of resistance has not been remained unheard and unanswered; and a new era envisioned by Bama will surely herald to epitomize fraternity, equality and liberty in society.

Works Cited

Althusser, Louis. "Ideology and Ideological State Apparatuses." *Lenin and Philosophy, and Other Essays.* Trans. Ben Brewster. London: New Left Books, 1971. 127-188. Print.

Bama. *Karukku.* Trans. Lakshmi Holmstrom. Ed. Mini Krishnan. New Delhi: Oxford University Press, 2011. Print.

19

Transforming Pain into Resistance in Omprakash Valmiki's *Joothan: A Dalit's Life*

Jyoti Arora Sharma

Cultural plurality, exploitation, repression, caste-based discrimination, repression and heterogeneity have always been the central themes in Indian Dalit literature. Dalits are always considered sub-humans or animals who are deemed to bear sufferings without any protest. Indian states are gripped with racial-prejudices where Dalit and marginalized people have been exploited. Omprakash Valmiki's autobiographical novel *Joothan: A Dalit's Life* explores the problems of Dalit communities. It is a story of subjugation and repression of Valmikis who are also called as Chuhra with contempt in some parts of India. This autobiography unmasks the hellish life of the people of this caste.

"*Joothan*" word is literally called the scraps of food left on a plate as garbage for the family pet or stray animals. The scraps of food after eating are generally called Joothan and this novel is based on this theme. Omprakash Valmiki's autobiography *Joothan* was first published in Hindi in 1997. It was translated into English in 2003 by Arun Prabha Mukherjee who is a professor of English at York University in Canada. This novel is based on caste-system. Sen contends that caste is "an ever-present feature of communal and sectarian violence" (Sen 209).

J*oothan* is the story of Dalit exploitation and the setting of the novel is in a village in Gaya District in Bihar, India. The Chuhras, the most exploited class used to live segregated in this village: "Our house was adjacent to Chandrabhan Taga's gher or cowshed. Next to it lived the families of Muslim weavers. Right in front of Chandrabhan Taga's gher was a little johri, a pond which was created as a partition of between the Chuhra's dwellings and the Village" (Valmiki 1). The people of this caste were deprived of all kind of facilities. These people were called most inferior and they had no facilities. They lived alone just because they were called the mean and abject. Their girls and women also had worse situation in their homes. The women's chastity and respect was not of prime importance and that was due to economical problems faced by them as even newly-wedded women had to go to open sky to relieve themselves:

> All the women of the village, young girls, older women, even the newly married brides would sit in the open space behind these homes at the edge of the pond to take a shit. Not just under the cover of darkness but even in daylight. The purdah observing Tyagi women, their faces covered with their saris, shawls around their shoulders, found relief in this open air latrine. They sat on Dabbowali's shores without worrying about decency exposing their private parts. (Valmiki 1)

Omprakash Valmiki's novel depicts a beautiful story about the caste discrimination. The life in the jhuggi basti where Omprakash Valmiki used to live was very hard. The people of this community had to work hard throughout the day and despite of it they had to live from hand to mouth: "Our family lived in the Chuhra basti. Five brothers, one sister, two cha-chas, one tau lived separately. Everyone in the family did some other work. Even then we didn't manage to get two decent meals a day." (Valmiki 1-2)

This novel is based on especially two castes in the novel. One is upper caste known as Tyagis, the upper caste in the village and other bhangis or Chuhras called by these upper class people. The people of this upper caste were dominant in the village and the sweeper class worked under them. The latter class people generally used to live in mud-walled cottages. These people earned their livelihood by doing some inferior kind of work. Most of the people were either scavengers, grass-cutters, washer-men, water-carriers, barbers or leather-workers.

The lower castes people had to work for upper caste people and they worked like slaves under them. They had no right to ask for their wages in return. If the upper caste people have pity on them, only then they get something but they had no courage to speak in front of them for their rights. They get not even a single penny after the work for the whole day. They could not muster courage to refuse for this unpaid work which also gave them nothing but humiliation. People were not known by their names instead they were called by their caste: "We would often have to work without pay. Nobody dared to refuse this unpaid work for which we got neither money nor grain. Instead we got swarm at and abused. Omprakash calls it not a life: "What sort of a life was that? After working hard day and night, the price of our sweat was just joothan". (Valmiki 10) They did not call us by our names. If a person were older, then he would be called "Oh Chuhre". If the person was young or of the same age, then 'Abe Chuhre' was called." (Valmiki 2)

The novel focuses on the grave problem of untouchability in this novel. The people of this caste were called untouchables and they were not the part of the social system as they were not allowed to participate in any social work. So all the social works were only limited to the high class. They were, that's why, segregated from the village and lived apart in a separate basti. If anybody from the high caste unfortunately touches them, then they were beaten black and blue and the immediate bath was must for purgation as one was considered polluted by touch from this lower caste:

> Untouchability was so rampant that while it was considered all right to touch the dogs and cats or cows or buffaloes if one happened to touch a Chuhra, one got contaminated or pollution. The Chuhras were not seen as humans. (Valmiki 2)

The children of this caste were deprived of basic amenities of life and that's why there were no provisions for their education in the village. There was a different kind of class for them and that was also only for boys. A Christian priest named Sewak Ram Munshi used to come to teach reading and writing to Dalit boys only. The girls were not allowed to go to attend class. It was only Omprakash from his family who used to go to attend the class. Other brothers were set to work.

The real story of exploitation of Ompraksh starts when One day Sewak Ram Munshi and Omprakash Valmiki's father take a revolutionary step and enroll him to the Basic Primary School in the school. Om's father's name was Chhotan Lal. He had to listen a lot from the society. People comment on sending him to school:

> "What is the point of sending him to school?
> When has a crow became a swan?" (Valmiki 6)

He had to beg to the teacher to get his son admitted in the school. He said to the teacher Harphool Singh, "Materji, I will be forever in your debt if you teach this child of mine a letter or two." (Valmiki 2) But admission in the school of a low caste boy was not so easy task. The teacher puts him for next day for many days and it took a long time and only after it he got admitted. Heart-rendering story of Omprakash Valmiki's school experiences now begins from here. He had to sit segregated from the other children as there was fear of their getting polluted:

> I had to sit away from the others in the class, that too on the floor. The mat ran out before reaching the spot I sat on. Sometimes I would have to sit away behind everybody, right near the door. And the letters on the board from there seemed faded. (Valmiki 2-3)

The caste-based discrimination did not spare him in an educational institution also. Even the teachers were the supporters of it. School children call Omprakash 'Chuhre Ka' (the son of a scavenger) in the school and there was no objection from the teacher. Students thrash him without any rhyme and reason just because he belonged to the lowest class in the village. Discrimination, on the basis of caste, is clear from this horrible experience of school: "During the examinations we could not drink water from the glass when thirsty. To drink water, we had to cup our hands. The peon would pour water from way high up, lest our hands touch the glass." (Valmiki16)

This caste-discrimination reminds one of Arvind Adiga' novel *The White Tiger* where Balram Halwai goes to school with his nickname Munna and his class teacher finds this name unsuitable for him. When the teacher asks his name and he tells "Munna", then the teacher remains aghast:

> Munna? That's not a real name.
> He was right: it just meant "boy".
> "That's all I've got, sir", I said.
> It was true. I would never been given a name. (Adiga 10)

Next questions of the teacher make the reader to think how the low caste people or lower employed people have no time for their children. The women in these families are always down with one or the other disease and cannot give time for their children and men are always busy to somehow earn bread for their family. This conversation makes the situation more pathetic:

> "Didn't your mother name you?
>
> "She's very ill sir. She lies in bed and spews blood. She've got no time to name me."
>
> "And your father?"
>
> "He's a rickshaw-puller sir. He's got no time to name me." (Adiga 10)

Thus, the novel *The White Tiger* also tells the story of a new school going boy who is warmly accepted by his teacher but here in the novel *Jooothan* the story is drastically different. Omprakash is admitted in the school somehow but he is not able to learn something from the school. Two other children of the low caste were in the class. They were Ram Singh who belonged to Chamar or leather-worker class and another Sukhhan Singh who was a Jhinwar (basket-maker). So, now these were three children who became the toys for entertainment for other children. They were insulted and humiliated by students and teachers equally. They were being mocked on their dress whatever they wore: "If we went outwearing neat and clean clothes we had to hear their taunts that pierced deep inside like poisoned arrows. If we went to the school in neat and clean clothes we had to hear their taunts." (Valmiki 2-3) Not only boys but the school headmaster also did not spare them. He was also a tyrannizer. He called Omprakash one day and he makes Omprakash realized that he belongs to a low class and then passes an order that does not suit for a teacher: "All right... See that teak tree there? Go climb that tree. Break some twigs and make a broom. And sweep the whole school clean as mirror. It is often all, your family occupation" (Valmiki 4)

This exploitation does not end here and the headmaster orders him to sweep the rooms, verandah and playground the next day also. This kind of task was not fit for a boy still Omprakash did it somehow thinking that he will get a chance to sit in the class third day. But now the circumstances were not favourable for him and third day he heard the loud thundering voice of the headmaster, "Abey Chuhre ke, motherfucker, where are you hiding... your mother... Go sweep the whole playground... otherwise I will shove chilies up your arse (anus) and throw you out of the school." (Valmiki 5) This was the third day of his exploitation and while he was sweeping the playground his father coincidentally passed that way and saw his son in that bad situation. He lost his temper and he burst on the headmaster but it made no difference to the headmaster, instead he warned his father too, "Take him away from here. The Chuhra wants him educated... Go, go... Otherwise I will have your bones broken." (Valmiki 6) Adiga also depicts the same butt: "The Autobiography of a Half-Baked Indian. That's what I ought to call my life's story" (Adiga 8)

The main theme around which this play revolves is a word 'jootha' or 'left over'. The low-caste people of this village were fed on the Joothan (left-over food). The high class people of this village exploited and tortured the low-caste people and gave them only the left-over food that was destined to be thrown in dustbin.

During the occasions of marriage, pattals (plates made of leaves) were used in the villages to eat food. When the people had eaten their food and there was something left on the pattals, the people threw them in dustbin. The Chuhras of this caste had to depend on the food left on these pattals thrown by people. These pattals were also given to them with arrogance and these people used to eat Joothan with great pleasure: "During a wedding when the gusts and the baratis, the bridegrooms' party, were eating their meals, the Chuhras would sit outside with huge basket. After the baratis has eaten, the dirty pattals or leaf-plates were put in the Chuhras' basket, which they took home to save the Joothan, sticking to them. The little pieces of pooris, bits of sweetmeats and a little bit of vegetable were enough to make them happy. The joothan was eaten with a relish. The bridegroom's guests who didn't leave enough scraps on the pattals were denounced as gluttons." (Valmiki 6)

On the wedding occasion of Sudhdev Singh Tyagi's daughter, Omprakash's mother begged for some sweets from Tyagi in the hope that she may be able to feed her family with some sweets: "Chowdhriji, all of your guests have eaten and gone. Please put something on the pattal of my children. They too have waited for this day." (Valmiki 6) Sukhdev Singh did not give her any sweets and pointed at the pattals and said: "You are having a basketful of joothan. And on the top of that you want food for your children. Don't forget your place Chuhri. Pick up your basket and get going." (Valmiki 10-11) Omprakash was a boy then and he also felt so hurt and insulted that he could not forget these words his whole life: "These words of Sukhdev Singh Tyagi's penetrated my breast like a knife. They continue to singe me to this day." (Valmiki 11)

As there was no provision for education for the low caste people, hospital facility was also not there for Valmikis in the village. Omprakash had to see the death of his elder brother just because there was no provision of medication and treatment for them in the village. After his brother's death Omprakash's family had to see very tough days. When Omprakash had problem in his studies due to financial problem then his widow bhabhi offers her only anklet to sell so that Omprakash peruse his studies without any objection. Omprakash's father is moved on it and says: "No bahoo, don't sell it. I will arrange somehow and send him to school. Don't you worry. You have just the one ornament. How can we sell that too? Go and keep it." (Valmiki 14) Ultimately, he had to succumb in front of circumstances and the anklet was pawned to Vaidya Satyanarayan Sharma. In this way Om was admitted in sixth class in the school.

There was not only financial problem alone that was faced by this family. Even the society did not accept them. Another incident also took place in his life. One day Om wanted to get his uniform ironed and only a dhobi could do it. He knew his classmate was a dhobi but when he goes there he finds disappointment waiting for him:

> 'Abe Chuhre ka, where do you think you are going?' His son was standing near him.
>
> I said, 'I need to have the uniform ironed'.

> We don't wash the clothes of Chuhra-Chamars. Nor do we iron them. If we iron your clothes, then the Tagas won't get their clothes washed by us. We will lose our roti.' (Valmiki 17)

The novel also focuses on an evil of false religion. The high class students from the village school used to tease Omprakash just because he was a non-vegetarian and he ate pork. The high caste students and people in the novel on one way mock at the lower class and on the other way, they are always hungry to eat pork. In the novel many children of high caste "came in the darkness of night to the Bhangi basti to eat pork." (Valmiki 18) A money-lender named Teja Tega like pork and liquor very much. He used to give money on high interest to people and demanded Pork and liquor in return. He gave loan only to them who gave him pork and liquor. Omprakash's father had to give him pork and liquor in order to get money. He was looking like a dog while he was eating pork: "Sucking at the pork slices, his face has resembled a spotted dog's. His eyes red from drinking, had looked satanic. His interest rates were so high that one could spend a whole lifetime pay his interest, and the principal would remain untouched. Most of the residents of the Bhangi basti were drowning in debt." (Valmiki 18) the people of this basti had no image or respect of their own: "Most people of our basti suffered everything in silence. Honour and prestige had no meaning for them being threatened and controlled by the higher ups was an everyday's occurrence for the basti dwellers." (Valmiki 18)

Another problems faced by the people was really grave. Low caste people had to do the scavenging work and rainy season was like a curse for them as they had to sweep the lanes filled with mud and excreta of the human beings: "Our arms and legs would get smeared with dirt. The feet became mangy. The space between the toes filled up with reddish sores started itch. Once they started to itch, they would itch nonstop." (Valmiki 19) The rainy season came like a curse for them as they got no pure and clean water from anywhere and they had to drink dirty water of the single well available in basti for this low caste: "There was one well in our basti. People had raised money to get it cemented. Both the plinth and the parapet of the well were quite high. Despite this safeguard, the water in the well was full if long worms during the rainy season. We had no other alternative but to drink that water. We did not have the right to take water from the well of Tagas." (Valmiki 19) This Bhangi basti contained almost all mud houses. These houses were the centers of the constant fear of the loss of their lives: "We had to stay awake during these rainy nights. A fear constantly dogged us: who knew when a wall might collapse... That night a huge piece of our baithak in our basti. People were screaming and shouting (Valmiki 19)

There was no way left for these people to stay in Bhangi basti. They had to take shelter in Mamraj Tyagi's baithak. The scene of their stay is very pathetic as they had nothing to eat except rice. In the baithak, Om's mother cooked rice. The smell of rice permeated the whole baithak. Rice was eaten and mar (rice-water) was drunk with relish. The mar was a big thing for them and they liked it very much. Om was badly rebuked by his teacher when his teacher told him that in the epic *Mahabharata* Guru Dronacharya had to give the flour-mixed water to drink to his son Ashvatthama just because they had no milk. Omprakash could not stop himself at this occasion and he said: "I had the temerity to stand up and ask Master Saheb a question afterwards. So Ashwatthama was given flour mixed in water instead of milk, but what about us who had to drink mar? How come we were never mentioned in any epic? Why didn't an epic poet ever write a word on our lives?" (Valmiki 23) Omprakash's teacher, on hearing this, loses his control, screams and beats him badly:

> Darkest Kaliyug has descended upon us so that an untouchable is daring to talk back... Chuhre ke, you dare compare yourself with Dronacharya... Here take this, I will write an epic on your back (Valmiki 23).

Arvind Adiga also depicts the same butt in his novel *The White Tiger*. He considers his life a curse: 'Me and thousands of others in this country like me are half-baked, because we were never allowed to complete our schooling" (Adiga 8) Mulk Raj Anand's novel *Untouchable* also has the same theme of untouchability. This evil is prevalent in the society since ancient times. Mulk Raj Anand raises his voice through the character of Bhakha. When Omprakash was in tenth standard, he wants to score well in the exam so that he may score well in exam: "My mind was set aflame by his swearing. A fire had engulfed my inwards that day. The memories of these crimes of the Tyagis continue to smoulder deep inside me, emitting red hot heat". (Valmiki 57) But his chemistry teacher named Brajpal did not like a boy of a lower caste in his school and he lost all of his hope to secure good marks as he did not allow him to attend practices in his lab: "I felt that whenever I went to the lab for practical. Brajpal would keep me out on some pretext or the other." (Valmiki 65) Consequently, Omprakash was declared failure in the result. This narrow-minded teacher's cruel attitude brought a bleak future for Omprakash. He felt so dejected after this and lost his interest of study: "I no longer felt interested in studying. I couldn't make up my mind as to what to do next. I felt surrounded by darkness". (Valmiki 66) It was his older brother Jasbir further by saying: "Come on let this village go to hell. Come to Dehradum and study there. I will get you admitted to DAV College. Why are you worrying? You will definite pass next year". (Valmiki 66) He joined college but soon he abandoned his college and admitted in an Ordnance Factory as apprentice. His father's joy knew no bounds when he gets a news that his son has got a job. With this job he felt a bit relaxed as he got the company of books and received a monthly income of one hundred and seven rupees: "Books were my greatest friends. They kept up my morale." (Valmiki 79)

Thereafter the story of his success continued. He had the training for one year and after that he appeared for a competitive examination in which he got success. He feels elated: "The new surroundings and the new environment gave me new experiences. The hostel was huge, large enough to accommodate up to five hundred students. The rooms were very large and ten to twelve students shared a room. The students had come from different parts of the country." (Valmiki 84)

Omprakash had to face caste discrimination throughout his life. When he was in Mumbai the finds the people of Mumbai also they prey of caste discrimination. He finds them like the people of his village: "My village was divided along lines of touchability and untouchability. The situation was very bad in Dehradun and in Uttar Pradesh in general at time when I saw well-educated people in a metropolitan city like Bombay indulging in such behaviour, I felt a fountain of hot lava erupting within me". (Valmiki 95) According to Dirks, caste is "the chilling sign that India's relationship to history and tradition will necessary continue to be mediated by the colonial past." (Dirks 294) Bayly contends: "Caste as jati—to be seen as a concrete ethnographic fact of Indian life, a source of historic national strengths and organized self-improvement or "uplift." (Bayly 154) Omprakash Valmiki says that caste follows a person since his birth:

> 'Caste' is a very important element of Indian society. As soon as a person is born, 'caste' determines his or her destiny. Being born is not in the control of a person. If it were in one's control, then why would I have been born in a Bhangi household? Those who call themselves the standard—bearers of this country's great cultural heritage, did they decide which homes they would be born into? They turn to scripture to justify their position, the scriptures that establish feudal instead of promoting equality and freedom (Valmiki 134).

Works-Cited

Adiga, Arvind. *The White Tiger.* New Delhi: Harper Collins, 2009. Print.

Bayly, Susan. *The New Cambridge History of India: Caste, Society and Politics in India from the Eighteen Century to the Modern Age.* Vol. 3. Cambridge: CUP, 1999. Print.

Dirks, Nicholas B. *Castes of Mind: Colonialism and the Making of Modern India.* Princeton and Oxford: Princeton University Press, 2001. Print.

Valmikis, Omprakash. *Joothan: A Dalit's Life.* Kolkata: Samya, 2003. Print.

20

Representation of Caste in *Untouchable* and *The God of Small Things*: A Comparative Study of Bakha and Velutha

SURUCHI SHARMA AND KUSUM KANGER

Being rooted in the consciousness of the time a work of art is also a significant social document of the age in which it is written. The Indian Novel in English has come of age taking in its stride variegated themes with multiple mellifluousness and myriad of meanings at times. Through this literary device various social issues and challenges, despite their historical tinge, have created ripples in the minds of the reformers on the one hand and the victim of numerous evils on the other.

The present paper attempts to make a comparative study of two great novelists, who through their writing have shown how despite of being of two ages their concern for development is full of anguish. Mulk Raj Anand, a great social historian and a chronicler of the pink decades and Arundhati Roy the famous Booker Prize winner, a product of the much talked of the developed, voice their protest against the development at the cost of the hoi polloi who brought that development. Their works bear the stamps of the ages they lived in and stipulate how the materialistic advancements called development have deprived common folk of their basic rights of livelihood.

Bakha is the angry but subdued hero in Anand's 1935 classic Untouchable, who is severely limited by his own small intelligence in understanding the full extent of his social marginalization, suggesting that untouchables are incapable of becoming agents of their own emancipation because they cannot intellectually identify the systemic sources of their own oppression, mired as they are in the " experience of untouchability " so damned to remain an outcaste despite stirrings deep inside his soul. More than sixty years later, in her international bestseller *The God of Small Things*, Arundhati Roy aestheticizes the untouchable character Velutha, a paravan, endowing him with a body made " beautiful by his labor" who cherishes a desire to 'relive' as a touchable. He dares to have physical relation with an upper-class woman (unthinkable to Bakha) which ultimately costs him his life. Therefore, one notices a sea change in their attitude, psychology, behaviour, intellectual growth and consciousness as demonstrated in the growing intensity of anger and protest in these characters belonging to the same class.

In the novel *Untouchable* Mulk Raj Anand highlights the social evil of untouchability. The novelist highlights this evil by describing humiliation of Bakha, the sweeper boy. Anand has located the protagonist, Bakha, in a fixed reality in the hope of capturing the essence of the sweepers' existence. The one-day action of the hero is intended to represent a fairly complete sociological experience. An uneducated young man of eighteen years, he was not dull-witted. Like others of his community he was subjected to humiliation and indifference by high-born Hindus. He was aware of his low position and also conscious of his inability to offer resistance against the inhuman treatment ruthlessly meted out to him. He was born in a sweeper-family, so he was never provided proper upbringing to become a civilized man. Bakha's day dawns to the harsh tune of his father's abuses intended to whip him up to work. He does not dislike work and needs no goading. Bakha accidentally touches a Hindu and this starts off reactions. He is introduced symbolically as a child of modern India and the impact of new influences has caused stir in him. Anand has located the protagonist, Bakha, in a fixed reality in the hope of capturing the essence of the sweepers' existence. The one-day action of the hero is intended to represent a fairly complete sociological experience. Mulk Raj Anand has himself amplified the whole idea thus in *The Story of Experiment With a White Lie*: "I glimpsed the truth that the tragedy of my hero (Bakha) lay in the fact that he was never allowed to attain anything near the potential of his qualities of manhood" (Anand 12).

A similar incident occurs a little ahead in the main street where Bakha goes again to sweep the market road and the temple courtyard. He wants to purchase four anna's worth of cheap sweetmeat, after weighing the consequences of doing so both in philosophic and rational terms. Anand has masterly presented this scene, which contains Bakha's suppressed feelings and emotions before buying sweetmeat: "'"Eight anna in my pocket', he said to himself, 'dare I buy some sweets? If my father comes to know that I spend all my money on sweets'; he thought and hesitated, 'but come, I have only one life to live'; he said to himself, 'let me taste the sweets; who knows, tomorrow I may be no more'" (*Untouchable* 51).

Bakha asks for jalebis worth four annas to a Bengali sweetmeat seller. The shopkeeper weighs jalebis with great alacrity and hurls the packet at Bakha who catches it reluctantly: He caught the jalebis which the confectioner threw at him like a cricket ball, placed four nickel coins on the shoe-board for the confectioner's assistant who stood ready to splash some water on them, and walked away, embarrassed yet happy (*Untouchable* 52). Bakha's annoyance knew no bounds at the contemptuous behaviour of the shopkeeper but he finds himself unable to raise his voice against this callous behaviour. The germs of revolutionary feelings are germinating here in Bakha's mind as a sequel to these insults. This is not the end of these incidents but the worst is yet to come. Prior to this stage, Bakha is seen to have mirthfully accepted his given lot.

Another serious incident happened when Bakha touched a Lallaji. This produces an endless torrent of vulgar abuses from the touched man. Bakha's intention was not to pollute the Lallaji. He feels sorry and begs his pardon but in vain. It collected a big crowd, which continued to scold him mercilessly. In due course of time, encouraged by the crowd, Lallaji at once gave a sound slap on Bakha's cheek as a reward for what he has done. Dr. G.S. Balarama Gupta has rightly observed here when he says: "The climax of the novel, the incident where in Bakha 'touches' the Lallaji, is especially significant for the slap dealt on Bakha's face is symbolic not only of all the cruelty to which untouchables are subjected, but of the scornful treatment meted out to the underprivileged all over the world as, for *instance the Negroes in the U.S.A.*" (Gupta 28). Bakha stood still his turban fallen on the ground and his poor jalebis scattered in the dust. At this critical juncture nobody was bit kind to him except a tongawalla who tries to console Bakha. He was also very much angry with Lallaji for his inhuman as well as brutal behaviour. Just after this serious incident, Anand has vividly described Bakha's revolutionary feelings, which emerged in him as a result of utter humiliation. The following passage shows a radical change in protagonist's personality:

> He stood aghast. Then his whole continence lit with fire and his hands use no more joined. Tears welled up in his eyes and rolled down his cheeks. The cumulated strength of his giantbody glistened in him with the desire for revenge, while horror, rage, indignation swept over his frame (*Untouchable* 55-56).

The scene of the cruel crowd and the man who hit him flashes before his mind. Bakha, immediately realizes his actual position in the world. He automatically raises very pertinent as well as debatable questions before us to be sympathetically pondered over: "The cruel crowd: All of them abused, abused, abused, why are we always abused? They always abuse us. Because we are sweepers. Because we touch dung. They hate dung. I hate it too. That is why I came here. I was tired of working of the latrines every day. That's why they don't touch us, the highcastes" (*Untouchable* 56). Bakha was highly grateful to the tongawalla for he has been kind to him. In his opinion, the Muhammadans and the Sahib are better than the Hindus because they do not mind touching anyone. After long consideration, Bakha expresses his factual position and worth, in the following passage:

> It is only the Hindus, and the outcastes who are not sweepers. For them I am a sweeper, sweepers—Untouchable, Untouchable, Untouchable. That is the word—untouchable. I am an untouchable. Like a ray of light shooting through the darkness, the recognition of his position, the significance of his lot dawned upon him (*Untouchable* 57).

This is not the end of Bakha's insults but another more humiliating event than the previous one awaits him. He goes near the temple-door and catches just a glimpse of the dark sanctuary and its idols. He is moved by the songs of the worshippers. After some time, he is highly surprised to hear the priest's noise—"polluted, "polluted". Another priest shouts now from near the temple that he too has been polluted by the contact of Sohini, Bakha's beautiful sister. On being asked by her brother, she hesitatingly told him that the priest, Pundit Kali Nath had made improper suggestion to her when she was cleaning the latrine and held her by her breast. In India, superstition has been playing havoc since the dawn of the human civilization and still our country is in its vicious grip. According to Hindu religion a temple can be polluted by a low caste man coming within sixty-nine yards of it. Bakha went mad on listening to the pathetic story of his sister. His revolutionary feelings, indignation and anger can implicitly be seen in his own words:

> He felt he could kill them all. He looked ruthless, deadly pale and livid with anger and rage.... The man must have made indecent suggestions to her. I wonder what he did. Father of father! I could kill that man... Brahmin dog! Bakha exclaimed, "I will go and kill him" (*Untouchable* 68-69).

It appears as though Bakha has to live on insults. After sending Sohini home, he goes out to fetch food. There is orthodox housewife shouting with fury that Bakha had defiled her house by contact. She promptly scolds him and hurls some chapaties down from the fourth storey of the building. It came on the ground and scattered in the dust. Bakha picks them up and walks off with disgust overwhelming him. The last incident, which provokes Bakha's mind, happened when a little child of higher caste was wounded with a stone in the match, which was being played between 31st Punjabis and the 38th Dogra boys. Bakha being an intelligent boy has already forbidden the child to play. Bakha himself took the child in his arms with profound sense of love and sympathy and went to his house. When Bakha carries the child to his house, the Babu's wife gets very much angry with him for he has polluted her son. She even thinks that Bakha himself has hit her boy and so starts abusing him vehemently. Had there been another person of higher caste in the place of Bakha, he would have highly been admired for this act of kindness. Unfortunately, he deserves only the step-motherly treatment of the woman, which further sours his mind. Prof. R.S. Singh has rightly observed here:

> They refused to recognize his sentiments and even his acts of kindness. Even when he saved the child from accident and brought him back to his mother, he was not praised for endangering his life to help the child. On the contrary, he was condemned for polluting the child lifting him in his lap" (Singh 40).

The approaching evening presents three solutions with which the book closes. Anand does not introduce any tricky situation, but creates one of the most memorable scenes in the recent Indo-Anglian fiction. Having been turned out by his angry father, Bakha meets three men with different solutions to his deep-rooted problem. First, Hutch in son the padre of the Salvation Army proposes to baptize Bakha in order to remove the stigma of caste. But Bakha instinctively turns to Gandhi who identifies himself with the untouchable by declaring that he wishes to be reborn as an untouchable. But Bakha feels something mystical about the Mahatmaji's solution. The final solution is of poet Iqbal Nath Sarkar who tells about water closets and main-drainage all over the country, which means a definite destruction of the soulless system of caste. He is of the opinion that the introduction of flush-system will finish all the troubles of both untouchability and untouchables. The creation of *Untouchable* by Anand is the rejection of casteism as a heinous practice involving man's inhumanity to man. The novel is a crusade not only against the evil effects of caste system, but it generates the element of compassion among readers for the protagonist also. Bakha is a perfect individual whose excellence is flawed by his low caste for which he is definitely not responsible. All the episodes of Bakha's humiliation reveal how unjustly the untouchables are treated by caste Hinuds. Thus by creating a powerful character like Bakha, Mulk Raj Anand hits at the evils of the society and advocates for the social justice to the down—trodden section of Indian population. Arundhati Roy's famous Booker Prize winning novel, *The God of Small Things,* apart from dealing with a number of postmodern issues like history, politics, religion and biology, is also concerned with the theme of untouchability. Untouchables exist at the bottom of India's rigid social order known as caste system. Arundhati Roy has very potentially portrayed this problem and has tried to establish the fact that in spite of the development of science and technology in the country, thinking of Indians has not broadened accordingly and they could not easily tolerate the progress made by a Dalit.

The story of the novel *The God of Small Things* is set in the town named Aymanam in Kerala, depicting the time period from 1969 to 1993. Though the story basically depicts the history of a well-to-do Kochamma family, while describing the socio-cultural milieu of the town, the novelist has laid bare the evil consequences of untouchability in the post-colonial India. The caste described in the novel is Paravan to which the young Velutha belongs. His

Father Villya Paapen was a toddy tapper and he too, was the victim of caste discrimination but he dare not speak even a single word against it because during the colonial period the conditions were worse and a very inhuman treatment was given to untouchables. Remembering those days, Mammachi, the mistress of Kochamma family once told about her girlhood days:

> When Paravans were expected to crawl backwards with a broom sweeping away their foot prints ... were not allowed to cover their upper bodies, not allowed to carry umbrellas. They had to put their hands over their mouth when they spoke, to divert their polluted breath away from those whom they addressed (Roy 73-74).

Even now in early seventies of 20th century they are "not allowed to touch anything that touchables touched" (73). Arrival of Britishers to Malabar worsen their condition as a number of people from the castes like Paravan, Peiya and Pulya converted to Christianity in lieu of a little food and money but unfortunately they were neither accepted by high class Christians nor by the upper caste Hindus. Respectable status remained a dream for them and they were segregated as 'Rice-Christians'. Even independence of India could not prove to be beneficial for them because they remained devoid of the benefits given to the Scheduled Castes as on paper they were Christians. Therefore, they had to bear the curse of untouchability. Velutha, the protagonist of *The God of Small Things* is committed to be an educated, skilled carpenter, in spite of the handicaps his father faced during educational journey of his son. He got such an inmate technical mind that he could easily set all the machines including radios, clocks, water pumps, etc., right within a short span of time. It was his misfortune that he was born to a Parvan family otherwise "he might have become an engineer" (75). In a way, his caste proves to be a barrier in the fullest development of his capabilities. Velutha, an untouchable works at the Paradise Pickles and Preserves factory owned by Chacko, Ammu's brother. Ammu, a touchable woman is attracted towards Velutha because of his outstanding intelligence, skills, sudden smile and a touch of humanity he had. Her life, in itself, is a tale of suffering and agony as neither the members of her family nor the relatives and neighbours like her decision of living with her parents after her divorce. She is also the victim of whimsical society. Her marriage to a man of her own liking and the subsequent divorce made her a kind of outcaste. Her presence and the presence of her children Rahel and Estha, is avoided by people living around her. Obviously, she begins to feel neglected and gradually turns irritating. In such condition it is Velutha who offers what is denied to her and her children. He gives company to the children in spite of the fact that children are prohibited to go to his house. Ammu's attraction towards him is quite spontaneous and natural and she used to meet him near the bank of the river in the darkness of night. She does not care about his caste rather looks at his human qualities. Her dreams also have him, though in a disguised form of a cheerful 'one arm man' with which he held a lamp. "He had no other arm with which to fight the shadows that flickered around him on the floor" (215). He swam in the sea but with no "foot prints in sand, no ripples in water, no image in mirror". He was in fact, "The God of Loss", "The God of Small Things", "The God of Goose Bumps and sudden smiles" (217). Here the one-arm man symbolically stands for an incapable man who in spite of his will to fight, is unable to combat against the hostile factors that check his progress in life. He is unable to use the utmost of his powers and only half of his potentials could be utilized by him. The shadows that flickered around him and "the shadows that only he could see" stand for the forces of society which hinder his way only for his being an untouchable. When he dares touch a woman from higher caste, whole of world gets topsy turvy. His godly qualities though retained but he is called "The God of Small Things." In a way his untouchability is such a bane for him that his human qualities appear to be insignificant in comparison to his caste identity. His deeds no doubt are praiseworthy and indispensable for the members of upper caste but he does not get proper respect and congenial treatment in society.

The love affair between Ammu and Velutha develops day by day. The two abandoned souls meet in a deserted house of Kari Saipu on the other side of the river. They begin to derive pleasure of the company of each other from the small things like devout praying mantis, the pair of small fish those bite Velutha and cause a tickling, while he is in the streams of river and also the clumsy caterpillars and the helpless beetles. They laugh at these small things because no other philosophy can justify their love and the pleasure that they are driving from their meetings. Eventually, their secret relationship is discovered and its news is first given by Velutha's father himself to Mammachi. Baby Kochamma's reactions, after knowing about the love affair are quite natural and truly represent the established hierarchical order of the society in which the identity of an untouchable is considered negligent. She betrays Velutha to save her family name. In the whirlwinds of circumstances he is proved to be a man who committed a crime. He is charged falsely for being a victim for Sophie Mol's death, attempting rape on Ammu, kidnapping Rahel and Estha, etc. Even the political activist comrade Pillai does not come to the rescue of Velutha. The Police Inspector, a representative of higher caste is also against Velutha after seeing the illicit relation between Ammu and him. His attempt to get the statement of children changed to save the reputation of Baby Kochamma clearly reveals that his purpose is not to trace the truth rather it is to protect touchables at the cost of an untouchable's life. Therefore, Velutha was beaten brutally by him and his men and with the severe injuries he died. The novelist Arundhati Roy had described very realistically the miserable condition of Velutha:

> Blood spilled from his skull like a secret. His face was swollen and his head looked like a pumpkin, too large and heavy for the slender stem it grew from. A pumpkin with a monstrous upside down smile. Police boots stepped back from the rim of a pool of urine spreading from him, the bright bare electric bulb reflected it (319-20).

To conclude, Velutha in *The God of Small Things* can be rightly called as the re-incarnation of Bakha in a sense that both of them are flat characters created by their respective authors. Their predicaments, their longing for equality, their skills, their rebellious attitude, their lot and their dreams have a very close affinity to each other. Both of them are the male protagonists of their novels, belonging to a low caste, sharing the same burning problems leading to agony and misery. Their agony crossed all human boundaries. They are Dalits. They are sweepers. Both Bakha and Veutha are one in line with innumerable millions who have been at the receiving end of a hierarchical social system. That resulted into segregation, self-denial, self-alienation and isolation of the entire class. They are the tragic heroes and outstanding figures out and out.

Works Cited

Anand, Mulk Raj. *The Story of Experiment with a White Lie.* New Delhi: Arnold Publishers, 1981. Print.

____. *Untouchable.* New Delhi: Arnold Publishers, 1981. Print.

Gupta, G. S. Balarama. *Mulk Raj Anand: A Study of His Fiction in Human Perspective.* Bareilly: Prakash Book Depot, 1974. Print.

Roy, Arundhati. *The God of Small Things.* New Delhi: India Ink Publishing, 1997. Print.

Singh, R. S. *Indian Novel in English.* New Delhi: Arnold-Heinemann, 1977. Print.

21

'Myth, Masculinity and Memory': An Autobiographical Study of Baby Kamble's *The Prison We Broke*

Shankar Lal Seemawat

In the title of the book *The Prison We Broke* (original written in Marathi as *Jina Aamcha*) written by Baby Kamble, the word *Prison* is very crucial which suggests the creative nature of the writer. The word has been punned deliberately to create literal meaning of prison as a limited space provided to women in general and Dalit ones in particular (they are asked to be involved in kitchen, cooking and child caring only) or fictional world created around them to restrain them in false ideological conception of values, culture, religion and society. Since the practice of writing autobiography is considered an independent and respectable mode of expression, so the paper would focus on how distressing effects of the caste system on the social and cultural status of Dalit women on the basis of myths, masculinity as the source of power and authority and only men can write in case of Dalits as Gopal Guru says:

> It is not only in the political arena that Dalit women face exclusion. In the cultural field, for instance, Dalit women have criticized their male counterparts for dominating the literary scene. Dalit male writers do not take serious note of the literary output of Dalit women and tend to be dismissive of it. Dalit women rightly question why they are not considered for the top positions in Dalit literary conferences and institutions (Guru 83).

Here, Baby Kamble recovers memory to expose the Mahar's pitiable situation in Maharashtra. This text provides a realistic picture of the oppressive caste and patriarchal beliefs of the Indian society. She is tried to depict the life of her community and people showing that how brahminical domination had turned the Mahar into slaves. Dalit women writers wanted to define themselves and not be trapped in framed images that others, including male Dalit writers, had created regarding them. The paper would also make attempts to reflect that Dr. Ambedkar was the most educated Dalit and therefore he could lead them to the truth. It is he who asked the Dalits not to believe in gods and goddesses. In general, most of the Dalit autobiographies corroborate the conditions of contemporary Dalits in the different Indian States. All the authors depicted their deprived conditions of food, shelter, settlement, and culture within and around the Indian society. Besides, Omprakash Valmiki, Vasant Moon, Baby Kamble, Siddalingaiah, Bama and Gunasekaran could be ranked as the "civil-heroes" of a deprived community. They also gave their traumatic memories of apartheid, abuses, assaults, discriminations, injustices, and atrocities. In the process, the study delineates the socio-economic, traumas, and self-elevation. It is important to note that such an autobiographical mode has subtle license to provide Dalit feminists a powerful weapon to channelize their inner immense literary capability to thrash the long lasting norms of misconceptions based on illogical or outdated hypocritical values. This mode was more authoritative in its truth and realistic portrayal than other tools such as novels, plays or poems, since here they could incorporate a retrospective glance at the life and personality of a person, one in which the facts carry less importance than the veracity and profundity of the experience. The 'true' autobiography, tells us not merely of remembered deeds and thoughts, but is for both author and reader "a spiritual experiment, a voyage of discovery. True autobiography can be written only by men and women pledged to their innermost selves beyond fastened truth, beyond the likeness, the autobiography has to give that unique truth of life as it is seen from inside, and in this respect it has not submitted arrival.

Literary means of autobiography is an account of a person's life written by himself or herself. The term autobiography appears to have been first used by Southey in 1809. Autobiography speaks not only about writers and incidents but also about their experiences. Roy Pascal defines: '*Autobiography is historical in method and at the same time the representation of the self in and through its relations with the outer world'* (Pascal 8). It is clear that an autobiography is the true representation of the extraordinary, renowned and popular men's life, achievements and experiences. But in the case of Dalits, ordinary men and women, who do not hold any prominent position in the social history and politics write autobiographies. They keep aside the established style of writing autobiographies. Moreover, it is important to see why the 'community' is given more importance than the 'self' in the Dalit autobiographies. In Indian context of Dalit autobiography it includes both annals of a man's life and a philosophical history in a retrospective mode mainly based on her/his memory. In this respect, Pascal further says:

> Every experience is a nucleus from which energies radiate in various directions. In any worthwhile life there is a dominant direction that is not accidental; therefore ultimately the life is a sort of graph linking the experiences (Pascal 17).

African American Literature created advancing wave fronting the United States of America during the twentieth century as a voice of protest against racial discrimination. Similarly, Dalit literature also documents the socio-cultural political factors of the exploited mass in India. African Americans were prevented from enjoying life because of their race. The Harlem Renaissance during the 1920s-1930s institutionalised the African American literature as a subject of academic inquiry and ensured that the writers and their readers were keenly aware of the circumstances in which they worked. Whether the writers embraced the tradition or resisted its premises, their work extended its contours. *The Continuum Encyclopaedia of American Literature* says:

> ...the first two centuries of the African diaspora's sojorun in the U.S. were marked by the dominance of the SLAVE NARRATIVE and African American FOLKLORE, both of which continued to flourish and influence African American literature and politics long after the end of slavery. This does not mean, however, that these two creative forms represented the totality of African American literature. (Steven 15).

Making sense of autobiographies is necessarily a culturally conditioned and socially reflexive process. Martin Barker, Comic: Ideology, Power and the Critics, explains: "*the first function of language is to establish social relations between human beings in society"* (B Martin 265). As a medium, autobiography authentically establishes the individual relationship of Dalits and non-Dalits. All the writers are integral part of the Indian society. The driving force behind contemporary Dalit literature is the thought of Dr. B. R. Ambedkar. The immense potential of Dr. Ambedkar and his philosophy was not restricted to himself or any one particular individual.

Most of the sources and incidents used in their autobiographies are the productions of Indian society, which are the objects of the research that bound up with the socio economic of state and society. As Oliver Mendelsohn and Marika Vicziany say:

> ....for the present purposes Indian poverty can more be usefully defined as the sum of low standards of nutrition, health, housing, general material consumption, and formal education. By these criteria, the Untouchables are overwhelmingly poor people. The principal source, as opposed to the measure, of Untouchables' poverty is their relationship with agricultural land. There is a relentless logic that flows from their being an agrarian people without strong land assets (M Oliver & V Marika 30).

Quest for identity is an important aspect of the Dalit autobiographies, which represent the struggles of the Dalits for social equality and justice. The Dalit autobiographies in general are the narratives of the caste history of the Dalits. In the process of writing their caste history, the narrators interrogate the mainstream culture, religion, polity and the bases of exploitation. In so doing, the Dalit narratives construct an alternative history by liberally drawing from their culture, language and myth. Beginning in the 19th century it was the high-caste Hindu women, who started writing autobiographies, which were located in the new emerging material and social condition resulting from reforms and legislative innovation in the public sphere. Women's autobiographies then become a cultural site, where tensions were articulated resulting from colonial modernity. The dominant ideology of 19th century cultural nationalism celebrated India's spiritual superiority over material West but remained silent over caste/gender based humiliation. The autobiographies of upper caste women have to be located within this framework. The question of caste was invisible in their writings. Sharmile Rege has drawn attention to this erasure:

> Brahmin women's autobiographies have been narratives of upper caste women, their struggles with tradition and their desire to be modern. It is this 'self' that claims to be universal, modern unmarked by caste through its journeys of companionate marriage, modern institutions and marital discord. This claims of the upper caste women's autobiography to represent modern Marathi/Indian women serves, on the other hand, to render invisible their complicity in privileges of Brahminical patriarchy; and on the other, it classifies the narratives of women whose self-definition is located explicitly in caste as a relational identity, as if it were the 'other' of modern and feminist' (Rege 50).

Baby Kamble raises certain important issues like caste discrimination, women subjugation and the influence of Dr. Ambedkar on Dalit women to get themselves educated both socially and culturally. Kamble writes about caste discrimination that the poor Maharswentunder. Mahars were treated as untouchable servants 'yeskars'. By doing yeskar jobs, the Mahars would get bhakris (leftover food) which they eat after drying them in the sun. Mahars are not allowed to use the regular road that is used by the upper castes. Kamble writes, "*When somebody from these castes walked from the opposite direction, the Mahars had to leave the road, climb down into the shrubbery and walk through the thorny bushes on the road side*" (Kamble 52). Women's autobiographies were defined by feminist critics as texts with reference to life. *'Difference' becomes an important term to situate the concept of gendered narrative with reference to women's autobiographies and subject position. Difference was confined not just to sexual difference but there was "pluralisation of difference*" (Anderson 117) across race, gender, ethnicity, class and sexuality. Autobiography has been one of the most important sites of feminist debates because it demonstrated that there are different ways of writing the subject that are often experimental and challenged the existing critical boundaries. She notes that after Phule and Shahu Maharaj, it was Dr. Babasaheb Ambedkar who provided the intellectual and ideological foundations for a sustained critique of the caste system and that under the leadership of Dr. Ambedkar, Dalit protest acquired the form and force of a militant political movement and challenged the very foundations of Hinduism. Kamble raises certain important issues like caste discrimination, women subjugation and the influence of Dr. Ambedkar on Dalit women to get themselves educated both socially and culturally. In this autobiography, Kamble speaks out for the women of her community, presenting an unflinching portrait of its women, subjugated by both caste and patriarchy. Especially newly married younger women suffer the worst fate. Usually married off at the age of eight or nine, immature, even without knowing what a husband meant yet the child has to go her in-laws' house to lead a married life. However, for the girl marriage meant nothing but calamity:

> When the bride arrived at her in-laws' house, she would be asked to make two basket full bhakris. The poor child would sit down to make them but she could not able to do that properly, may be bhakris burnt in some places and remain uncooked in some. Then the sasu would call all her friend for the presentation of the tiny-burnt bhakris, Attyabai, come and see what happening here is. Didn't you think that I'd brought the daughter of a good woman into my house? Look at the bhakris this slut has prepared. She cannot even make a few bhakris properly. Oh, well, what can on expect of this daughter of a dunce? (Kamble 94).

Baby Kamble has lived in the same social structure of Hindu society in which woman is considered as subordinate to the husband. She was subjected for her husband's doubts and harsh beating. But her autobiography deals with grandparents, parents and her community people. The age old tradition like Redejatra and certain religious conventions are the integral part of her autobiography. The tone of the autobiography is egalitarian and it is not influenced by masculinity. The adversity is an equal challenge for wife and husband. They started vegetable merchandise in their locality and added provisions like oil, salt and such other stuff. Her husband used to look after the business in the morning till she finished her household chores and once she came he left for the market to buy provisions. They played the role of business partner rather than one substitute to another. As far as the composition of autobiography is concerned, we find that Baby Kamble was not requested to compose it, on the other hand it was her inner inspiration which made her to express about her community people. She describes an anecdote of Dr. Babasaheb Ambedkar's speech at Jejuri. For Baby Kamble conversion is satisfying the logical rationality and wining the struggle of emancipation which was not possible for them in the circumference of Hindu religion. Hindu religion is bunch of ugly customs, exploitations, superstitions and detachment from education for the downtrodden. Buddhism has the potentials to give them recognition as human beings and rights of equality along with education. According to the then tradition, Kamble was not very much free because she was somebody's wife. Her husband often had control over her. She did not have freedom to do anything if she wished to do. Whenever she happened to go against the patriarchal norms, she was brutally beaten up by her husband. She suffered a lot at the hands of her husband. *The Prisons We Broke* reveals in detail how Kamble was a victim of her husband's male chauvinistic mentality. She remembers:

> Once we went to Mumbai to attend a meeting, we travelled in a general compartment that was very crowded and some young men happened to stare at me. My husband immediately suspected me and hit me so hard that my nose started bleeding profusely. The same evening we returned and he was so angry that he kept hitting me in the train (Kamble 155).

Her autobiography deals with these two contradictory approaches for two religions in which the logical rationality, self-awareness and struggle for emancipation are important aspects. In short we can say that the basic difference between these two autobiographies is that the former finds romance and trill in the conversion whereas the later deals with the utter need of conversion as means of emancipation for each and every type of adversity in the life of downtrodden. Though the Dalit autobiographies are full of agony and angst, they are aimed at awakening the Dalits and raising their consciousness. The Dalit autobiographies are not merely the writings of vengeance to spread hatred against the caste Hindus but also to promote the heritage of the Dalits. The Dalit autobiographies are aimed at rebuilding society to promote honour, dignity, justice and equality. The subjectivity of the Dalit autobiographies needs to be understood in terms of the communal self:

> The identity of a person will be based on the location to which he/she belongs. Accordingly, the person will undergo the experiences in life. In order to understand the life-experiences of a person several disparate identical criterion can be put to test. It can be caste, class, ethnicity, language, religion, region, gender etc' (Kumar 2).

The Effect of Ambedkar's speeches is seen in the last part of Kamble's text, when Rani Sahiba organizes Mahila Mandal in Phaltan, she called Brahmins, Maratha and Mahar women for this Mandal. The second round meeting was organizing in dining hall where all the Brahmins and Maratha women occupied the chairs. Unfortunately, Mahar women stood on one side at the same time when Rani Sahiba and her followers move towards stage; suddenly Thakubai shook shoulder and told her:

> Your women are not allowing our women to sit on the chairs. Our Ambedkar has told us to demand our rights. I am going to forcefully remove your women from the hairs and sear my women there. The Rani Sahiba was taken aback for a moment. But she immediately arranged chairs in the front for all of us (Kamble 133).

Baby Kamble's narration of various incidents vis-à-vis the Dalit women suggests that the nature of the problems faced by the Dalit women in India essentially differs from those that the upper caste women face. Since the nature of the problems differs, the solutions to the problems of the Dalit women too differ. As a staunch follower of Dr. Ambedkar, Baby Kamble illustrates how education and self-assertion redeem the Dalit women from the kind of the domestic and social problems such as caste discrimination and gender violence that the Dalit women confront in their day-to-day life.

Finally, I would argue that *The Prisons We Broke* is very important text because it draws the progress of the Mahar community from pre-Ambedkar days to its rapid transformation through education and mass conversion. Dalit Literature represents a powerful, emerging movement in the Indian literary tradition. In the last part of her book Kamble talks about the responsibility of the present society to look Dalits as human beings and treat them with dignity and respect. Even now discrimination is not completely wiped out from our society. There are a lot of villages which should be brought into the light of main stream and the educated people should work for them. By inscribing subaltern past, the texts call for an understanding of subalternity which pushes the limits of literature and literary produced at the institutional site of university. The texts represent the complex relationship of social location, experience and history. To conclude this paper I would like to say that, the situation of Dalit women in India needs special attention. They are one of the biggest socially segregated groups anywhere in the world. There is no doubt about the traditional taboos are same for Dalit men and women. However, this is not a move in the direction of sudden shift in ideological gear but initiates a process whereby an engagement with Dalit women's life-narratives can move in the radical direction of reading literary representations as "*metaphors of revision, rewriting and reclamation*" (Waugh 59) to produce new liberatory revisions of history. The book is the first work that comes under Dalit literature that is written by a woman. It is because of that itself, the book deals with the two major problems of the society: firstly, the exploitation and oppression of the Dalits by the upper caste Hindus, secondly, the discrimination done towards women in a patriarchal society irrespective of her caste. In this way this becomes a socio-biography, not merely an autobiography of self as an individual experience. Thus above paper focused that how the Dalit autobiographies are became historical documentations of self-assertion, self-respect, liberation and empowerment of the Dalits.

Works-Cited

Anderson, L. *Autobiography*. London: Routledge, 2007. Print.

Barker, Martin. *Comic: Ideology, Power, and the Critics*. Manchester: Manchester UP, 1989. Print.

Guru, G. *Dalit Women Talk Differently. Genderand Caste*. Ed. A. Rao. New Delhi: Women Unlimited, 203. 80-85. Print.

Kamble, B. *The Prisons We Broke*. Trans. M. Pandit. Hyderabad: Orient Longman, 2008. Print.

Kumar R. *Dalit Personal Narratives: Reading Caste, Nation and Gender*. New Delhi: Orient Longman, 2010. Print.

Mendelsohn, Oliver, and Marika Vicziany. *The Untouchables: Subordination, Poverty and the State in Modern India*. New Delhi: CUP, 2007. Print.

Rege S. *Writng Caste/Writng Gender: Narrating Dalit Women's Testimonios*. New Delhi: Zuban, 2006. Print.

Steven R. Serafin and Alfred Bendixen (eds) "African American Literature." *The Continuum Encyclopedia of American Literature*. New York: The Continuum International Publishing Group Inc., 2003. Print.

Waugh, P. *Revolutions of the Word: Intellectual Context for the Study of Modern Literature*. Ed. P. Waugh. London: Arnold, 1997. 57-62. Print.

22

Dalit Repercussions in Mahasweta Devi's Short Story *Outcast: Four Stories*

SUSHIL SARKAR

"Without contradiction there is no progression. Attraction and Repulsion, Reason and Energy, Love and Hate, are necessary to Human existence" (Marriage of Heaven and Hell-02) says Blake which means much not only to the mankind rather, of course, it refers contradictory binaries to maintain equilibrium in the society. That's why from the time immemorial, the words 'Rich' and 'Poor', 'Brahmin' and 'Sudra' are two opposite binary entities of society and at the same time two opposite poles of mankind. As Sudhir K. Arora states "As long as the monster capital is there, it will create a gulf and separate the two, showing them the two different paths which never meet each other" (Adiga 124). Hence one is unable to live without other and these two polarities run parallel without meeting each other. The "Intellectual hatred is the worst" (Adiga 124) which functions always among the rich and upper section of the society against the deprived classes. Writer-activist Mahasweta Devi's words can be mentioned here, who says: "The tribal and the mainstream have always been parallel. There has never been a meeting point. The mainstream simply doesn't understand the parallel..." *(Imaginary Maps II)*. In the capitalistic society rich always desires to be rich and to be positioned in the centre, not in the margin and poor always will be positioned in the margin, not in the centre. If the poor becomes rich who will work for the rich? In the Marxist theory one is capitalist and the other is proletariat, one is dominant and the other is dominated. Karl Marx reacted against this capitalism and purged his innermost feelings as a theoretical doctrine named as Marxism or better known as Communism.

The adaptation of lower classes in literature is not a new trend. The representation of marginalized people in Indian Writing in English is started by Mulk Raj Anand in his book "*Untouchable*". Afterwards this kind of 'Dalit' theme in literature is sketched by Arundhati Roy, and in the contemporary postmodern period Arvind Adiga, Rohinton Mistry, and translated literature Mahasweta Devi, of course. Dalit is a Sanskrit word which means to split, crack or open. Untouchables, split, depressed, underprivileged, downtrodden, underdogs and 'Harijans' ("God's people") are called Dalits. Dr. B.R. Ambedkar in Indian Constitution gives special provision for those depressed classes entitled as 'Scheduled Caste' or 'Scheduled Tribe'. The themes of exploitation, injustice, inhumanity, hatred etc. are the typical features of Dalit texts. And the heroes or the heroines of the texts cannot openly react against these so called long lasted socio-economical drawbacks. The passivity or the helplessness condition of fate is the inevitable phenomenon of the Dalit hero or heroin's ultimate destiny. The condition of these people is similar to that of the condition of African black people, apartheid or the Australian's aborigines or Canada's first nations. In India, Dalit is concerned with the Schedule Caste or Schedule Tribes who are somehow or the other way exploited in respect of race, caste, class or gender. The racial discrimination caged them in the zoo of casteism after the sixty years of India's independence. As Mahasweta Devi states:

> In these thirty one years after independence, I have not seen our own people attaining true independence in anything-in food, water, land, loan and bonded labour. A pure, white and sun like rage against the system which had made this independence impossible is the inspiration behind all my works. I believe that all parties right or left have failed to keep their promises to the common people. I have no hope of this conviction being shaken during my lifetime. Thus I have written only about humanity to the best of my ability so that I do not have to feel ashamed to face myself." (*Agnigarva*).

What is the criterion to be a Dalit writer? Will the author be a Dalit by birth? Or will the writings be Dalit in theme? However, Mahasweta Devi is not a Dalit by birth but her writings expose the theme of poor Dalit, tribals and marginalized sections of the society and their dispossession and displacement from the mainstream. She is social activist and an eminent Bengali writer who has hundreds of books in her credit and all these books are translated into English and many foreign languages by various researchers and writers and critics. The texts of Mahasweta Devi, certainly deal with the rootlesness, land alleviation, peasants' movement, insurgency, poverty and above all dire helplessness existential dilemma of the tribals and dalits of the society. Mahasweta Devi also awarded many prestigious awards for her creative output in her texts. She is not only championed for the representation of underdogs in her texts rather her creative writing has been published in various newspaper or journals all over the world in an iconoclastic way. All the texts are reflection of miserable socio-economic condition of depressed classes of the society. And for that she becomes global writer and familiar with every reader from first world to third world countries. She was awarded Sahitya Academy award in 1979, in 1996 prestigious Jnanpith award and in 1986 Padmashree award also. Mahasweta Devi's 'Bangla' short stories and novels depict the tribes of Eastern part of India, many writings were historical in theme and in subject matter and that's why Gayatri Chakraborty Spivak describes all these as "history imagined into fiction" (*Breast Stories* 77). She doesn't adopt the history written by dominant group of the Indian historiography rather she takes the alternative history from the tribal/dalit society which is in a word may be available in the tribal oral historical form.

Mahasweta Devi in her short story *Outcast-Four Stories* sketches the victimized fate of four different women—Dhouli, Sanichari, Josmina and Chinta respectively. These four women are marginalized, downtrodden female heroines, more clearly in an Indian term Dalit female protagonists. Each and every character of the story represents the true suffering of poor people by the feudal laws. These women are primarily exploited being the deprived section of the society and secondly being women they are being exploited by the patriarchal as well as by the mainstream of society. Thirdly the protagonists of the stories are somehow or the other way such as Dhouli, Sanichari and Josmina, everyone is ostracized from their own tribal society/dalit society because they save themselves and their families from the dire poverty, assume the profession of prostitution. So this is not only the fate of Mahasweta Devi's heroines, in reality this kind of violence or trafficking of women is happening everyday and Mahasweta Devi frankly delineates all in her texts.

The first story of the text *Dhouli* starts with a dusad (Untouchable) lower caste tribal girl. She got married at an earliest period of her life with the help of Hanuman Mishra, a local landlord of the village where douli's family works as a bonded labour under same village 'Jotedar' Hanumnji Mishra. After the unexpected death of dhouli's husband, dhouli also becomes a bonded labour of Mishra family. She is seduced by the Mishrilal, the son of 'Jotedar' Hanumanji Mishra. Mishrilal continuously seduced her and tried to intercourse with her just to gratify his physical thirstiness. The son of the landlord, Mishrilal promises douli to marry her as he is not at all bothers about caste of dhouli, a Dalit and bonded slave of his own family. He pursues dhouli for impuring her through physical intercourse. Being undone, dhouli cannot revolt rather answers in a passive tone and replies: "What can I do? Nothing. Deotas like you always get what you want! Go ahead, take me dishonor me."(*Dhouli 10*). As a frequent seducing and false promise dhouli becomes pregnant and in his impregnated condition junior Mishrilal denied to marry dhouli. As "…there were several illegitimate Mishra children growing up in the dushad-ganju-dhobi quarters" (Dhouli-14). Mishrial got married another woman of his own community just to get rid of a Dalit woman's responsibility. Dhouli gives birth of a child as she wants to keep her motherhood intact and sacred. The story doesn't ends at this point only as the limit of exploitation doubled in the later part of her life. To save her newborn child from starvation, dhouli starts to sell her body to sensual counterpart of the society and becomes a branded prostitute. And she fells "How simple to sell one's body in a loveless exchange for salt, corn, maroa. If she had known it was that easy, she would have done it much earlier. Her son too would have been well faced healthy" *(Dhouli 28*). In the village meeting, it was decided that dhouli will not be allowed doing prostitution in that village and if she does, her house will be set on fire. As the verdict was declared by the senior Mishra, the head of the village, "Dhouli cannot practice prostitution in that village. She can go to the some town, to Ranchi and do her whoring there. If not her house will be set on fire and mother daughter child will be burnt to death" *(Dhouli 31*). The central character of the story Dhouli is herself the resident of 'Other' world and where she is ordered to go for practicing prostitution belongs to 'Other'. In this 'Other' world the light never penetrates as it is always darkening by hydra headed monster.

The second story is named after an Oraon girl Shanichari, the central character of the story *Shanichari*, after driven out of their village and inhospitable forest takes works in a brick kiln at Barasat in West Bengal. But the owner of the brick kiln Rahamat always harasses her sexually by continuous seducing, "Rahamat would dress Shanichari good clothes and nice jewellery, rub fragment oil in her hair and then tear into her ruthlessly" (*Shanichari 51*). There her condition becomes worst than earlier. A woman, Gohuman tricks Shanichari whose sole purpose is to sell the women to rich persons and trafficking innocent women she spreads this racket and makes money from it. This woman trafficker Gohuman promises Shanichari "malik will take care everything" (*Shanichari 108*). Not only that Gohuman befooled Shanichari by her false promises but ultimately Shanichari realizes later that the reality is absolutely different. It becomes clear from the conversation of Hiralal who says "Why don't the girls come back? A monstrous city, Kolkata. Devours everything around it… turns some girls into whores, sells off the rest" (*Shanichari 109*). Gohuman sells Shanichari to the brick kiln owner where she had been impregnated by lecherous Rahamat. And when Shanichari becomes pregnant Rahamat changes her sex partner and depute another tribal women to quench his lustful physical urge. The tribal society doesn't permit that kind of premarital sex and bastard child of their own tribal woman. This also happens to Shanichari also. So she has been marginalized three times, being women she has been exploited by the male counterpart of the society such as owner of brick kiln, Rahamat. Secondly being oraon girl she has been marginalized by upper caste of the society and finally by her own Oraon society, marginalized by the marginal. When Shanichari returns back at her own village, she and her new born child become outcast. Mahasweta Devi points out her finger to the society which is directly responsible for making a women whore and an innocent child outcaste by her own Oraon society. In that respect, Shanichari is here commodity who is sold in the market like other things having exchange value. The comodification, a prominent feature of postmodernism can be applied to the three female protagonists of

Mahasweta Devi's stories. The body of the female protagonist has been sold in the open market to live her livelihood. After the breaking the virginity of Shanichari by Rahamat and impregnated dhouli by Mishrilal, they become an outcast by their own tribal society. As branded outcast have do nothing to do except adaptation of whoring to alleviate dire poverty. The body of the dhouli and Shanichari are commodities as having exchange values. Out of these 'exchange value' they wring the sustainability of existence. Dhouli and Shanichari themselves are as symbol of 'use value' and the money they earn from it as 'exchange value'. So women are just merchandise and commodified. Without land, without food they become prostitute as hunger lead them to be such commodity through whoring. As Mahasweta Devi in an interview says:

> In Hyderabad, there is a special area where buyers from Middle East buy women in the name of marriage. Parents flock there because they are poor, they cannot give their daughters food and clothing. The basic reason is poverty…. As long as eighty percent of the Indian population lives below the poverty lines, this cannot stop. Decolonization has not reached the poor. This is why these things happen. Women are just merchandise, commodities" (*Imaginary Maps XX)*.

Dalit society faces this existential dilemma in their lives. To survive in a cruel and heartless world, the Dalit doesn't able to cope with the harsh realities and treatment against them. After the decolonization of India the condition of the outcaste, peasants, lower classes, and women remains the same. Dhouli and Shanichari want to live in the world with little aspirations but to exist in the world for them is an irony of life. The heroines of the stories don't commit suicide but decide to subsist in the world as the outcastes assuming the role of prostitution. Where is the marginal empowerment? Where is the Dalit empowerment? The empowerment never comes in their life, in their society? They cannot even lead a normal life as the violation of human rights is a part of their existence. Hence Mahasweta Devi's texts emphasize that the Dalit identity always in a crisis. The British left India looting India and India's wealth ruthlessly for a long time before India's independence. India got independence becomes decolonized country. But tribal, Dalit and outcast remain in the same condition as they were before. Nowadays the elite Indians become British-like.

In the third story *The Fairytale of Rajabasha*, Mahasweta Devi depicted a tribal couple, Sarjom and Josmina who live below poverty line but after their newly married life, they are very happy with their limited aspirations. This story stars with the description of their marriage ceremony where both of them are found in happy mood. And the happiness of them after marriage is described by the author vividly "Josmina collected roots and tubers from the forest. Living off just there and ghetto made makai, she looked gorgeous. A new mother, the curves of josmina's body filled out like gushing Koyena in the months of rain. There was much happiness and peace in the first chapter of rajabasha" (*Josmina* 59). At the same time "It was so refreshing to bathe in the waters of the Koyena. So peaceful to boil some makai at the end of the day and cook ghato in the evening. To sprinkle salt on it and at off leaf plates. So pleasant to sit by the banks of the river, washing pots and pan while chatting to girls you have known all your life" (*Josmina 78*).

But this Dalit couple was sold in Punjab by the village landlord, Nandalal Sahu to Niranjan Singh, a Punjabi agriculturalist just to fulfill his first wife's desire "A pucca brick house" (*Josmina 59*). This Punjabi agriculturalist, Niranjn Singh shifted them in Punjab to work in his farmhouse where he treats them like 'jungle janawar' with abhorrence and hatred. Not only that Niranjan Singh exploits Josmina sexually and physically and forced them to work '16 to 18 hours labour' rater abuse them in front of their children. He forcefully appointed them to "Keep the buffalos, cows and bonded labour under lock and key" (*Josmina 68*). Somehow they managed to come back to their own tribal village but their dreams were shattered when they discover that Josmina had been impregnated by the Punjabi and bearing the child of the same Punjabi who raped her many times. Josmina knows well that their tribal community will never accept this sin and for that sin her husband will be ostracized from their native village. So, Josmina drowns herself in the Koyena River where in her girlhood she enjoyed the idyllic beauty of the river amidst the lap of nature in her past days. The tragic fate of Josmina snatches her life and she becomes the victim of circumstances.

In these stories, the condition of the Dalit society in the Indian subcontinent remains in the same obscure stage as it was in the primitive age. The rays of modernity still now unknown to them. The story of Josmina, Shanichari and Dhouli prove the critique of that silence subaltern discourse. British left India but elite Indians assume the same role of British such as dominator, oppressor, and seducer. Dalit are always passive, tolerant and masochistic, whenever their awareness of 'cultural resistance' will arise they will undoubtedly take place in mainstream. But the social, political and economical conditions always lead them in the verge of their inability to raise voice. Till now the Dalit oppression is being practiced in different parts of India by mighty rich and powerful persons in different names under the canopy of social system. The Dalit will remain Dalit as far as the 'Super exploitation' (Spivak) exists in the society and it will not come to an end as it is "Parable of India after decolonization" (*Breast Giver 78*) and there is not God for the poor, '*Gariber Bhagban nai go Maa*' (Chinta).

Work Cited

Devi, Mahasweta. *Outcaste: Four Stories. Trans.* Sharmistha Dutta Gupta. Calcutta: Seagull Publishers, 2012. Print.

Blake, William. *Marriage of Heaven and Hell in Poetry and Prose.* London: Oxford University Press, 2012.Print.

Devi, Mahasweta. *Imaginary Maps.* Trans. Gayatri Chakraborty Spivak. New York: Rout ledge, 1995. Print.

Chattopadhaya, Debasish. "Frames of Marginalization in Mahasweta Devi's Outcast; Four Stories. *Neither East North West-Postcolonial Essays on Literature Culture and Religion.* Ed. Kerstin. Stands. Sweden: Soderton Hongs kola University College, 2008. Print.

Devi, Mahasweta. *Breast Stories.* Trans. Gayatri Chakraborty Spivak. Chicago: Chicago University Press, 2008. Print.

Arora. K. Sudhir. *Arvind Adiga's The White Tiger: A Freakish Booker.* New Delhi: Authorspress, 2011. Print.

http ://www.jstor.org/about/terms.html.

23

Who Knows the Forest Better Than We Do: An Eco-Dalit Approach to C. K. Janu's *Mother Forest*

DR. ZAINUL ABID KOTTA

I don't know whether there is a single term in English to describe the ecological and human rights concerns of the oppressed Dalit community in India. I think such a term is the need of the hour, hence I use the term eco-dalit to bring these people's concern in to the academic limelight and future deliberations, following the term eco-criticism and eco-feminism that are currently used worldwide today. The Dalit community in India faces multiple complexities including the shortage of food, governmental negligence, land encroachments, sexual abuse, untouchability (at least in some part of India) etc. along with myriads of identity issues. A common word, encompassing all the concerns, is inevitable to read and interpret the literatures written by Dalit activists. This essay is an attempt in that direction.

The opening page of *Mother Forest* starts with the beautiful and eulogizing note about the nature that no one knew the forest like they (the tribals) did. The note added that the forest was mother to them, and that more than a mother because she never abandoned them. It shows that the forest was everything to tribal folks. It was their mother. The forest community cannot think about a world in which they are far away from their mother forest. The tribal identity is inseparably associated with forest and its dynamism. Nowadays the whole world understood the importance of nature and the forest. Janu represents them and she is one among others, who fought for the reoccupation of the land that once belonged to them. She has started massive protests in a stage when her own life became topsy-turvy by the ruling class. The vision of Janu is an attempt to transform the world into a place, where the oppressed can live fearlessly as the others do. Janu is an acclaimed fighter for Dalit cause: for the life and land. She wants to make her people respected by all. The two entwined issues, caste and land, are the interminable identities of her community. Janu's *Mother Forest* is an autobiography in two senses: her own as well as her community's. Janu's work questions the hegemonic structure of the patriarchal society in which both the mother and the forest were subjugated to extreme form of assault. As Chinua Achebe talked about Martin Luther King did, she wanted to create awareness among her own community about their emancipation from the manacles of the caste oppression. *Mother Forest* was based on an interview V. Bhaskaran made with Janu. It was rendered to English by N. Ravishankar. The full title of the book is *Mother Forest: The Unfinished Story of C. K. Janu.*

The term 'Eco-feminism' is related with the French writer activist Françoise d' Eaubonne. Many consider her book, Le Féminismeou la Mort (1974) as the official opening of the movement. Eco-feminism argues that women and environment are equally exploited and dominated by the patriarchal societal structure. Eco-feminists believe that there is a strong historical connection between women and nature. According to them the traditional 'female' values of reciprocity, nurturing and cooperation etc., are present both among women and in nature. Both women and nature are united through their shared history of oppression by a society adhered to patriarchal values of the society. Greta Gaard and Lori Gruen in their path breaking book *Eco-feminism: Toward Global Justice and Planetary Health* accuses capitalism for its intrinsic need for the exploitation, destruction and instrumentalization of animals, earth and people for the limited purpose of creating wealth. The issues discussed in *Mother Forest* instinctively elaborate the idea that capitalism destroyed the forest and its people.

It was Vandana Shiva, the Indian physicist and environmental activist, who gave this theory a more dynamic and philosophically strong stand point. According to her, women have a special connection to the environment through their daily interactions, and this connection has been ignored. She says that women in subsistence economies, who produce wealth in partnership with nature, have been experts in their own right of holistic and ecological knowledge of nature's processes. However she makes the point that those alternative modes of knowing, which are oriented to the social benets and sustenance needs are not recognized by the capitalist reductionist paradigm, because it fails to perceive the interconnectedness of nature, or the connection of women's lives, work and knowledge with the creation of wealth. (http://en.wikipedia.org/wiki/Ecofeminism?oldid=632926450)

Janu's life is sketched in the minds of Keralites with utmost transparency. She was not much illumined by the media until the Adivasi Gothra Sabha lodged its final strike at Muthanga, in tribal dense Wayanad District of Kerala. A tribal activist born in the Adivasi Adiyar tribe she was working through the Kerala Krashak Thozilali Union, an organization whose presence was felt throughout the tribal pockets of Kerala. In 1992 she formed the Aadivasi Vikasana Pravartaka Samiti, which was hailed by many as the harbinger of a new platform for eco-dalit activism. As far as the tribals were concerned, forest was everything that fulfilled their dreams and desires. The outside encroachers colonised and usurped their lands and thus cut their daily bread. Their women were sexually abused. Their men were cheated by giving them tobacco and other narcotic things. Forest produces were plundered. As a result of this onslaught on their life and energy, those people were forced for bonded labour in the local Jenmi's (landlord) fields. In *Mother Forest*, she narrated the sad plight of her community Adiyar, who were compelled to strenuous works and resulted in deep fatigue both mentally and physically, and the unnatural and inhuman behaviour of the upper caste Warriors to them. Even the unmarried girls were forced to work from dawn to dusk. Nobody was dared to protest. The landlords put them in debt trap, and there was no way out. They were treated as animals and the landlords made them believe that even food was their sheer magnanimity. The illiteracy and landlessness along with the futile lip service of the politicians made their lives unbearable.

Janu identifies the significance of education in the pursuit of excellence, though she was critical of the education that breeds patriarchy. *Mother Forest* introduces one Sibi was who taught the Adiyars the art of reading and writing. "When our people went for party procession they used to bring back pamphlets, I read them too" (Janu 24). Janu was not given formal education in her tender years. She diagnoses the real issues of the community with a clinical precision. She was doubtful about the intention of her own party workers towards the Adivasi issues. Finally, she had realized that the illiteracy and resultant negligence would, definitely and crucially, would make her community still more backward. She strongly thought about a new awareness and education that is modern and simultaneously planting its roots on Adivasi sensibility and sentiments. There is another teacher named Mary Kutti, mentioned by Janu, who had expressed strong pity and sympathy towards her. Janu had served as a maid in that teacher's house. There is a wonderful analogy in the novel related with a mirror. The symbolic representation of the mirror gives the critic a delicious dish of multiple peripherals. The mirror in the autobiographical writing speaks about a lot of things. It echoes the old proverbial statement that if one has a good friend, he doesn't need a mirror. Mirror is the microcosmic reflection of ones's own image. Here the forest is treated as an image of self-identity. Janu faces the difficulties created by the external society when she looks at the glass. When Janu was a small girl she didn't see her image in the mirror. "There were raised spots at some places on the mirror like unfurled umbrellas. I couldn't see myself in such spots" (Janu 56). This mirror is nothing but our society. When she came back from Vellamunda, a place in Wayanadu, she found some pieces of mirror stuck on her wall. She can't found her full image, her image was fragmented. The mirror image in the work unambiguously argues for a revised sensibility of awareness for self-gratification and fulfillment. But the antithesis of her experience leads the reader to an unforeseen conclusion and enigma. It's similar to an Eliotian concept of broken images.

> What are the roots that clutch, what branches grow
> Out of this stony rubbish? Son of man,
> You cannot say, or guess, for you know only
> A heap of broken images, where the sun beats...
>
> (*The Waste Land*, lines 19-22)

Like other writer activists, she was trying to create an identity that is being defined neither by the conventional patriarchy nor by the Party to which she had affiliated herself in the past. Another powerful symbol employed by Janu in her writing is the comparison that she made of her life to that of a cattle life. Conventional political parties treated the tribals as space fillers for their mammoth conferences. The speakers in those conferences made tall claims that they were working and striving hard for the uplift of the poor and the tribals. Janu used to attend the rallies and protest marches organized by the communist parties in her early youthful days. But later she identified that her community was treated as instruments or as animals by almost all political parties. The journeys to the rallies were exactly like journeys for being slaughtered. "We left in the afternoon in a big Lorry covered on all sides with bamboo meshing we must have looked like cattle being taken to the cattle market" (Janu 27). Three important words are there: bamboo, cattle and market. The first word stands for their adherence to nature, the second word for the deplorable life situation and the third for their destiny. Every aspect of a typical Adivasi life was demonstrated by the political activists to make the former impressed that the party was trying their level best for the uplift of the community. Janu picturises an incident: *"A very old woman of our community was called on the stage and presented with a packet. Never know what was in it or why it was given?"* (Janu 28) She was unaware of two things: why the packet and what it contained.

Janu then brings our attention to one of the major issues the tribal community worldwide experiences—sexual exploitation. The tribals were exposed to worse forms of sexual abuse in India also. Young girls were terrorized and were exposed to brutal forms of sex abuse by many upper caste communities. Organized rape was used as a weapon for terrorizing and for usurping their land illegally. Big capital inflow was assured by the multinational companies to evacuate the Adivasis from their centuries long inherited land for building large scale business and real estate enterprises. In many cases the Adivasi communities were blocks before them. It was sad to note that even political parties were halted before the big dons and they became the mediators to protect the interest of the latter. That is one instance. Another one is that the party men used the tribal girls for satisfying their sexual greeds, under the pretext that they were protecting them. The first was an open assault, but the second was so pathetic and hideous. Janu tells us the party men used the Adivasi women and immature girls for sex, and their children were searching for the names of their father. *"Quite a few women in Thrissileri and Thirunelli gave birth to the babies of party men. There are hundreds of children whose father's names do not appear in the records"* (Janu 35).

Once she identified the double standards of the party men, she decided to say goodbye to the party, and in 1992 she formed Aadivasi Vikasana Pravartaka Samiti. Other significant images in *Mother Forest* are the beetle and the match box. Both are symbolically significant in their lives. It shows the knowledge of an average tribal about her surroundings. When she was young, she used to catch beetles on the Gingili flower and put them into match box. If one raised the box to one‘s ears, one could hear it humming. "The Gingili flower beetle can survive in the box for many days without food and never stops humming, which is but sad hum" (Janu 55). The images of the beetle and Gingili flowers show the pain of her own people. The flower metaphorically stands for the forest and beetle for the tribal. The black colour of the beetle conveys the colour of those people, along with the message of endurance of the people it represents. They are happy in the forests and their needs are met there. They are in direct communication even with wild elephants. They have immense knowledge in the medicinal value of the herbs. They were compelled to protest when they felt that they had nothing to lose since everything theirs were taken by the so called literate and educated outsiders. Their struggles were brutally handled by the police and the media. Janu was devilishly beaten, by the police when she was agitating at Appootti in 1994, and resultantly remained in the hospital for weeks. The autobiographical work *Mother Forest* thus opens a new world of understanding before the sensible readers.

Works Cited

Achebe, Chinua "Martin Luther King and Africa." in *Modern Prose and Drama* (Ed.) Kotta, Zainul Abid. New Delhi: Oxford University Press, 2014. 17-22. Print.

Gaard, Greta (2011). "Ecofeminism Revisited: Rejecting Essentialism and Re-Placing Species in a Material Feminist Environmentalism". *Feminist Formations* 23 (2): 26-53. Print.

Janu, C.K. *Mother Forest: The Unfinished Story of C. K. Janu.* New Delhi: Kali for Women, 2004. Print.

Kumar, N. Prasantha. "Ideology as Articulating Identity: The Politics of Resistance in Mother Forest". Malayalam Literary Survey: A Quarterly Publication of Kerala Sahitya Akademi, Ed. R. Gopalakrishnan Vol. 31 No. 4-33 No. 2-2010 Oct-2013 June Thrissur: 36-39. Print.

Raj, M. S. The Representation of an Ecotone in "When the Lost Soil Beckoned: Life Sketch Narrated by C. K. Janu." *Malayalam Literary Survey: A Quarterly Publication of Kerala Sahitya Akademi.* Ed. R. Gopalakrishnan Vol. 31 No. 4-33 No. 2-2010 Oct.-2013 June Thrissur: 58-61.Print.

Shiva, Vandana. *Staying Alive: Women, Ecology and Development.* London: Zed Books. 1988. Print.

http://en.wikipedia.org/wiki/Ecofeminism?oldid=632926450. Web

24

Tribal Ethnicity: A Reading of Mahasweta Devi's *Chotti Munda and His Arrow* and *Bashai Tudu*

Tuhin Majumdar and Nandini Maity

Marginalization of the tribal people could be seen in vogue in the historical writings as well as the theoretical framework of the intellectuals. Popular intellectuals of the academic circle such as Eric Wolf's 'people without history,' E.P Thompson's 'unsung voices of history,' Genovese's 'objects and subjects of history,' Ranajit Guha's 'subaltern,' Lacan's 'others,' Sharia's 'hybrid histories' and many other intellectuals continuously question the validity of the existing orthodox historical discourses of the marginalized down through the ages.

The mainstream society carries on a continuous, harsh and systematic attack on the social system of the tribes, their culture, their tribal identity and their way of life. The debts of mainstream India to the efforts and struggles of the tribes during the colonial regime and even in the pre-colonial days should be acknowledged by re-writing the history of our country. The history of their struggles is not only documented in their scripts but also in their folktales, dances and songs that passed on from one generation to the other. In short, they are 'othered' and treated as subalterns. It is also that, in the constitution of the 'Other,' great attention was given to the absolute obliteration of the textual ingredients with which these subalterns could react, could claim their place in the mainstream society, literature and culture-not only with the ideological discourses and scientific production but also by the more powerful institution of law. These marginalized people, that is, these tribes who are thought to occupy the lowest strata of the Indian society, are continuously marked out by the epistemic violence. In the opinion of Foucault and Deluze, these oppressed and 'othered' tribes, if given a chance and a road leading to the solidarity of their identity through alliance politics can speak out their subaltern consciousness and understand their condition. Thus starting from the colonial days the Indian history have served to create the foundation of these exclusion of groups resulting in different forms of splits often evinced in these binary and hierarchal terms; local-outsiders, majority-minority etc. Their exclusion from society resulted in deprivation, marginalization and identity losses. It is for these reasons that the poets and writers of these regions are anxious for the preservation of their language, culture and traditions and also their demand of autonomy.

What Mahasweta Devi wanted to do through her works, is to focus on the ethnic identity of the tribal of Bengal. Ethnicity means the ways in which a group conceptualizes their relation to the mainstream society. It brings together the people who have a common history, culture, tradition and community feeling; and shares a common religion, linguistic background and most significantly with a strong sense of regional belonging as if they are from the same stock. From historical times people used to associate themselves with a particular region and culture through the processes like integration, acculturation etc. the rise of the spirit of ethnicity or assertion of ethnic identity among various sects of the society enable the people to aspire for asserting their own ethnic selves. In every almost every state in our country we find that these ethnic groups suffer from an identity crisis because of their marginalization by the mainstream society leading to their lack of sufficient exposure. The zeal for establishing an independent ethnic identity gives rise to a nation within a nation through various strategies like various forms violence against the authority and ethnic struggles; they strive hard in order to preserve their ethnic culture and tradition and prevent them from being one with the dominant culture of the mainstream society. According to A. K. Baruah, "...identity is directly related to the emergence of educated elite in the concerned community." Such an educated elite community takes over the dominant hegemonic position. According to H.N Das, the issues such as the desire of expressing oneself, the deliberate discrimination and marginalization and injustice, the desire for economic, social, political and cultural development are the solely responsible for the growth of these ethnic groups and the ethnic struggles and movements in West Bengal very much discernable in the novels of Mahaswata Devi. The general tendencies of the mainstream society are to brand all the desires and aspirations of these ethnic groups as anti-national without analyzing their needs, merits and demerits. This paper has attempted to bring up the issues related to the struggle of the tribes in Bengal to establish their ethnic identity, portrayed through the works of Mahasweta Devi. There is also an issue which is not very overtly depicted as whether the problems of identity crisis of different ethnic groups of Bengal are evolved or are deliberately created. Whatever may be the reason Mahasweta Devi wants to state this fact that building of a nation state is impossible without recognizing the specificities of the component parts of each and every corner of the country. The Political leaders can play a significant role in resolving the conflicts of the mainstream society and these ethnic groups by bringing integration and not a forced assimilation by fulfilling the needs and basic demands of both the classes.

Mahasweta Devi considers her writing to be a significant part of the struggle against the repression and exploitation of the people of the backward classes, especially the tribes of India. Most of the books of Devi are translated by the postcolonial Marxist feminist, Gayatri Chakravorty Spivak. Through Spivak's translations Devi has become one of the renowned literary figures worldwide. The translated feats are a discourse of the dispossessed and downtrodden marked by a desire to find a suitable language for the new territory of human life hitherto neglected, unheard and was characterized by a suffocating silence. Most of the works of Devi are about the lives of the tribal people of India, their incessant struggle against domination and exploitation of the authority. These stories of Devi have a proximity and loyalty that cannot be found in the works of even the tribal writers though there is a trend of writing among the Dalits drawing motivation from the Dalit Panther movement. Devi's commitment for writing about the oppressed and the marginalized cannot be questioned. Yet sometimes she makes the emphatic statement that we can do nothing to bring an end to the ceaseless exploitation of the tribal people under the unbending system which does not know to compromise. She tries to raise the consciousness of the society by pointing out that these oppressed people are bound to disappear if social inequality is not droved out immediately.

Devi's historical fictions are in close proximity to the subaltern historiography. The long-established national history is loaded with silences and absences. These absences are a result of the continuous deprivation and marginalization. Rewriting of the national history is an endeavour to fill these fissures by making an honest effort to bring the periphery to the centre. Devi attempts to depict the other side of the national history by portraying in her narratives the struggles of the peripherals against domination and biasness of the mainstream Indian society. By depicting the tribals in almost all her celebrated work, she focuses on the very aspect of the absence of their stories in the recorded national as well as literary history. By giving the central position to the struggles of the tribes in her works, she reinstates the Dalit history into the postcolonial and national historiographies.

Devi has enthusiastically devoted herself to the liberation of the tribal people from the stigma of caste discrimination. The curse of racism that has made the very existence of the tribal people a miserable one is an overarching system in the responsibility of the elite classes of India. This system has been in vogue right from the colonial times in India. That is why Devi has tried to present an alternative history by exposing the drawbacks of the colonial as well as postcolonial history of India in order to show the dehumanization of the tribal masses at the hands of the colonizers and the post-colonial comprador bourgeois. What Devi tries to do through her work is subverting the notion of caste system which she believed creates an unbalanced equation and thereby challenge the rigid customs and conventions of the mainstream Indian society. The farmers, the *adivasis* and the other people belonging to the lower classes in India embody a charade which has been exposed by Devi in order to rectify the system thereby bringing about a change. In her masterpiece *Chotti Munda and His arrow*, the writer has rediscovered a tribal history in the complex system of the colonial and post-colonial era." I am talking about a place of great caste difference… but with the tribals they were one in everything" (Devi xiii).

"I had but that one arrow" (Devi, *Chotti Munda* and His Arrow 289), says the Chotti Munda, the protagonist of Mahasweta Devi's novel. Here Chotti talks about the 'magic' arrow, the symbol of wisdom, tradition and pride of the society, threatened continuously with the possibility of destruction as its age old structure disintegrated due to the onslaughts of 'national development'. This novel of Devi is multilayered. It encompasses a large span of time in the life of Chotti, the protagonist, during which India sees the colonial rule, the fight for freedom, the independence and finally the unrest in the 1970s. The writer delves deep into the then social system and brings out the intricate complications of the exchanges at social and economic level based on power relations. This novel also locate the changes in the daily lives of the marginalized communities when moves from a pre-colonial to a post-colonial period. It centers on the life of Chotti, the renowned archer, an ideal and wise leader and a role model to his fellow comrades. This novel raises various questions regarding the position of these tribes on the map of national identity. Further, it also raises questions regarding their rights of owing lands, their human rights for survival, protests against 'musemization' of their ethnic tradition and try their best to justify their strong resistance against the elite mainstream culture. Thus Gayatri Spivak aptly opines: "This is the first novel where Mahasweta articulates tribal history with colonial and postcolonial history" (Preface to *Chotti Munda and his Arrow* vii). After the publication of Chotti, this book depicting tribality liberates itself from the burden of being simply an Indian history. *Chotti Munda* frequently produces subaltern solidarity: Tudu, Munda, Oraon, and the Hindu tribes must join hands. In the present times such solidarity has been given a name—Dalit.

Caste, from the historic times, has always been one marker of the people in the Indian society. Caste system, in the past and even in the present, has been a strong means of social control by elite class. Caste is quintessentially rooted in religious belief. *Chotti Munda* vehemently criticizes the egregious caste system that has become an intricate part of the social system over times. The setting of this work of Devi is built up on the village of Chotti which symbolizes 'tribal aspiration' against the tremendous odds of preconceived notions, social customs and prejudices prevalent in the society for ages. Through her fictional world

Devi has made the readers to realize and thereby raise their voice of protest against the ruthless manner of oppressing the tribal masses. She articulates:

> These people do not find anyone writing about them, and they do not have script… this is unwritten history. I had to learn it by being with the people. They compose the stream of events into song... their history is like a big flowing flower going somewhere, not without a destination... tribal world is like a continent handed over to us, and we never tried to explore it, know is mysteries, we only destroyed it. (*Chotti Munda and His Arrow*, xi)

In *Chotti Munda and his Arrow*, Devi has incisively brought into the light the attitude of the feudal lords in India. They believed whole heartedly in the divine right to rule the people belonging to the lower castes. This right goaded the landlords to exploit the landless peasants and the tribal people. Bhabha is of the view that, "subaltern classes are not unified and cannot unite until they are able to become a State" (qtd in Vandhana 5879). What Devi has done is highlighting this very notion of Bhabha by studying the ways in which these tribal masses as *Dusdad, Ganjus, Charams* throw out the differences of the caste system and heartily welcome the marginalized and outcastes of the Hindu society into the mainstream social life. These long marginalized tribes unite forces in order to challenge the divine right and confront the suppression. What Devi found out after personally interacting with the tribes is that they are extremely peace-loving people in contrary to being uncivilized or barbaric as presented frequently by the elite society.

Devi addresses the existing system with all its drawbacks and brings into focus the tyranny of the human beings which works as fuel to the fire. She attacks this kind of hidden ideological workings through her novel *Chotti Munda*. It is because of these subtle ideological workings, the people like Tirathnath (another character in this novel), work for the elite class without a word of protest. The writer views it as a way of 'indirect exploitation.' The extent to which this indirect oppression works can be felt when the mentality to treat the tribal people as social outcastes is seen to be implemented by the schools. Thus it is evident that these schools along with other such institutions functions in accordance to the government and its prejudiced belief system. So the schools can be viewed as one of the 'Ideological State Apparatuses' as was put forth by the postmodern-Marxist, Althusser (Vandhana 5887). In this context Devi highlights the point where the workings of ISA are thoroughly discernable. She states, "A Munda'll go to government school here! Diku boys won' study then, and t' master chases off even t' boys of Chhagan's caste. They say, Low caste, do low work, why d' ye need to study?" (Chotti *Munda* 150-206).

Thus in her magnum opus *Chotti Munda and his Arrow*, what Devi has done is rebuilding the history of the tribes in the mazy systems of the pre-independence and the post-independent governments. To uphold the cause of the tribal masses Devi asserts:

> ...thus came *Chotti Munda*. In it, so many experiences, I had stored them so lovingly-Chotti is my best beloved book. I had such a great asthirata in me, such a restlessness; an udbeg: I have to write, somehow I have to document this period which I have experienced because it is going away, it is vanishing... it is cultural, it is economic, it is connected with the land, with everything, they want to rob the tribal of everything. (*Chotti Munda* xiii)

Another noteworthy work where Devi speaks of deprivation, marginalization and discrimination based on caste system is *Bashai Tudu*. It stresses that the existing disparity between the "haves" and the "have-nots" is nothing new. The resistance of Bashai and his fellow comrades is noteworthy as he fights of reclaim their rights and the rights of his people, the *adivasis* who are mostly landless laborers. Bashai is seen to continually challenge the elite Institutions and the social Establishments and becomes the leader of four major movements in the 1970s. In order to wipe out the threatening elements in the periphery, the administrative authority sets out a 'noble mission'. These authorities design some shrewd means in order to disrupt the forces of Bashai and his *adivasi* comrades but instead of being able to break the joint force, their plans boomerangs on them. Under their ideal leader, Bashai, the tribal force seems to disrupt the administration of the metropolis. Bashai's protests can be viewed as 'little narratives' which counter the 'grand narrative' of the nation by continuously wiping out its totalizing boundaries and threatens the dominant ideological schemes, by applying which national essentialist identities are given to the imagined communities. Thus the outer identity of India as a democratic non-violent secular state is smashed by the clashes of the two forces of the 'haves,' the administrative authorities and the 'have-nots,' the forces of Bashai Tudu.

What makes this particular work of art a unique piece is the fact that the whole narrative is carefully woven as a double helix. This work revolves round the life of Bashai Tudu, the protagonist, who is wanted dead or alive by the police and also the administrative body of the city. Bashai proudly declares his own identity as an *adivasi*, "I am Bashai the Santal, one of those who go about almost naked, and feed on mice and snake when there's a famine" (Devi, *Bashai Tudu*). Throughout the novel Bashai is reported dead a couple of times but resurrects mysteriously thereby emerging as a legend and bringing hope among his people. Bashai keeps on resurrecting in order to remind the metropolis that he is an epitome of struggle for the due rights of his people. What Devi does is redefining the center as the legend of undying Bashai Tudu destabilizes the dominating metropolitan discourse. Thus Devi's protagonist, Bashai Tudu evokes the suppressed and neglected voice of the subalterns and finds a significant space in the domain of historical fictions.

Through these stories the author tries to give voice to these 'peripheral people' continuously suppressed by the present reality. The subaltern communities are always subject to the control by the social authorities, even when they try to voice their protests against the authorities. It has been noticed by the subaltern historians that the Indian history is basically under the dominance of the elites. The Divine right of ruling the subalterns has been ideologically constructed by the elites over time. This is why all the great achievements in the history of India have been attributed to the elites, institutions of the state authorities, their activities and ideas. Ranajit Guha, the renowned subaltern historian, calls the history of Indian nationalism "a sort of spiritual biography of the Indian elite" (qtd in Mcleod 109). It ignored the peasants and tribal rebellions that preceded the formation of Indian National Congress. In this context, Ranajit Guha proclaims in the chapter "On Some Aspects of the Historiography of Colonial India" from the book *Selected Subaltern*

Studies: "The historiography of Indian nationalism has for a long time been dominated by elitism—colonialist elitism and bourgeoisie nationalist elitism. Both originated as the ideological product of British rule in India...." (Guha 37). Further, in the similar book, Ranajit Guha writes *in extenso* in the chapter "The Prose of Counter Insurgency":

> When a peasant rose in revolt at any time or place under the Raj, he did so necessarily and explicitly in violation of a series of codes which defined his very existence as a member of that colonial, and still largely semi-feudal society. For his subalternity was materialized by the structure of property, institutionalized by law, sanctified by religion and made tolerable-and even desirable-by tradition. To rebel was indeed to destroy many of those familiar signs which he had learned to read and manipulate in order to extract a meaning out of the harsh world around him and live with it. The risk in 'turning things upside down' under these conditions was indeed so great that he could hardly afford to engage in such a project in a state of absent-mindedness. (Guha 45)

According to Guha the histories that are presented to us are biased as these fail to capture and explicate the contribution of the common people. The subalterns problematise the ideological construction of elitist history and make a deliberate endeavour to draw the attention of the readers to the contribution of the marginalized people in the building up the history of the nation.

There are several tribes in West Bengal and throughout India following the indigenous lifestyle. These tribal people are considered the children of the forest whose coexistence with the nature characterize their way of life which seems to be far out-of-the-way from the mainstream social life. Mahasweta Devi gives voice to this marginalized world and her historical narratives give us more than an insight into the deeply-felt perceptive world of the common folk leading a life of struggle and misery.

Works Cited

Ashcroft, Bill. Gareth Griffiths, Helen Tiffin. *The Post-colonial Studies Reader*. Taylor & Francis. 2006. Print.

Devi, Mahasweta. *Bashai Tudu*. Trans. Samik Bandyopadhyay and Gayatri Chakravorty Spivak. Calcutta: Thema. 1990. Print.

____. *Chotti Munda and His Arrow*. Trans. Gayatri C. Spivak. Malden: Blackwell Pub, 2003. Print.

Guha, Ranajit, and Gayatri C. Spivak. *Selected Subaltern Studies.* New York: Oxford University Press, 1988. Print.

McLeod, John. *Beginning Postcolonialism.* Manchester University Press. 2000. Print.

Sharma, Vandhana and Quleen Kaur. "Articulating Tribal History: The Fallouts of Caste in Mahasweta Devi's *Chotti Munda and His Arrow*" *European Academic Research* 1.12 (2014): 5876-5902.Web. 22 July. 2014.

25

Perambulation of Caste Hierarchs in Siddalinagaiah's *Ooru Keri*

BIJENDER SINGH

> Man is born free but everywhere he is in the chains.
>
> (Rousseau 2)

Poverty proves a paralyzing factor in our life. On one side there is phallocentric chauvinistic society and on the other there is caste and the later one is an overt suffocating and exploitative factor. Dalit writers fag in articulating their bad experiences and ground realities of their lives and project the heinous picture of the society and the predicament of the Dalits. Dalit narratives, written in autobiographical, biographical or any genre, are the coherent and important heritage in Indian Dalit literature. The ditch of caste exists not only in the minds of high caste people; it is equally among the Dalits also. Nobody remains behind to take advantage of the availed opportunity whether the person is Dalit or non-Dalit. Women Dalit writers like Urmila Pawar, Baby Kamble, Bama, P. Sivakamai etc. have raised their voice to eradicate triple exploitation of women and the men Dalit writers have generally protested against discrimination, injustice and tyrannies of the caste hierarchs. Every Dalit autobiography has such voices as Raj Kumar says:

> The fact that every title of Dalit autobiography has subtitle that refers to an untouchable life makes it clear that it is not yet time for any Dalit autobiographer to celebrate his/her freedom, the most desirable part of one's life. The search is still on. (260)

Siddalingaiah is very famous Dalit poet and writer who is the founder of Dalit Sangarsha Samiti and he is a former member of the Karnataka Legislative Council. He earned his Ph.D from Bangalore University. He is currently the President of Kannada Book Authority, Bangalore. Siddalingaiah's *Ooru Keri: An Autobiography* came in a Kannada magazine *Rujuvatu* as an article and it was translated by Dr. D.R. Nagaraj and appeared in the magazine section of *Deccan Herald* during 1995. It was published in five parts in 2003 in a book. It is the finest example of Dalit autobiography in which he has not only depicted the real pictures of his life but very ugly faces of penury and Dalit humiliation in the state of Karnataka. There is no one to help the poor and Dalit people in the society. If they remain uneducated, the caste plays a vital role in their illiteracy.

Ooru Keri means "neighbourhood". Keri is a name of a colony where Dalits live and this colony is segregated from the village and thus, these people are socially cut from the higher castes of the village. Siddalingaiah's father Dyavanna was a farm labourer and he got very low-income. His mother also worked as a sweeper in a Dalit hostel in Srirampura. Both, his mother and father had to see very bad days in their life. As Siddalingaiah's mother was a sweeper in a Dalit hostel in Srirampura, she brought the food home left behind by the hostel boys and it was eaten by her family members with great relish. Not only this, many other Dalit families were fed on the leftover.

The first chapter in this book is "Ainoru's Fields". Ainoru was a landlord and he had a beautiful house and a huge pore well with bump-set cabin. It was a reserved well and Dalits were not allowed to take water from this well. They had to go to very far off places to fetch water. Siddalingaiah had never eaten sumptuous food cooked in his own home. He got good food always from others. One day he was eating stale citranna and poori, he could not forget its taste: *"I had never tasted these delicacies before*" (2-3). There are many instances of leftover in Dalit literature in which Dalits have been depicted to eat left-over or to run for receiving it. Another example of leftover depicted by Siddalingaiah is:

> That was a time of drought everywhere. People had to struggle even for a morsel of food. Some threw ceremonial fests to appease the rain god. During fests, the Holeyas were made to sit in a corner. We were noticed only after people of the upper castes had been served. I felt contented with whatever little food came my way, and wouldn't think much about the discrimination. (7)

Siddalingaiah has to conceal his poverty in his school. He did not take free study material in the school just to conceal his caste but one day when his mistress saw his father's poverty-stricken face and pitiable plight; she immediately gave him free study material:

> My father's tattered clothes, his submissiveness, and his unshaven, pleading face proclaimed his poverty. Madam immediately called for the books and pencils meant for poor students and gave them to me. Her affection increased after she came to know that I was the son of an utterly poor man. (31-32)

Siddalingaiah has narrated very ugly pictures of Dalit society. The women and children of the Dalits had a stigmatized life and their poverty stricken faces automatically tell the tale of their agony. The wives of the Dalit reproached them saying why they married them if they had nothing to feed them and Dalit people were helpless and hopeless in front of their present circumstances. This autobiography tells the stark reality of life that money makes the relationship, not the people. When people failed to feed their members of family then their wives and children did not behave well with them. Children started beating their parents also when they found nothing to eat. There is an instance of a boy named Ramu who disliked his father just because he could not give him sufficient facilities of life. When people ask him about his father's health he comments: *"He isn't dead yet"* (37). Siddalingaiah's family had to live in slums and they had to collect tuber, yams and greens to prepare dinner. His father was in huge debt and he often failed to pay his debts. Due to his debt he was badly beaten by two men and thus, his clothes were torn:

> Bringing loans was, to him, as easy as drinking water. But he found it very hard to repay them. One day two toughs beat him on the street. He was wailing and trying to escape. He was injured all over his body and his clothes were torn. The toughs were agents of the moneylender. They had assaulted my father because he hadn't repaid a loan in time. (37)

Siddalingaiah also had seen bad days in his life like his parents. He joined Gopalaswamy Iyaer Hostel and his life took a turn hereafter. He was inspired by the speeches of Kannadigas and Tamils. He also started delivering speeches on Ambedkar and caste system and won many prizes but he sold all of his prizes and clothes and bought books. He started challenging Hindu beliefs and he started saying publically that god does not exist. In one of his speech he put off the light which was considered as a symbol of existence of god and challenged the god: "If God does exist, will it stop me speaking" (81) and he got the first prize in this competition. During one of his speeches when he said that caste system should be abolished, one Hindu person opposed this. A student said to the speaker if caste was not an issue, were they ready to marry their girls outside their caste. At this opponents became so outraged that they assaulted whomsoever they found there:

> They used knives, daggers... All those who were dark got beaten up then. One of my Veerashiva friends was dark. The opponents hit him despite his pleading that he was a Veerasaiva. His clothes tore, and they felt sorry when they saw that he was wearing a sivalinga and had spoken the truth. (93-94)

Siddalingaiah had to face untouchablity also in his life. One day he went with his grandmother in a wedding and his hand brushed against the clothes of an upper caste man. That man lost his temper and his grandmother saved him somehow from the wrath of that man. Siddalingaiah was a bibliophile and tried his best to get new books to read and he got books by working in the houses, factories, and by delivering speeches. *Ooru Keri: An Autobiography* is the reflection of Siddalingaiah's life in his village and slum of Bangalore. It has been described in Shankarrao Kharat's autobiography, *Taral-Antaral* when his father, Ram's sister died and he got the news by a letter; there was no any person in his family or community who could read this letter. The teacher who read this letter, he did not sympathize on the news of demise of his father's sister rather he took undue advantage by getting cut the woods by him. Not only this when Omprakash's father wants to admit his son in a school in *Joothan* he gets a very bad response from the Dalit people and the school administration. Laxman Gaikwad also faces the same problem in *The Branded* and in Rohinton Mistry's *A Fine Balance* there is a great revolt among the Hindus when Dukhi Mochi makes his sons tailors instead of cobblers.

Thus, education is sometimes considered useful only for the high caste people and the people of other castes are expected to serve the upper castes. Siddalingaiah got education and he started reading the letters without demanding anything, he got food and some money also in return. He narrates: *"I would then get, besides a generous amount of eats, some money as well. For the handful who got love letters, I was equal to god."* (33-34). Thus, education is must for the sustenance of life and the social image of a person. It is as indispensable as air and food for all.

Untouchability is not rampant only in the illiterate minds, the roots of untouchability are also found in the educated people's mind also till date. Siddalingaiah tells an instance of his college life when he studied in Government Arts College in Bangalore and one of his non-Dalit lecturers took him for a Lingayat and asked him to bring water but when he came to know about his caste he stopped asking him for that: *"He had mistaken me for a Lingayat. I was liberated from the task of fetching water after he came to know my caste."* (76) In Omprakash Valmiki's *Joothan: A Dalit's Life* he is not first easily admitted in the school and when admitted he has to sweep the school by the headmaster's order. Even when he reads in high classes he is not allowed to attend practical classes by his teacher just because he is a Dalit child.

Siddalingaiah tried his best to transform the society and bring equality for Dalits. He had to take many pains and he had got even threatening of murdering him but he remained firm in his decision. The caste-conscious people always try to oppress and suppress Dalits. Siddalingaiah says that Dalits should be aware and conscious for their rights of equality. They can achieve their rights through struggle and boldness. Omprakash Valmiki always keeps fighting against the oddities of life and keeps studying and raising his voice against the caste discrimination. He tells in his autobiography *Joothan: A Dalit's Life* how he and the people of his caste are forced to eat left-over to satisfy their hunger. Dalits like Gunasekaran are not allowed to participate in music competitions but it is their hard work and struggle that makes their survival possible in Dalit community.

The canker of caste bursts even in the educated people though in lesser degree but they are also not free from this cruel clutch of caste.

Gunasekaran's father was a teacher but he knew all the reality of caste system and he never dared to speak against the injustice and discriminations done to them. Some people sometimes even go to the extent of changing their caste. Gunasekaran also wants to convert himself to Islam: *"I have experienced harassment in the name of caste and have often thought about converting to Islam"* (4). Gunasekaran has further fears that if he converts into Islam the Muslims of India are similarly infected by this disease of caste: "*Even if we asked a Muslim household for water, they too would ask us: 'Who are you?' before they offered us water*" (20). Gunasekaran also says: *"Inside the village we had to address the upper caste person as, 'Ayya' and 'Sami'. The women were referred to as 'Nachiyar' or 'Aachi'. One had to call even those who were younger in age only thus. No one can call the upper caste boys or girls by their names"* (42). Baby Kamble also had to drop her study after fourth standard and she was married when she was a child. She had to face cruelty of her husband named Kondiba Kamble. She recorded all of her bad experiences in scrap paper which were published by an American researcher Maxine Berntson as *Jina Amucha* (1982) and it came as *The Prisons We Broke* in 1986.

To sum up with, caste sometimes seems a curse. High caste or a low caste, both are not good for a good society. To identify a person by its caste is very derogatory. God has made males and females but caste hierarchs have divided this society into innumerous castes on the basis of works and economic status. Those who got power and penny flew away from the range of this grinding machine of casteism but those failed to achieve that they grinded between the strong stones of caste-system. Other way to escape from this system is to get a high education. Some children from these socially ostracized castes got good education and became, more or less, liberated from the cruel clutch of casteism. It is rightly said: *"If the Dalits are not educated, they will be exploited and harassed in many ways"* (Murhari 1). Dalit writers raised their voice through their writings. They have their way to express their horrendous experiences of caste-ridden social system. There are many different genres through which they have raised their voice against this system but autobiography is very influential among them and *Oori Keri* is the best example of caste discrimination.

Works Cited

Bharathiraja, S. *A Study of Social Realism in the Select Indian Dalit Autobiographies.* Annamalai University Ph.D Thesis. February 2012. Print.

Gunasekaran, K. A. *The Scar.* Chennai: Orient BlackSwan, 2009. Print.

Kumar, Raj. *Dalit Personal Narratives: Reading Caste, Nation, and Identity.* New Delhi: Orient BlackSwan, 2011. Print.

Murhari, Banshelkikar Yashpal. Breaking Tenets: A Study of Stigmatized Lives in *[O]oru Keri* and *The Scar.* IRWLE VOL. 7 No. 2 July 2011. Web

Pawar, Daya. *Baluta.* Mumbai: Granthali Prakashan, 1995. Print.

Siddalingaiah. *Ooru Keri.* New Delhi: Sahitya Academi, 2003. Print.

Rousseau, Jean Jacques. *The Social Contract.* Cosimo Inc. 2008. Print.

Valmiki, Omprakash. *Joothan: A Dalit's Life.* Kolkata: Samya, 2003. Print.

26

Decadent Brahmanism in U. R. Anathamurthy's *Samskara: A Rite for a Dead Man*

Jyoti Arora Sharma

Udupi Rajagopalacharya Ananthamurthy was born in a small village on December 21, 1932 in an orthodox Brahmin community whose grandfather was a priest. He did his schooling from a Sanskrit school but later he did his doctorate in English from the University of Birmingham. He is a pioneer writer of Kannada and English language. His body of work is a critique of his community and its biases. He has received Padma Bhushan and Jnanpith awards and he was nominated for the Man Booker International Prize in 2013. He has been the president of Sahitya Akademi, the vice-chancellor of Mahatma Gandhi University and the chairman of National Book Trust India. He has worked as a visiting professor in many renowned universities in India and abroad. His famous work *Samskara* (1965) deals with the theme of cremation of a dead iconoclast whose body keeps rotting while the people squabble over rituals of cremation and a debate ensues on this matter. *Bharathipura* (1971) is a story of a wealthy young *landowner* who tries his best to abolish the oppression and exploitation of low-caste people. *Bhava* (1994) is a story of two men and their sons. Their attempts to trace the painful chains of memory find the links to certain answers irrevocably broken. Mishra says about the Dalit writers:

> These writers make use of the language of the out caste and underprivileged in Indian society, Shame, anger, sorrow and indomitable hope are the stuff of Dalit literature. Because of the anger against the age-old oppression, the expression of the Dalit writers has become sharp. (Mishra 2-3)

Anathamurthy's novel *Samskara: A Rite for a Dead Man* is about high and lower caste, tradition and modernity, oppression and rule and dharma and adharma. The novel is about a small village Sarasvatipura in the Western Ghats of Karnataka. There is majority of a Brahmin community named Madhwas. The people have a traditional mindset and they perform all the rituals and rites prescribed for the Brahmins. The village is guided by a learned and devout Brahmin Preshacharya who has read Vedas in Kashi Vidyapeeth. He is a learned man who has full authority on Vedas, Upanishadas and Hindu scriptures. His aim of life is to attain *moksha* or salvation. He marries an invalid woman named Bhagirathi and does his duties as a very devoted husband: "He bathed Bhagirathi's body, a dried-up waste pea-pod, and wrapped a fresh sari around it; then he offered food and flowers to the gods as he did every day, put the flowers in her hair, and gave her holy water…"(1). Her wife keeps saying him to remarry so that he may be able to extend his progeny. She remains unhappy that she is unable to give her husband an heir: "Being married with me is no joy. A house needs a child. Why don't you just get married again? Praneshacharyan would laugh aloud. A wedding for an old man? (1). People sometimes feel losing interest in their life or they feel that they have lost their self-respect and they go on to say like Daya Pawar who in his autobiography, *Baluta* says: "Sometimes I used to feel that I have lost all my self-respect just for a morsel of food" (Pawar 72).

The agarahara becomes the centre of people's attention because a wealthy Brahmin named Naranappa starts living with a concubine named Chandri, a low-caste woman. He starts eating meat and behaves which is not fit for a Brahmin. One day Naranappa, with his friends, catches sacred fish form the temple tank, cooks and eats them. After this incidence the Brahmins of the village rise up against him. They excommunicate Naranappa from their caste and treat him as an outcaste. One day Naranappa visits Shimoga and he comes back Duravasapura with high fever and dies after suffering from fever for four days: "He came back from Shivamogga and took to bed in a fever. Four days of fever, that's all. He had a painful lump on his side, the kind they get with fever." (3)

After his death, his concubine, Chandri comes to village guru Praneshacharya and she informs her about the death of Naranappa.

Chandri as she is a Dalit woman and if he talks to her, he will be polluted and he will have to take bath before eating his meal: "Chandri was Naranappa's concubine. If Acharya talked to her he would be polluted; he would have to bathe again before his meal" (2). But he has no option but to hear her and the news that Chandri gave to him was very shocking to him. They converse:

> 'What's the matter?'
>
> 'He… He…'
>
> 'Chandri shivered; words struck in her mouth. She held on the pillar.'
>
> 'What? Naranappa? What happened?'
>
> 'Gone…' (2)

As soon as Praneshacharya learns about this news he immediately rushes to other people to inform so that they may not eat even a bite of food as per custom of the village: "Garudacharya was eating rice mixed with *saru* to his mouth. Praneshacharya said to him: "Narayana. Don't. Garuda, Don't eat. I hear Narappa is dead." (3) It was a very critical time for the village people as they were not allowed to eat during the time when somebody is dead. As soon as Garudacharya gets this news he does not accept his food: "Dumbstruck Garuda threw down the mixed rice in his hand on the leaf before him, took a gulp on consecrated water and rose from his seat. He could not eat even though he has quarrelled with Narappa, severed all relations with him and shed his kinship long ago." (3) But it was a good thing that there was no such kind of prohibition on the children: "Garudacharya said to his wife Sitadevi. It's all right for the children. They can eat. Only we adults shouldn't till the funeral rites done". (3) Naranappa is considered as an enemy but Garudacharya forgets all of his enmity when he dies. He says: "Alive, Naranappa was an enemy; dead a preventer of meals; as a corpse, a problem, a nuisance." (3). There arises a piquant situation as in this condition Narnappa was neither a Brahmin nor a low-caste. There arises a dispute over the cremation of his dead body. The people were not ready to accept Narnappa as a brhamin. They go for their village guru for the solution of this problem. All wait for his decision: "Don't be in a hurry. Wait till Praneshacharya gives you a decision. Don't agree too quickly to perform the rites." (4) They argue over this issue: "The real question is: Is he a Brahmin at all? What do you say?—he slept regularly with a low-caste woman…(5)." Their village guru had a respect in his village and all the people wait for his decision earnestly. They have faith on their vedic professor Praneshacharya as Garudacharya says: "We don't have to advise great Praneshacharya. He knows all about alliances and misalliances, has studied it all in Kashi and he knows all the scriptures, earned his title Crest-Jewel of Vedic Learning (6)."

At another place Durgabhatta says: "Agreed, Acharya. The Brahminism of your entire sect is in your hands. Your burden is great. Who can go against what you decide?" (6) All of these people knew well how Naranappa lived: "Only another Brahmin has any right to touch his body. If we let someone else to do it, we would be sullying our Brahmanhood. Yet I can't tell you go ahead with the rites. We all saw how he lived. What shall we do? What do the law books say?" (9).

Even Brahmin women were not ready to hand over the dead body to the low-caste people: "Anasuya nagged him. Wasn't Naranappa my own maternal uncle's son? Sinner he may be. But if any low-caste man is allowed to pick up his dead body, I'll die of shame." (32) Shankaraya, the priest of Parijatapura tells an interesting ideology of the birth of the Brahmins. According to it, 'a snake is also a twice born,' if you happen to see a dead snake you have to perform the proper rites for it. You shouldn't eat till you have done so. (19). Later this twice birth theory was explained like this:

> Twice born; Dvija, the epithet applies not only to brahmins and the other two upper castes (kshtriya 'warrior', vaisya 'tradesman') but also to birds, snakes, various grains, and tooth etc., anything that may be said to have two births (e.g. birds and snakes are born as eggs and reborn from them). Snakes are considered sacred and therefore should be cremated ceremoniously. (151)

He is neither Brahmin nor an outcaste and the inhabitants of Saravastipura are confused over the matter of Naranappa's funeral. Some of his Brahmin relatives want the norms of Brahmins to cremate Naranappa's body but other people argue that he has relations with Dalit woman that's why he should not be cremated like Brahmins. When they are confused they want solution from Praneshacharya for this problem. He consults all of his religious books but fails as solution of such kind of problem has not been discussed in the religious books also. He goes to the Hanuman temple in the forest but he fails to find the solution of this problem also. When he leaves the Hanuman temple he finds Chandri in the forest who falls at his feet. She requests him to help her so that her Naranappa's dead body should be cremated. While he lifts her, his hands touch Chandri's uncovered bosom. He is mesmerised by her beauty and he fails to control himself and he has sexual intercourse with her. When he returns the village he finds that his ailing wife has passed away due to plague. After her funeral he leaves the village as he is repentant of what he had done with Chantri. He moves from one place to another place for the redemption of the sin but he realizes that only being away from the village will not bring out any solution of his problem. He determines to clean the pollution of his village and restore the lost glory of Brahmins.

Naranappa is a Brahmin by caste but he has been degraded to a low-caste because he has his relations with Chandri. Praneshacharya has tried to reform Naranappa but he could not reform him.

> But Naranappa hadn't walked the path, he had turned a deaf ear to all counsel. By sheer power of example, had even stolen Praneshacharya's own words and Sanskrit pupils. Guruda's son Shayam, Lakshmana's son-in-law Shripati. Naranappa had incited Shyam to run away from home and join the army. The Acharya, wearied by complaints, had gone to see Naranappa one day. He was looking on a soft mattress, and showed some courtesy by getting up. He didn't take counsel well, and talked his head off; sneered at the Acharya and Brahmin ways" (Mukherji 43).

Praneshacharya knew that the Dalit women bend before the Brahmins. Dalits are poverty-stricken and there is prosperity and happiness in Brahmins" houses. Natarajan says: "The novella establishes Pranesha's singularity and his merit through the hard work he performs feeding his invalid wife, cooking and cleaning" (Natarajan 160).

Conclusively, the village guru, who has gone to the temple to do justice for Chandri and Naranappa; he did more injustice for Chandri by losing his self-control. He has gone for the people of his village who have faith in him but he also could no justice with them also. He had to go to forests after the funeral of his wife. He wanders here and there but he finds solace nowhere. He craves for something that he missed somewhere. He feels a voidance in his life. To do justice with himself, he returns to the village and this is the place where this novel meets an end.

Works Cited

Mishra, Kishore Jugal, "A critical study of Dalit literature in India", http://litteritt.blogspot.in/2012/09/dalit-literature-reading.html

Murthy, Anantha. *Samskara.* Translated by A. K Ramanujana, New Delhi: Oxford University Press, 2004

Mukherji, Meenakshi. *Realism and Reality: Novel and Society in India.* New Delhi: Oxford University Press, 2009. Print.

Natarajan, Nalini. "Gender, Caste and Modernity: A Reading of U.R. Ananthamurthy's *Samskara* in its Intellectual Context" in Rajan, Rajeshwari Sunder's Signposts: Gender Issues in Post-Independence India". Rutgers University Press: New Jersey, 1999. Print.

Pawar, Daya. *Baluta.* Mumbai: Granthali Ptakashan, 1982. Print.

27

Shoulder for the Dalits: Voicing the Voiceless in the Select Poems of Jaydeep Sarangi

MOHINI GURAV

Dalit literature or literature about the Dalits—an oppressed Indian class under the Indian Caste system—forms an important and distinct part of Indian literature. Dalit literature emerged into the forefront and as a prominent voice after 1960, starting with the Marathi language, and soon appeared in languages like Hindi, Kannada, Bengali, Telugu and Tamil languages through narratives such as, poems, short stories, and most importantly autobiographies, which stood out due to their stark portrayal of reality and the Dalit political scene. Dalit writers belong to a historical, social, and political background that spreads throughout India from Gujarat, Tamil Nadu, Maharashtra, and Andhra Pradesh to Bengal. It could be said that Dalit literature achieved a firm foundation in the mid-20th century, but its framework was established in the early 19th century. Today, Dalit writers have their own literary foundations and publish numerous journals. They also have a number of political organizations. The most prominent of these is the Dalit Panthers (begun in the 1970s), which has borrowed much of its ideology from America's Black Panthers. Here, after all, is a society based on terrible persistent inequalities, social servitude and economic bondage. At the centre of the serfdom, and legitimizing it, is the systematic and religiously sanctified discrimination against the Dalits, India's former 'untouchables'. The form or style of Dalit literature covers a wide range of literary genres. The overall message is about community not individuality, revolt not passivity, progress not backwardness. The shared political position of these authors is against the hegemony of upper and middle-class Hindu beliefs and for the power of the human being against oppressive social rules. Because of this, cultural concepts such as religion and identity are called into question. The language of these texts is very faithful to local, spoken dialects, and high-flown language is not seen to have adequate political power. Dalit literature has, since its inception, been translated into several Indian and European languages without compromising on the quality of rebellion that first characterized it. Such literature defies the idea that practice and theory remain separate. The strength of the term Dalit, originally used to ostracize a section of Indian society, enabled a successful literary movement that has overthrown social prejudice and won worldwide acclaim.

Legally, the notion of untouchables and discrimination against the Dalits are prohibited under the Indian Constitution under a 1955 civil rights act and the 1989 Prevention of Atrocities, or POA act. The act was written explicitly to outlaw physical and verbal abuse against Dalits, but hasn't had the desired effect. The real flowering of Dalit writing, however, begins in the 1970s when a number of younger poets and short story writers emerged. Namdeo Dhasal, Arjun Dangle and J.V. Pawar took the initiative of establishing a new militant Dalit organization called Dalit Panthers in Bombay in 1972. They began to describe the reality of Dalit life. These descriptions of slavery and oppression as well as the open and hidden forms of caste discrimination in the contemporary world, were unlike anything that had been written before. With the rise of autonomous Dalit movements in South India in the 1970s and after, Dalit literature made its presence felt in Karnataka, Andhra Pradesh, Tamil Nadu, Kerala and Bengal.

Jaydeep Sarangi is a bilingual writer, academician, editor, translator administrator and author of a number of significant publications on post-colonial issues, Indian writing in English, Australian literature and Dalit literature in reputed journals/magazines in India and abroad. Jaydeep Sarangi extends his help to the dalits by giving them voice through his poems and through his different literary activities. He is also working with the other contemporary Dalit writers and with the Bangla Dalit Sahitya Sanstha. This Sanstha, is an organization of movement of Dalit literature and culture of Bengal. People who believe in cultural and literary identity of Dalits as one different from the mainstream are generally associated with this apolitical organization having been working throughout West Bengal for last one and a half decade. There are other organizations as well.

We must not forget that Dalit is not a caste but a realization and is related to the experience of joys and sorrows and struggle of those in the lowest stratum of the society. Dalit literary corpus is a window on culture—a Dalit culture that is the culture of exclusion and exploitation. Those who shoulder Dalit poetics walk through long corridors of ignited discourse through which there is often no return; but return with the coloured wings of successive images and idioms. Let us proclaim, his grail is Dalit. No one can deny the Sun rising. For Sarangi: 'Right' is a euphonious equivalent of 'might.' Recently he has come out with a book entitled *The Wheel Will Turn.* The book is a serious collection of translated poems of Manohar Mouli Biswas. *The Wheel Will Turn* is far more than a wonderful collection of moving and powerful poems. It is an expression of true freedom, a freedom that a few years ago seemed impossible and unachievable. The dalits of India have been oppressed and denied the chance of rising above their birth origins for centuries, perhaps for over a thousand years. Relegated to extreme poverty, extreme hard work, with no chance of education, and quite often dying from starvation has been the lot of these human beings. Things are finally changing very slowly; the Wheel will now indeed turn. This title refers to the *Wheel of Dhamma or Justice*, which may have become stagnant for a while leading to oppression of the powerless, but will turn to re-establish a just society (5). He has translated Bengali Dalit poems/stories into English as well as edited a number of anthologies of translations of Bengali Dalit writings. Many of his poems translated in English refer to contemporary Bengali Dalit writers like Jatin Bala, Manohar Mouli Biswas, Manoranjan Byapari and Kalani Thakur. He gives shoulder to these people in need by translating their works and making it available to the world to read it in English. His translated work in English helps the readers to know about the struggle of the dalits in West Bengal. His dream is to see that Bengal literature does not just remain confined to West Bengal but the voices should reach the world. Through his conversations with different activists from different regions he makes an attempt to find out the differences and similarities in the conditions of the Dalits in different states.

He tries to find out ways of emancipating the dalits from the clutches of slavery and domination. To name a few he has interviewed Manoranjan Byapari, Kalyani Thakur and Manohar Mouli Biswas from Bengal, Bama from Tamilnadu, Harish Mangalam from Gujarat and Sharankumar Limbale from Maharastra. Sharing the experiences with these activists helps him to ponder upon the ways these people have adapted to emancipate the dalits.

Jaydeep Sarangi writes in Bengali and English. He has been anthologized widely in several shores. The journey of "the bilingual bard" begins "*From Dulong to Beas*" and continues till Perth, where he has been awarded with visiting fellow/writer to the University of Wollongong, Australia and the Westerly Centre at the University of Western Australia. He has been invited and honoured by universities abroad and most of his lectures were on delivered on Dalit literature. His latest collection *Silent Days* was released at Australia. His poems can be read loud and clear. His poetry convinces and impresses the readers. It is the poet's readiness to allow voices to be heard from all contending perspectives. His poetry has a social function apart from aesthetic value. Jaydeep Sarangi defines poetry as an engagement that invites him to react with certain things of life. He writes because it makes him happy. Here is one of his translated poems from Bengali to English:

> Take a small part of me and scatter everywhere
> Invisible self, I will touch all five senses.
> No more rejection from your quarter—why?
> You will witness
> How I shall become human blood.
> I'm no longer, where I live,
> Evolving every moment.
> I construct me to make myself a human being.
> I try to write, writing beguiles me
> I speak, what I can't.
> So many things remain under the cover.
> I destroy and preserve my heart
> Day and night
> With a little palpation of the untouchable dust. (*TWWT*)
> ("Dalit Mirror" Manohar Mouli Biswas)

His translated poems talk about the themes and thoughts from the new point of view. The voices of the dalits in different languages sound the same all full of bitterness. The sufferings and the problems remain the same so the expressions though represented in Bengali sound the same. Jaydeep Sarangi brings it to us in English to make the readers aware of the sufferings of the dalits. Jaydeep Sarangi's latest poetry collection '*Silent Days*' represent some of the voices of dalits and tribals. Poetry is eyes to Jaydeep Sarangi which capture each rainy moment of life's acts.

Silent Days is a wonderful collection of 50 poems along with a foreword by Laxmi Kannan. From native explosion, it has become a new form of Indian culture, and voice in which he is accepted in the outside world. Indian culture, customs and traditions have lot of influence on his writings. His poems reveal his creativity and artistic nature. Indeed a powerful work vibrant with description that is alive. His poetry is about universal truth, reactions to situations and experiences leading to outburst of feelings. He has an eye for detail and captures what he witnesses around. This can be seen in the form of poetry, the flow of his soul. This flow carries personal, social, political, mythlogical, native poems, sporting activities, celebration of small, the small things happening every day, life under stress, life in metropolitan cities, relationships, representative voice of the dalits and the tribals which have distinct voices etc. Indianness is at the core of his poems which shows India through its language, imagery, sensibility of anything. There are poems which defy boundaries with universal subjectivity and cadence.

One of the Senior Indian Poets Keki Daruwalla applauded his work as "*Jaydeep Sarangi gives a fresh paint to everyday living. 'Small rivers' near tribal villages are his haunts. His language can be unorthodox, where a rock can turn into a 'reckless flow', but his poems are a rewarding read, with the scent of herbs through the pages.*" (Back Cover, *Silent Days*) His poetry provides a mirror to the society and the different activities performed by the people. The activities of the aborigines and the dalits have always remained a different kind of attraction to him. Their bows and arrows attract him to work for them. The land and forest haunts him and he gets carried away to them. The land, forest, bows and arrows attract him and take him to their side. His supportive words shoulder the Dalits. In his poem "*I'm on Your Side*" he says:

Your bows and arrows attract me to work
Your land and forest take me to your side,
You are a vision. (Silent Days 17)

Jaydeep Sarangi has received appreciation globally for his collection *Silent Days*. One of the leading writers from Australia Dennis Haskell, the Director, Westerly Centre, the University of Western Australia has appreciated and applauded his work as:

> *The myriad of experiences thrust on us in every moment of contemporary life exercises Jaydeep Sarangi's poetic mind, and produces poems full of questions and hopes but also recognitions of limitations. The wish to break away, to take flight from moment to moment meets a realistic awareness of links to the land of red soil.* (*Silent Days*, Back Cover)

Jaydeep Sarangi considers himself to be a writer rooted in the rural landscape. Indianness is an inherent and integral to the poet's core as we move from one poem to another. Indianness affords certain joy of recognition to the native readers and opens the treasure of poems to the foreign readers. He shares Indianness globally. Most of his poems deal with the landscape, red soil and possess Indian sensibility. The earthiness of his poetry exhibits itself in descriptions.

He is allured by the red soil and he knows he is already enrolled to be there among the hunting—freak tribal children. Even though he is far away in city area for work still he cannot forget the freak tribal children. He assures the readers that his thoughts and heart is enrolled among the hunting-freak tribal children even though physically absent. The tribal children make him feel integrated with them. The soil holds the tradition so that things cannot fall apart. His longings to be there are portrayed through one of his poems *"The Red Soil Allure"*:

Longing for the red soil
Corrodes me day by day
Like the ticking of a clock
Tick tick tick…
I know, I'm enrolled among the hunting—freak tribal children
(Silent Days 14)

Poetry survives in spite of all mechanical, prosaic, hectic schedule of the day because it restores peace and order in his mind. According to him literature is a social commitment with a social purpose. His supportive words assure the aborigines that he is with them even though he is in a home away from home. His being conscious and aware about the sufferings of the Dalits is evident when he calls the "aborigines" as "saviours of history". He is aware of their sufferings through readings. He is a true poet holding on all the issues of society to his heart and looking for solutions to these problems. He is away from the scenic surroundings; the red soil and green forest where the saviours of history live in close proximity with natured he is far away dwelling in city still he remember them. In one of his poems "*In a Home away from Home*" he says:

> "People call you "aborigines",
> We call you the saviours of lighted History" (22)

Jaydeep Sarangi's writings come from the margins of the caste code dictated for many centuries. He uses his voice not only to expose the atrocities faced by the dalits but also to represent the anger that boils within them as a reaction to these prejudices. His sober observations are both penetrating and piercing that can be seen in his poems. He is greatly influenced by the great Dalit Writer from Maharashtra Arjun Dangle. His desire to bring about the change, passion to fight against the injustice done to the dalits and to emancipate the marginalized, dalits and the Subalterns is at the core of his poems as he mentions him in one of his poems "*Homeless in my Land*" he says:

> I sit under a banyan tree
> I read Arjun Dangle aloud!
> How nice it is to think, time is ripe
> Things to follow as history completes the full cycle
> My silent pen becomes my sword. (40)

Jaydeep Sarangi uses his poetry as a sword to fight against inequality based on caste discrimination. Arjun Dangle born in Mumbai in 1945 is an important name in the politics and Dalit literature of Maharashtra. A founder member of the militant Dalit Youth. He has made lot of contributions and translated his writings of Dalit into English. One of his famous book is "*Poisoned Bread*" (Transalation from Modern Dalit

Literature) 2009 It also shows how Dalit Literature moves beyond the usual discourses of literary modernity. He talks about the struggle of class identity "*Singing woes of land lost / They mould their class identity / Torch of expression blazes bright / In every Dalit's wordy pool.*" (*The Torch 55*)

Their bitterness is totally understandable through poems They have been subjected to the worst atrocities. A young man's thumb may be amputated just so that he does not become a better archer than a lad of the upper class. He, thus, observes the suppressed voice of the Dalits, their self-experience of injustice and atrocities and their furious expression on the Brahminical traditions. The dalits are economically exploited, socially condemned and educationally ignored. He talks about how this class is neglected. It portrays how discrimination can be seen at every level. Jaydeep Sarangi says: "*She counts darkness/ Dalit Writes Some claim. "We are not Dalits" "We are Socialists" None has read their tales of pain/ Not even the Gods"!* (*Why This Neglect* 60)

He is a poet with a powerfully social conscience whose humanism is expressed in form that is reminiscent, subtle and oblique. He has the sensibility of a modern poet whose self confronts the fallen world and stands in contrasts to the ideal world. His poems have the voices of an empowering outcry that fostered a pioneering revolution at many socio-political and cultural levels. Jaydeep Sarangi is greatly influenced by the "Ideology of Subaltern Theory" and suggestions made by Gayatri Spivak as she suggests that the Subaltern is denied access to both mimetic and political form of representation. Jaydeep Sarangi too feels that the subaltern should speak for their rights and not merely be silent sufferers called as Subaltern. He believes that the work of the poets and writers is not just to write stories and verses about them but to invoke the readers to emancipate the downtrodden from the clutches of different dominations. Jaydeep Sarangi has edited few books on marginal writings and desires to bring about a change in the minds of the readers which for sure will awake their sensibilities to rise above and be human He exemplifies this in his poems which show the endurance in the course of this ordeal. The lines in the poem "*Towards the Center*"' read:

> The margin is unfamiliar like any wild flower/ unseen and not named yet /Though we are struggling in our long walk to the spotted discourse/

> We stay together /we unburden our pains and sorrows of our long history and associated memory. Are we there to record them? Will we consider them as important? Can a rickshaw puller speak out/The untold legacy of subjugation? SILENCE People exchange series of lies/ Promises are forgotten/ As a method in madness. We are crawling for a walking stick! (32)

Jaydeep Sarangi voices out the Silent suffering and unheard agony through his marginal writings His poems implicitly make an attempt to lend a walking stick to the staggering downtrodden to rise up and fight for their rights. In one of his poems "*A Rose is a Rose*" he reminds us of 'decolonizing the minds a post colonial theory by Thiongo, Ngugi Wa, Poet feels that decolonization of minds can bring in real purity of hearts and body. Decolonisation of self can regain one's self and identity. *"Brutal within is voiced / When her innocent body crumbles/ She bleeds/ As the nation under a colonial rule./ Our youth is touched / With blood at their mouth.* (A Rose is a Rose 20) We face so many problems in our country which make us helpless and mere spectator and impose a question to the youngsters and the citizens. Are we truly decolonized? If so why is this purity of mind not seen and why so much of suspicion with fear? Why this feeling of being alien and unsafe in our own land?

Jaydeep Sarangi displays his alertness to immediate surroundings, to pitiable conditions of the people and raging problems of the country. He is influenced by great personalities which connect him with their ideologies. He too wishes to walk together with them to fight the struggle against injustice and inequality and eradicate the discriminations based on caste and class. His poems communicate his feelings and tradition in a global language to reach out the vast reading world. It's a gentle soothing delight to the soul. A powerful tool that aids the Sarangi in doing so is the language used—militant and blunt. The language is mostly colloquial. At times, unconventionally militant similes, metaphors and analogies used seem to befittingly paint his social experiences, experience of the self, as well as that of subaltern populations, as devoid of dignity, frustrating, repulsive and torturous. His new outlook which is intended to give a new society, its new literature and aesthetics, has many fresh and humane concerns.

Jaydeep Sarangi's poems offer a ray of hope to those oppressed by the harshness of life's reality. They have an enigmatic and at times ethereal quality drifting into the mystical. Jaydeep Sarangi is a poet of many a themes and one finds a wide range of subjects and variety in his poems. His voice is an emerging forceful voice in Indian English Poetry by virtue of compact expressions, individualistic style, varied themes, lucid, cadence and topical relevance. He lends his shoulder to help the dalits and voices the voiceless. His poems will for sure have a positive effect on the sensibilities of the readers and encourage them to come forward for a noble cause to save mankind and emancipate them from all kinds of dominations and bondages. This is a welcome addition in the vast collection of Indian English Poetry.

Works Cited

Biswas, Manohar Mouli. *The Wheel Will Turn.* Ed. Sarangi, Jaydeep. Cyberwit.net: Allahabad, 2014. Print.

Dangle, Arjun. *Poisoned Bread.* Trans. from Modern Dalit Literature, Orient BlackSwan: Mumbai, 2009. Print.

Sarangi, Jaydeep. *Silent Days.* Cyberwit.net: Allahabad, 2013. Print.

____. *A Door Somewhere?* Cyberwit.net: Allahabad, 2014. Print.

Spivak. Gayatri. *In Other Worlds: Essays in Cultural Politics.* N.Y. Methuen, 1987. Print.

Thiongo, Ngugi Wa. *Decolonizing the Mind.* Delhi: Worldview, 2007. Print.

http://en.wikipedia.org/wiki/Dalit_literature

http://www.englisharticles.info/2011/01/11/dalit-literature/

28

Cruelty of Casteism: Pathetic Reality of Dalits in Mulkraj Anand's *Untouchable*

PRITI SHARMA

Indian society since time immemorial has experienced the cruelty of Casteism. Indian society is a caste-based group where the upper caste exploits the lower caste. Dalit's who are considered as the lower ranked caste is in a worst condition and are continuously exploited by the upper caste of the society. The present powerful impression and ideological assumptions and the old rotten system about caste have doomed the life of poor Dalit's. Through this paper I have attempted to discuss the object misery of Untouchables and inhumanity of upper caste. "Untouchable" by Mulk Raj Anand's novel presents the Dalit's sufferings, struggle, and exploitation at the hands of the Hindus who are the upper caste people. In the novel *Untouchable*, it reflects protest and resentment and has exposed the hypocrisy of the cast Hindu who boast of their nobility and blue blood. In *Untouchable*, Bakha a younger sweeper from the outcaste's colony of a north Indian Cantonment town bears daily torments like missionary tries to persuade him to embrace Christianity, he listens to Gandhiji, who advocates social reform and so on. In fact, *untouchable* is a contrast between rural and urban India and race relations. In the novel it is exposed that the caste Hindus are megalomaniac, egoist, Sinister, crooked and malicious. Though we are living in the age of technology and information and as today it's a modern India still the status of Dalit's is figured in a very sorrowful sate.

The term "Caste" is derived from Spanish and Portuguese word "casta" which means 'race, lineage or breed". Caste is a social stratification. It is characterized as an endogamy and hereditary social group limited to person of the same rank, occupation, economic position and having distinguishing it from the other such group. The word "Dalit" is rooted from the Sanskrit word "dal" which means broken, oppressed, ground-down, down-trodden, culturally subjugated and politically marginalized. They can be given a designation like Untouchable, Depressed classes and Harijans. Mahatma Gandhi named them as "Harijan" (The People of God). They are menial castes and so they are socially excluded and isolated from the rest of the society. Caste system plays a significant role in every aspects of Indian life and the upper castes that use the ideology of the caste system to economically exploit low—ranking landless labourers. Through this paper I have laid down my view points that has been expressed in Mulk Raj Anand's novel (1935) were the writer presents the very suffering, mystery, struggle, exploitation at the hands of the upper class Hindus.

We live in a modern society and lay several ideas and concepts on equality, freedom and rights to all caste, creed, race, and religion. But do we actually bring that to practice. The answer is A big NO as we can see the reality by seeing the status of the Dalit's which still in a worst and pathetic condition and has remained the same till now. Dalit's are being called as Untouchable which means that cannot be touched or touch others. In *Untouchable* there is a contrast between rural and urban India and race-relations where Bakha, a younger sweeper from the outcaste's colony of a north Indian Cantonment town. It is concerned with the experiences of Bakha, a social pariah, depressed and frustrated.

Untouchable presents an account of a single day in Bakha's life, a scavenger boy of eighteen and the central character of the novel. His occupation or his usual daily routine is cleaning of toilets which indeed marks him an outcaste and so a victim of humanity. He sweeps and clean gullies for exchange of handful food for his family. He is not allowed to touch the higher class sophisticated Hindus. Even he was not allowed to make entrance or even his appearance visible in the temples. *Untouchable* illustrates a day of great difficulty for Bakha and accidentally he touches an upper caste Hindu and so earns a slap and rebuked for making the man polluted. Even when he was cleaning a gutter for a lady on the same day she rather did not like to offer the food in his hand rather threw the food on him. A priest tries to seduce and molest her sister on the very same day and when he peeps into the temple to see what is happening the Brahmins screams, "polluted, polluted". Even he was blamed for harming or injuring a young boy after a hockey match. Even his father tells him how once when Bakha was ill with fever and how he couldn't go to chemist shop to buy medicine for fear of defiling the place and had to stand by the road side imploring passer-by to fetch it for him. As the day goes on, it becomes worst and worst for him. These entire episodes conspire to crush Bakha's self-confidence to force him back into his hopeless caste position. The conditions were not in favour, he was thrown from home by his father and so he turns to become frustrated and tormented by the societal issue on caste and occupation.

He thinks that his life is full of miseries, thorns, suffering and exploitation. The action of the caste Hindu by simply touching by the low caste person Bakha is considered to be a sin. If by mistake touching of the upper people led them to purify or sanctify them. At this anger of Bakha reveals as he says:

> ...all of them abused, abused, abused why are we always abused? The sanitary inspector that day abused my father. They always abuse us. Because we are sweepers, because we touch. They hate dung. I hate it to. That's why, I came here. I was tired of working on the latrines every day. That's why they don't touch us, the high caste... I am a sweeper, sweeper-untouchable I am an untouchable! (*Untouchable* 58-59)

His anger can be revealed before his father after bearing the insult of his sister, who has been seduced and molested by a Pandit of the temple. He is filled with anger at the time of his sister molestation. Bakha's way his feel, his act, and his reaction is revealed when he says: *'They think we are mere dirt, because we clean their dirt. (Untouchable 89)* Bakha, the untouchable lad and so a life of an untouchable like Bakha is full of miseries, anxieties, suffering. Bakha becomes a symbolic figure who represents universal exploitation of the untouchable (the pariah, the underdogs, or the down-trodden). We could see the struggle for survival of the Dalit's at every step and how they are manhandled, suppressed, abused, rebuked, molested by the upper caste Hindu who thinks themselves as the emperor over the lowest caste people. E.M. Forster rightly says:

> The sweeper is worse off than a slave, for the slave may change his master and his duties and may even become free, but the sweeper is bound for ever, born into a state from which he can't escape and where he is excluded from social intercourse and the consolation of his religion. Unclean himself he pollutes other when he touches them. They have to purify themselves, and to rearrange their plans for the day. This he is disgusting as well as disquieting object to the orthodox a she walks along the public roads, and it is his duty to call out and warn them that he is coming... The sweepers were more sensitive looking and more personable than other servants and... had some skill as a poet. (*Untouchable* Preface 8)

A writer is always known for his vision that wants to disseminate, driven by his purpose to ameliorate the lot of poor, deprived, and driven by his purpose to ameliorate the lot of the poor, deprived and neglected. Anand being a writer condemned and disapproved the inhuman caste system. A writer raises true voice of these unheard people of the society and through his writing conveys the deplorable description of the destitute. An outcaste person lives a life which is meaner than an animal. Trauma and humiliation seem to ceaseless and endless for Bakha who represent the outcaste Hindus subjected to untold miseries. Anand condemned religious hypocrisy, fanaticism, superstitious, and bigotry. It is rigidity, religious bigotry and hypocrisy of Hinduism which has segregated the untouchable and exploited them ruthlessly.

Bakha is in oscillating in a state of dichotomy. He cannot get of tradition and he cannot resist the temptations of modernity. He feels like a caged bird that flutters its wings for a free flight. So, he decides to learn about Christianity and the philosophy of Mahatma Gandhi. He bears daily torments like missionary tries him to persuade him to embrace Christianity; he listens to Gandhiji, who advocates social reforms and so on. There is a quest in life of Bakha....... *thinking of everything he had heard, though he could not understand it all.* (*A History of Indian English Literature* 164)

The Dalit's remain to be the most oppressed section of the social order in India. The outcastes are used to live in dirty and filthy environment because they have inherited humility and servility as a consequence of thousand years of Hindu caste domination. Hindu society is divided into high and low caste communities. The social stratification of Hindu has rendered the Dalit's as untouchable. Our Indian Constitution has provided the right to equality, education, opportunity, social justice, but these still have not been socially practiced today. In the traditional and caste-ridden society, the Hindus treat the untouchable as scum of the earth. The untouchable are denied of their rights in the so called society of our modern India, world of information and technology. It vehemently denounces the caste system and exposes the callousness and hypocrisy of the caste Hindus who considered themselves the custodians of Hindu cultural heritage. Dalit's are pressurized, humiliated, tortured, abused, manhandled because of their lowest status in Indian social order of castes.

We see that in 1950's Untouchability is legally abolished from the Indian Constitution. Any discrimination of any kind in India today is forbidden by law. But still today the very caste system has not been totally disappeared or vanished from the society. Today even not only in villages but in towns and colonies we find that untouchability is not excluded from the minds of people. We are living in 21st century where science and technology has bought great changes and where people are educated. But still when it comes to caste the broad minded people became narrow minded. We should take initiative and step forward for the upliftment of the Dalit's and should promote them to a higher level of life. They should be provided equal opportunity, rights. If we want to see our nation developed for better we should vanish the bolt which is the huge rock of casteism in the path of development. Bakha represent the whole group of untouchable and shows their suffering in different fields and life due to their lowest status in the society. The untouchable should not be segregated and discriminated against the rest of society. They even deserve human love and sympathy and free air of equality and equal opportunity. We all should join hands to bring an equal society where people are not distinguished due to caste, creed, or race or colour but live together by the bond of brotherhood. Change is not the only thing but acceptance should be there in the minds of people for making it a better society.

Works Cited

Anand, Mulk Raj. *Coolie.* Penguin Books: New Delhi, 2000. Print

____. *Untouchable.* Penguin Books: New Delhi, 2011.Print

____. (Preface). Arnold Heinemann: New Delhi, 1934.Print

Naik, M. K. *A History of Indian English Literature.* Sahitya Academi: New Delhi, 2011. Print

29

Indian Nation as a 'Tradition': Raja Rao's *The Serpent and the Rope*

DR. PARMOD KUMAR

> I was born a Brahmin—that is, devoted to truth and all that. "Brahmin is he who knows Brahman" etc., etc.... But how many of my ancestors since the excellent Yagnyavalkya, my legendary and Upanishadic ancestor, have really known the Truth excepting the sage Madhava, who founded an empire or, rather, helped to build an empire and wrote some of the most profound Vedantic texts since Sri Sankara? (Rao 1)

Perhaps Raja Rao is the only writer to have written a novel with an autobiographical note like this. As he claims in the novel *The Serpent and the Rope*, Raja Rao was born in a traditional South Indian Brahmin family in the then Mysore state, and is proud of his birth. It is his birth as Brahmin that is central to his consciousness and it goes into the shaping of his entire work. This literary stance is unlike the Nigerian novelist Chinua Achebe, for example writing in English, Rao too once was concerned with the colonial language. In the foreword to *Kanthapura* (1938), published in London, he admitted the difficulties in using "a language that is not one's own the spirit that is one's own," and conveying "the various shades and omissions of certain thought-movement that looks maltreated in an alien language." Fundamentally, Rao seeks to project India more as a 'darshana' or perspective and each of his work in the post colonial phase points it to that direction. The present paper examines the case of *The Serpent and the Rope* more closely.

Raja Rao spent the early years of his childhood with his grandfather who was deeply religious. The Rao family originally belonged to Mysore, but migrated to the then Muslim state of Hyderabad due to the escapades of his grand uncle. He grew up in Hyderabad, where two languages Telugu and Urdu are spoken. Right from the birth Raja Rao has been on a prolonged exile both religiously and linguistically; he was the only Hindu student in the Muslim school, Madarasa-e-Aliya at Hyderabad and this alienation continues in one way or the other till date. He was later on sent to Aligarh Muslim University in North India where a cousin of his was working, with the hope that the change of atmosphere would do well to his weak lungs. As it turned out, it did good, but more on his mental plain. At Aligarh he met Eric Dickinson (a minor oxford poet) who brought out the artist in him, teaching him to 'love France' and appreciate Michelangelo and Santayana. Raja Rao returned to Hyderabad for his graduation. After taking Bachelor's degree from Nizam College, Hyderabad with History and English as special subjects which are typically Western, he was awarded the Asiatic Scholarship of the Government of Hyderabad for the study at abroad and set sailed for France in 1929. Soon after his arrival, he married Camille Mouly, a professor of French.

Apart from supplying the model for Madeleine, the heroine of his major work *The Serpent and the Rope* (1960), she played an important role in her husband's development as an artist. It is on her insistence that he published a few literary pieces, articles and a long poem in Kannada, and it was she who helped him to come out of his "rubbish Machvelian English,"[2] and to form his own style of translating Kannada into English. However after living together for ten years, their marriage got dissolved. After a long gap, in 1965 he married Katherine Jones, an American Stage actress. However even his second marriage which gave him his only son too broke up leading to his third union with another American woman. All these details are important for understanding and evaluating Raja Rao as a writer, for all these details appear in his work in some form or the other. He admits that he is autobiographical: "All writers write only autobiography."

What is evident that Rama does not make any crude declarations in the favour of his caste, and condemn the Sudras and untouchables, like Manu. There is no such necessity for him. His expostulation is like a King's request. A King's request is tantamount to order and no king would menacingly shout his orders. Rama was like a prince from his birth itself; his authority is always respected, and it is not at all necessary for him to assert himself time and again. Thus, we do not find him making direct insinuations against the lower castes in the novel. But his casual behaviour, his encounter with others and the Brahmanical (what he calls metaphysical) debates he conducts speak volumes of his strong attachment to the tradition of caste.

Ramaswamy, unlike Moorthy in the *Kanthapura*, does not say anything on the problem of untouchability, nor does he voice other problems that India was facing then. He simply glorifies India: "… India is Freedom", 'The Truth' (88). But he does nothing for the India that he extols in such great terms. On his return to France after his first 'pilgrimage to India', he goes on praising India in his own natural way: "We are sentimental people... we weep for everything" (62). To a question from Madeline, if he had hated the Europeans, while at India, he tells her that even the Englishman is more loved in India now, leave alone the Europeans, celebrating the broad-mindedness of Indians: "We forget evil easily. Naturally we love the good" (62). But all this is at a very abstract level. Continuing the discussion, when she poses two concrete problems, the problem of untouchability and the Indian patriarchy, in her words, "So that the pariah may have his separate well and the woman slave for men"—he is bewildered and hurt (62). In her remark he finds "an unexpected … new bitterness" (63). She finds him greatly hurt and is forced to change the discussion over to Georges. What is important in their discussion is that Rama does not contradict her; he does not show the idealism for the eradication of untouchability that Moorthy exhibits in the *Kanthapura.* Instead he is greatly hurt for such a remark. He is hurt because he thinks and acts like a caste Brahmin; therefore in the entire novel we do not we find any programme or an action from him for the 'annihilation' of untouchability or caste system—which is 'dualism' and hence 'anti-Indian'. Rama only professes 'Brahman'. What he wants from Madeleine is a silent ear for his one-sided abstract praise of India.

Rama upholds the tradition of caste throughout the novel. During the marriage ceremony of Saroja, when Little Mother expresses her anger over Saroja's in-laws, calling them "Low untouchables" and to Uncle

Seetharamu's dubbing them as "cadaver—eating pariahs", Rama maintains complete silence. The 'Brahman', 'the knowledge of the self', 'The Truth' in Rama does not take objection to such demeaning of 'the Self' in other human beings, neither does he find his relatives going against the *dharma*, 'the impersonal'. He does not pass any comments and does not dissuade them from using such language, because the 'Brahmin'—the caste in him approves the abuses. Thus, earlier too, he has not appreciated his sister Sukumari's interest in Marx and he found her enthusiasm for the eradication of caste and class strange and objectionable. His attachment to caste is so intense, that it not only influences his relationships with others, like with his fiancé Savithri, but is also solely responsible for the break-up of his marriage with Madeleine.

Madeleine is a lovely young French woman, with golden hair and her skin for an Indian like Rama "...was like the unearthed marble with which we built our winter palaces" (13). "Madeleine was like the palace of Amber seen in moonlight" (14). She is extremely happy with her marriage with Ramaswamy, and tries very hard to keep it going. She is in fond love with 'India' from where her husband comes: For her "... 'India is paradise' ", and is greatly delighted at the prospect of dying in India, by virtue of her marriage to an Indian (88). She has great veneration for her Brahmin husband, and immensely respects his sentiments. In short, she is a devoted wife. In the words of Rama, her husband:

> There was nothing I needed which she did not know beforehand, and bring to me: my medicine after lunch, my handkerchief when I started on a walk, my pencil, duly sharpened and laid on my notebook .... (77)

Her love for husband is so intense that as Annu Celly rightly points, it is she "...who makes all the necessary adjustments and compromises" (26) in their married life. She takes immense pride in bearing children for him, and hangs his mother's photograph in their room with great love and respect. When her husband's friend, Savithri comes to stay with them, she wholeheartedly welcomes her and was humble enough to say that she being a European is less civilized. Though she is a non-vegetarian by birth, she becomes a strict vegetarian after her marriage, and her austerity makes her husband comment that she is more Brahmanic than he himself.

This is only one aspect of her personality. Apart from being a devoted wife, she is also a strong individual both physically and intellectually. She loves long walks and it is she who carries the suitcases of her tuberculosis husband and is always willing to work outside the home as well as at home. We never hear her complaining about the work. She is intelligent and well read enough to hold discussions on difficult topics like religion and philosophy with Lezo, Georges and Rama, and is also frank and strong enough in refuting Lezo's advances. If she appears to Rama as a "running brook", Georges finds it "To be near her… is to feel intelligent" (151). She is not happy with her given identity as a European woman, nor is she satisfied with her Christian God. In the beginning of the novel we find her calling herself 'a pagan', and her search to know 'Truth', and from 'being' to 'becoming' continues till she finds solace in Buddhism. Her statement "Let me follow my own Gods" reveals her strong resoluteness to realize the meaning of life on her own (326). Pointing out this aspect in Madeleine S. Krishna Swamy says that "She does not need a mediator to reach her god nor does she feel she ought to be a medium to enable her husband to reach Moksha (39)". As Meena Shirwadkar points out: "She would rather have a god of her own (66)."

This second aspect of Madeleine's personality seems to bring about a strong undercurrent of resentment in Rama and hence he tries to defeat and annihilate her 'ego' throughout the novel. Their conflict has attracted the attention of many critics, and we have many interesting comments in this regard. S. Nagarajan points out that the conflict emanates from "two contrary world views, two contrary epistemologies" *(The Sewanee Review)* and But what is striking in these arguments is that all of them point to the differences at the level of worldviews, nations and cultures but fail to nail down the source of such conflicting worldviews. Rama himself answers this question: "Had I been less of a Brahmin, I might have known more of love" (400). In simple words it is the tradition of caste that is the real source of their conflict.

Right from the beginning of their relationship Madeleine is aware of the caste difference between them and her initial reaction to the tradition of caste is that of utmost veneration. She equates Brahmanism with India and feels proud of her Brahmin husband.

> Look at this pale skin beside your golden one. Oh, to be born in a country where tradition is so alive… even the skin of her men is like some royal satin, softened and given a new shine through the rubbing of ages. (19)

However, she fails to understand that the same caste which her husband and she herself so fervently admire would become the cause for the disintegration of their marriage. But soon, after her husband's first 'pilgrimage to India', she finds the seeds of their conflict in Rama's caste. Her casual statement that she has bought a dozen of towels so that his "Brahmanism, renewed and affirmed, can wash itself as often as it likes" reveals her apprehensions about the future and the role Brahmanism is going to play in her life (60). She silently accepts his one-sided praise of Brahmanism in the name of India. Her love for her husband allows him to be brutal with her. Rama makes her suffer intensely by attacking her belief in compassion and egalitarianism, in the name of 'Self, the Absolute, the Truth', a concept that Rama has time and again used to celebrate the triumph of Brahmanism over all religions including Buddhism, and other systems of thought, such as Marxism. Her personality is never respected and her husband never tries to disintegrate his ego in hers as he claims, because of his strong attachment to the tradition of caste.

Rama was married to Madeleine when he was twenty-one and Madeleine, twenty-six and as a consequence is constantly bogged with their age difference. He does not tolerate Madeleine being elder to him and that is why Madeleine at the time of divorce in a letter to Catherine advises Rama to get married to an Indian woman who is much younger to him. In Brahmanic tradition, the woman should be younger to her husband and in all respects be inferior to him and willingly annihilate her personality for the benefit of her husband's *'Moksha'*. Hence peeved at the age difference between them he relentlessly tries to subdue Madeleine and annihilate her 'ego'. In any discussion they have with each other, or in the company of others, he always tries to exercise dominance over her and presents her as a woman of confused soul, with hardly any talents. His motto: "But I am a Brahmin, and for me touch and knowledge go with the holiness of surrender, of woman not taking me there, but I revealing to her *that*" (66). He refuses to respect her personality, 'the Truth, the Absolute' in her. He vehemently ridicules Christ and Buddha as mere 'poets', knowing fully well that the latter has greatly inspired his wife Madeleine. These acts and his entire thinking are a result of his unequivocal attachment to his caste. The reason for the break-up of his marriage lies in the roots of the tradition of his caste. When Madeleine, greatly disturbed at the tensions in their married life, wants to know the reasons for the unwarranted turmoil from her wise husband, his reaction is typically that of a Brahmin. Their dialogue reveals his 'true' personality.

> "What is it separated us, Rama?"
>
> "India"
>
> "India? But I am Buddhist."
>
> "That is why Buddhism left India. India is *impitoyable*."
>
> "But one can become a Buddhist?"
>
> "Yes, and a Christian and a Muslim as well."
>
> "Then?"
>
> "One can never be converted to Hinduism"
>
> "You mean one can only be born a Brahmin?"
>
> "That is—an Indian", I added, as an explanation of India. (331)

He points out that India is the reason for their separation. But his India is Hindu-India, devoid of all religions except Hinduism. Like a typical Hindu nationalist, he ascribes a monolithic, Hindu upper-caste identity to India and denies the Sudra castes as well as other religions any place in it. When Madeleine tells him that she is a Buddhist he denies that it is Indian. This reaction stems from Brahmanism's antagonism towards Buddhism which waged a consistent ideological battle against Hinduism and the tradition of caste. His urge to 'become' a 'Brahmin' however strongly refutes Madeleine's becoming a Buddhist, not only because Buddhism negated Hinduism, but also as such his Brahmanism negates any form of "becoming", especially a non-Brahmin's wish to become a Brahmin. His statement that one can become a Christian or Muslim, but one can never be converted into Hinduism is an historical factual error. He categorically tells us that 'one can only be born as Brahmin' 'as an explanation of India'. He refuses to accept Hindu-India only "in time and space", as Madeleine points out, because the tradition of caste, which he is eulogizing in the name of India, is "contiguous with time and space" and "is anywhere, everywhere", including France (331). Thus the cause for the break-up of their marriage too is the tradition of caste. Commenting on the dissolution of their marriage in an interview with Shiva Niranjan, the novelist, Raja Rao makes interesting observations:

> But you see, the point is that in trying to become a Buddhist, she was unfair to her own *Dharma*, which was Catholicism. If she has been a good Catholic she might have been alright with Ramaswamy. (24)

He further states that he believes in 'authenticity', and opines that it is possible only when one sticks to one's religious faith, whatever it may be—be it Hinduism of Mahatma Gandhi or Islam of Maulana Azad. His firm conviction is that one must adhere to the faith in which one is born and since Madeleine has moved from her *Dharma* of Catholicism, there is no escape for her from suffering, and the divorce. In the first place the marriage between Rama and Madeleine was possible precisely because both had moved away from their *dharma*s. Rama's initial attraction towards Madeliene is like any other Western migrated Indian; being perhaps infatuated by her physical beauty—her golden hair and fair skin he marries her. In fact he frankly admits on his first "pilgrimage" back to India, that he never loved 'the Self' in Madeleine; "I knew I did not. I knew I could not love: that I did not even love Pierre [his son]" (24). Once the physical attraction is over he remembers his Brahmanic antecedents and is remorseful of the marriage, for such union is negated by his caste *dharma*. Thus, he time and again imagines how wonderful his marriage would have been if he had chosen a woman from his own caste—Rukmini or Kamudini or Subamma or Venkatalakshmamma, who would have served him with hot coffee at his wake up, and press his limbs. Thus, what Raja Rao actually means by authenticity is the caste tradition.

Rao's declaration that if Madeleine remained a Catholic, the marriage would have survived is far from reality; it could not survive because Rama time and again strives to defeat Madeleine's convictions by Brahmanism. Much before she became a Buddhist, he admits that he did not and could not love her, not even his own son from her. This is because Brahmanism is not only an ultimate ideal for him to achieve,

'The Truth', but also a concrete caste tradition based on heredity. Rama denies her the right to choose a religion, because it goes with the thinking of the novelist. Rao strongly denies Madeleine the right to choose and 'become', for such a right would go against caste-system which has placed him on the top of hierarchy, granting him all privileges possible on the earth.

Little Mother's real name is Vishalakshi, but as her personality is built around her title, the readers hardly remember her name. Vishalakshi is the daughter of a poor Brahmin clerk and is married to a man much older to her. She becomes a widow at the age of twenty-six, and is hardly elder (two or three years) to her step son, Rama Swamy who reverently calls her "Little Mother". She is younger to her step daughter-in-law, Madeleine, but neither she nor Rama Swamy appears to have taken note of that fact. She accepts widowhood as natural and never raises her voice against such cruelty. In that sense she is like Rangamma the benevolent, ascetic widow of Kanthapura. She accepts all values of the past. But, these values uphold the caste system. Her reactions in a hotel in Calcutta (the fish being part of Brahmin food—the episode is already discussed in this chapter elsewhere) and her utterances at Saroja's marriage calling her step-daughter's-in-laws as "Low untouchables" testify her allegiance to her caste. She thinks and acts like a traditional Brahmin woman, accepting patriarchy and caste system and superbly fits herself into the role of upper caste Indian women. Thus she is praised by one and all, and this is best expressed by Rama: "So rich and natural was Little Mother's silence that she often lay with her eyes closed, almost motionless" (34). If there is any woman in the novel, who has received Rama's utmost veneration, it is Little Mother. This is so because she symbolizes all the Brahmanic values that Rama upholds and celebrates in the name of 'Truth'.

The most idealized character in the novel among women who occupies a great attention from the writer and critics is Savithri Rathore. She is eloquently praised because her attitude to life goes well with the Little Mother's precept: "A woman has to marry, whether she be blind, deaf, mute or tuberculosis. Her womb is her life, and we cannot choose our men" (emphasis added, 258-59). Though she is a princess, and by caste Rajput different from Brahmins, though she is a student of Oxford and lived in the West for a quite some time, though she smokes, drinks and dances (she has even won a prize at Delhi Club for her boogie-woogie dance), she accepts like Little Mother, the traditional views of Rama, especially about women: "Men make her destiny. For a woman to choose is to betray her biology" (291-92). She believes in the Meerabai tradition of complete devotion to her man, and whole-heartedly accepts Rama's domination. She does not even take objection to Rama's declaration that "Eternity is only for men… women will die at the opportune time" (139). In contrary, she goes further and calls all women—'the disease'; "We are the fakers, the makers. We make the falsehood that is life, the trinkets. That is why man has such contempt for us" (360). Thus we find Rama, the proponent of tradition (and here it is patriarchy), appreciating her time and again in so many words: "To be a woman, she knew, was to be absorbed by a man" (187) and if with Madeleine everything was mere explanation, "With Savithri it was recognition" (340). He praises her because her spirit is kindred to his own "… a spirit Indian to the core (Naik 274)."

We do not find Savithri directly deliberating on the tradition of caste. But her preference for the role assigned to women by 'tradition' reveals her position on the caste system to some extent. She is a perfect Indian woman—"gentle, simple and very silent" (124). Rama appreciates this very silence, though he finds the root cause for such silence—the sorrow:

> She bore such sorrow, it seemed at moments, that she sang just to cover it up, or she would dramatize herself smoking or sit self-consciously as though to hide some unnamable disease that others could see and smell but she could not know (122).

He rightly identifies the cause of her sorrow in the attitude of 'total resignation of Hindu woman', but strangely this is what that brings them together. She completely accepts tradition. She admits that Rama Swamy is a Brahmin (that to a South Indian one) and superior to her with respect to caste and gender, though gender is predominant in their relationship. She smokes, dances and 'flirts' with men, but that is only an appearance in her effort to be 'modern'. In essence she is very traditional and accepts all forms of tradition including patriarchy and caste. She moves with

Muslims and communists, but never tries to assimilate the ideas of her friends. She is so greatly attached to tradition that though she is in deep love with Rama and gets married to him in a hotel room secretly, she goes on to get married to Prathap formally and pompously, for as a woman, 'who is a real woman', she cannot choose—because such an act would betray her 'biology'. Her *dharma* makes her abandon her Krishna, her Shiva, and marry the distasteful Turk, Prathap—a civil servant in the Government of India. We never find her speaking against caste system, and finally her marriage with Prathap from her own caste suggests her confirmity with the tradition of caste. As a staunch believer in tradition it can be expected that she would definitely uphold even the tradition of caste, though there are no instances available in the novel wherein she directly exhibited her casteism. However, what is interesting is that it is the tradition, which brings Rama and Savithri together, and it is again tradition which parts them.

Raja Rao celebrates tradition; things connected with the past—be it is from any region and religion. But his idea of tradition is based on selection and excludes many ancient traditional views. Being a firm believer in the caste, which he justifies in the name of tradition, he cannot afford to negate the traditions prevalent in other nations. Thus, he not only celebrates the imperiality of river Thames, but goes on glorifying the coronation of the Queen of England, quite contrary to the position he has taken on the British in his earlier novel, *Kanthapura*. This is a major shift in his thinking, and it continues till date. He praises the Queen, because in 'The King' (monarchy) he sees the 'Truth', the 'Self' and the 'Absolute'. All those born hierarchically hegemonic become adorable for him.

The city Bombay (which is called Mumbai today) does not appeal to the Brahmin in Rama; in his 'India' this 'barbaric' city has no place. "Bombay had no right to exist" (44). Rama however expresses a different opinion about another industrial city, Marseille and gives reasons for such a different opinion:

> Marseille is certainly horrible, with its wide dark windows and its singsong tramways, its underground world of ruffians, *Quemandeurs*, *bicots*, and its sheer smelly natural vulgarity; but at least it has the old port and the beauty of Notre-Dame-de-la-Garde. (44)

He appreciates Marseille for its Old Port and the beauty of Notre-Dame-de-la-Garde which is also old. What makes the difference between the two cities is not the people or their aspirations, but the two old structures. His love for 'India' does not provoke him to look into the reasons of 'vulgarity' of Bombay, and he goes on simply eulogizing a city which is not a part of India, for the simple reason that it has things of the past.

For Rama "… the past is necessary to understand the present" (199). He understands the present from the point of 'the past' for in his view, the past is the 'Absolute', the 'Truth'. It is beyond modification and change, and one cannot improve on the things of the past. Hence, for him Aurobindo becomes the Superman, and like Zarathustra, Stalin or Father Zossima, is the enemy of mankind for he tried to improve on the Advaita of Sri Sankara, which is more than ten centuries old. In the same breath, that he accepts the past as absolute he states with enormous appreciation that France is the country of Roman consuls, bishops, crusaders and princes; it is the country "…where Saint Louis trod… where Henry IV rode… where the great Mistral walked" … (124). He bestows similar praise on the River Cam. But what is missing is that nowhere does he mention either the people or France's contemporary ideas influenced by the French Revolution, which gave mankind the very important slogan of democracy—"Liberty, Equality and Fraternity". He does not talk about these contemporary French ideas, because, as Ambedkar points out, Hinduism negates the very idea of such humane values (Vol.3, 92), and Rama cannot think of Liberty, Equality and Fraternity—as these principles jeopardise his hegemonic place in the Indian society.

This being his stand, he does not see reason in any of the things he is talking about, but simply goes on showering appreciation on the things of the past. He applies the yardstick of judging things from the point of the past and his attempt to appear objective seems only pretence. He praises Sankara's Vedanta, while bestowing at the same time similar appreciation on the Queen of England and the monarchy unmindful of the fact that colonialism and casteism were responsible for the poverty and 'vulgarity' of India. He not only advises Savithri to obey tradition and get married to Prathap, but also strongly suggests that his beloved sister Saroja should get married in the same tradition, in spite of the fact that she detests her bridegroom—the 'ugly, big-lieutenant looking' Subramanya. True to the spirit of Advaitic tradition accessible to Brahmanis only, he demands that one should completely surrender oneself to his 'Guru'. Rao further explicates this idea in The Cat and The Shakespeare where he gives an analogy for such total submission of the kitten being carried away by Mother Cat holding its baby's neck in its mouth. Rama's reverence for the ancient things is so absolute that he goes to any extent to uphold the tradition; thus we find him praising even the practice of primitive peoples "… who took the first blood of menstruation for better harvesting of their fields" (50). However, what is strikingly important in his argument is that he seeks justification of Brahmanism based on 'past and tradition'. In this context, he cannot afford to glorify Brahmanism alone, and thus he goes on glorifying things of the past, irrespective of religions and regions, including the British.

In this discussion on tradition what emerges is that the past for Rao is authentic and absolute, and the present entails its mere continuation. Any deviation from the established tradition, an individual's will to choose, to be different, is viewed with suspicion. These are two important issues which pervade throughout the novel. Raja Rao celebrates India because it "…still has the most ancient civilization on earth" (189). India is 'different', far above all other nations because of its antiquity. However the debate does not end there. He presents this antiquity as Vedanta, to be more precise—as Sankara's Vedanta. He talks about the past, but does not include the contending schools of thought of the past in his discourse of tradition. Nowhere in the novel, do we find any mention about other religions, or other schools of thoughts even within Hinduism. He does not make any mention about important schools of thought like *Nyaya Vaisesika, Sankya* or *Charuvakas* who denounced the existence of God. He does mention Buddha, but his appreciation is limited by its level of abstractness—perhaps it is like Brahmins accepting Buddha as one among *Dashavthars*, but totally denouncing his egalitarian philosophy. Rao presents Muslims from a very communal point of view, as 'Turks at the door', and the Sudras and untouchables remain in his paradigm as

'Baligas, Rangis' and at best as Linge Gowdas 'but with folded hands and all'. The people, who constitute ninety percent within the Hinduism that he is talking about, are mentioned with least respect. Even with regard to Vedanta, his exposition is full of shortcomings and one-sided. He takes the names of Yagnyavalkya and Sankara but does not make mention of the ideological contradictions within Vedanta—the basic philosophical differences between *Uttara Mimmsa* and *Purva Mimmsa.* The only point he is interested in is Brahmanism.

Raja Rao presents Rama Swamy as the true representative of India: "My thoughts were, as you see, very Indian…" (36). We find Catherine defining him as "…not a man—man. He is an Indian…" (343). Rama defines himself as Indian at many places in the novel, and his friends and relatives of his wife in France praise him, because he is from India. He presents all his ideas as Indian, as if all Indians approve his opinions and carry the same sentiments and prejudices. He does mention his caste, but it is always kept at an abstract level and the concrete caste system remains camouflaged in his philosophical adventures. He presents his castiest understanding as the glorious Indian way of looking at life. In fact whatever he highlights about India is nothing more than a reflection of his Brahmanism caste moorings. To put it simply, he seeks justification of his caste in the name of India and tradition.

Raja Rao's whole thesis of tradition is based on the premise of antiquity. He demands that tradition *per se* must be followed, for it is ancient and handed down to the present from generation to generation. Like a typical nationalist he presents India as spiritual since time immemorial. But Chita Ankara argues that Rama, the epitome of Indianans, is a typical "Post Colonial" Hindu, and his Brahmanism or spiritualism is not the unsullied tradition of the yore (100). Rao simply accepts the colonial discourse of the artificial divide of West and East in terms of material/spiritual. He does not take into consideration the fact that during ancient times itself, there were many atheistic schools of thought, such as *Charuvakas, Sankya* and *Buddhism* which negated spiritualism and the very existence of 'God'. Rao also accepts the colonialist denunciation that India has no history. Hence we find Rama, time and again reiterating that "India has no history…" (102). "To integrate India into history—is like trying to marry Madeleine" (332). He further elaborates that "...Truth cannot have history" taking the colonial discourses on India for granted (102).

Thus, Raja Rao is very selective in his definition of tradition, totally excluding many major traditions. What Raja Rao praises in name of spirituality—the Brahman—is not ancient traditions but the modern colonialist presumptions. Rao's whole endeavour, we may suggest, is to celebrate the hegemony of Brahmins in the name of India and tradition. Thus Rama Swamy starts as a born-Brahmin, leads his life as a Brahmin and by the time the novel ends (even until the last page) he still remains a member of one particular religious community.

Works Cited

Ambedkar, B. R. *Dr. Babasaheb Ambedkar: Writings and Speeches.* Ed. Vasant Moon, Vol., Bombay: Government of Maharashtra, 1987. Print.

Celly, Annu. *Women in Raja Rao's Novel : A Feminist Reading of The Serpent And The Rope.* Jaipur: Print Well, 1995. Print.

Nagarajan S. "An Indian Novel". *The Sewanee Review.* 72.3 (1964).

Naik, M. K. *Raja Rao.* New York: Twayne, 1972. Print.

____. "The Serpent and The Rope: The Indo-Anglian Novel as epic Legend", *Critical Essays on Indian Writing in English* Ed. M.K. Naik et al. Madras: Macmillan, 1977. Print.

Niranjan, Shiva. "An Interview with Raja Rao." *Indian Writing in English.* Ed. Krishna Nandan. New Delhi: Heritage, 1979. Print.

Rao, Raja. "By Raja Rao" E. M. *Foster: A Tribute with Selections from His Writings on India.* Ed. Singh, K. Natwar. New York: Harcourt, 1964. Print.

Rao. *The Meaning of India.* New Delhi: Vision, 1996. Print.

Rao, Rao. "Trivandrum," Illustrated Weekly of India. 25 February 1962.

____. "Foreword" *Kanthapura* (1938). Madras: Oxford U P, 1974. Print.

____. *The Serpent and the Rope* (1960). New Delhi: Orient, 1968. Print.

Swamy, Shanta Krishna. *Glimpses of Women in India.* New Delhi: Ashish, 1983. Print.

Shirwadkar, Meena. Image of Woman in the Indo-Anglican Novel. New Delhi: Sterling, 1979. Print.

Wohl, Elizabeth. "Raja Rao on America". Span Jan.1973. Wohl, Elizabeth."Raja Rao on America". Span Jan. 1973.

Notes on the Contributors

1. **Dr. Sigma G. R.** is an Assistant Professor at Department of English in Cherthala NSS College, Alleppy district in Kerala, India. She has nine years of teaching experience both in national and international colleges. She worked for 3 years as a lecturer in English under Ministry of Manpower in Sultanate of Oman. Dr. Sigma's few poems were published by American Literary press in Wordchimes Anthology. She has also published few articles in Journals and Newspapers. She is currently working as an Editorial board member of TJPRC Journals and as a Reviewer in 'The Criterion' Journal.
2. **Dr. Sony Jalarajan Raj** is an Assistant Professor at the Faculty of Fine Arts and Communications, MacEwan University, Edmonton, Canada. Dr. Raj served as the Graduate Coordinator and Assistant Professor at St. Thomas University Florida, USA. He has been full time faculty member in many prestigious universities like Monash University, Australia; Curtin University, Mahatma Gandhi University and University of Kerala. Dr. Raj has worked in several news media channels like BBC, NDTV, Doordarshan, AIR, and Asianet News and he edits a journal 'Media Watch' He is a three times winner of the Monash University PVC Award, a recipient of Reuters Fellowship and Thomson Foundation (UK) Fellowship.
3. **Dr. Soumya Jose** is an Assistant Professor of English at the School of Social Sciences and Languages, VIT University, Vellore, Tamil Nadu. Her research interests include Post-Colonial Writings, African American Literature and Diaspora

Studies. She has published more than twenty-five research articles in various national and international journals.

4. **Dr. Archana Bhattacharjee** is an Associate Professor and Head in the Department of English, Kakojan College Jorhat, Assam which is affiliated with Dibrugarh University. She did her M.A. in English Literature from Gauhati University and M. Phil from Vinayaka Missions University, Tamilnadu. She has presented 66 papers at various National and international seminars and conferences both within and outside the country. She has published more than 30 research papers also in various journals and books. She is the joint editor of an ISSN journal "Emerging Echoes." She is also in the Editorial and Advisory board of four international journals. Her areas of interest are Gender Studies, Post-Colonial Writing, Indian Writing in English and British Literature.
5. **Dr. Himanginee Kaushik** is an Assistant Professor in RJLB Govt. Polytechnic College, Loharu. She has done her B. Ed (Spl.), M. Ed (Spl.) and M.A. in English from Kurukshetra University, Kurukshetra. She has done her Ph.D in English from M.D.S. University, Ajmer. She has published six papers in different international journals. Her areas of interest are Diasporic Literature, Gender Studies and Indian Writing in English.
6. **Imrul Kayes Alam Sarkar** (UGC-NET Twice) has done his graduation from Malda College and M. A. from University of Gour Banga, Malda. He has done his M. Phil from Visva Bharati University, Santiniketan. His areas of interest are Indian Partition Novels, Indian Diasporic Literature, British and American Literature.
7. **Dr. Narendra Kumar** (Triple Ph.D: English, Management and Education) is a principle at Rajasthan P.G. College, Chirawa, Jhunjhunu, Rajasthan. He has worked at many reputed institutes in Jaipur as an Assistant Professor and Head of Department like Shankara Institute of Technology, Sri Balaji College of Engineering & Technology and J. D. College of Technical

Education, Jaipur. He has command on English, Hindi, French, German and Russian equally.

8. **Patil Sangita Sharnappa** has served as an Assistant Professor in LBS Govt. First Grade College, University of Bangalore, Karnataka. She has more than eight years of teaching experience at U.G. level. She is pursuing her Ph.D at Tumkur University, Tumkur. She is a short-story writer. She has published her papers in the refereed journals. She has presented six papers at International Seminars/Conferences, nine papers at National Seminars/Conferences, one paper at Online Language Conference and participated in ten workshops.

9. **Dr. Sumitra Singh** is an Assistant Professor at Amity University, Noida, India. She is Editor of International Research Journal of Humanities, Engineering and Pharmaceutical Sciences. She holds Ph.D in Afro-American Literature. She has presented her research papers/articles in around 65 national and international conferences/seminars and workshops. She has published many papers in various national and international journals of repute.

10. **Md. Nazme Furkanul Hoque** is an M. Phil Research-scholar in the Department of English and Modern European Languages at University of Lucknow. He earned his Bachelor of Arts in English Language and Literature from University of North Bengal and Masters from CSJMU main campus in English Literature with the specialization on the works of the Romantics. His area of interest is South Asian Writing in English (including India, Pakistan, Afghanistan and Bangladesh), Feminism, Post-Colonial Literature and Literature in Translation. He is a bilingual poet and his poems have been published in the leading Bengali and English magazines.

11. **Dr. Anand Kumar** (M.A., B. Ed, M.Phil, Ph.D) is working as English lecturer at Mauri, Bhiwani. He is UGC-NET & JRF, CTET, STET, HTET and RTET qualified. He has worked as an Assistant Professor in J.V.M.G.R.R. Post Graduate College, Charkhi Dadri, S.B.C Engineering College at Rohtak, Vedanta

College at Kota, Rajasthan and R.P.S. Degree College Mahendergarh. He is working as a visiting faculty in various renowned Institutions. He has over five years experience in teaching at different degree, Engineering and Management colleges at both UG and PG level. He has presented his papers in many national and international conferences and seminars and published articles in the refereed journals and magazines. His areas of interest are Poetry, Literary Theory, Post-Colonial Writings, Indian Writing in English, Linguistics and Phonetics.

12. **Anita Gehlot** has done her M.A. in English from Jai Narain Vyas University, Jodhpur. She has done her M. Phil in English Language Teaching (ELT) from Banasthali Vidyapith, Jaipur, Rajasthan. She is a doing her doctoral research in Jodhpur National University, Jodhpur, Rajasthan. Her areas of interests are Indian English Literature, American English Literature, English Language Teaching and English phonetics and English Grammar.

13. **Udayan Gautam** done his M.A. from Rabindra Bharati University, Kolkata and is pursuing Ph.D on Dalit literature from Rabindra Bharati University, Kolkata. He has authored a number of scholarly papers on Subaltern Studies, Dalit Literature, Marxist Cultural Theories etc. and some of them have been either published or in the process of publication in journals of national and international repute. He has also presented papers in many esteemed institutes during seminars and conferences.

14. **Dr. Zainul Abid Kotta** is an Assistant Professor and Head in Postgraduate Department of English at Government College, Malappuram, Kerala, India. He has been a Syndicate Member and Academic Council Member of University of Calicut, the largest University in Kerala. He is a research supervisor at the Postgraduate Department of English, Government College Malappuram and eight research-scholars are working under his supervision. He is chief-editor of *International Journal of Advanced Research* (www.ijar.net.in). He is a regular contributor to research

journals and his edited works include *Modern Prose and Drama* (2014) published by Oxford University Press, New Delhi.

15. **Seema Rani** is an Assistant Professor in Maharaja Aggrasen Postgraduate College for Women, Jhajjar affiliated with Maharshi Dayanand University, Rohtak. She has completed her M.A. in English from Maharshi Dayanand University, Rohtak and M. Phil from Vinayaka Missions University, Salem, Tamilnadu. She is pursuing her Ph.D from Chhatrapati Shahuji Maharaj University, Kanpur.
16. **Vishali Sharma** is a Research Scholar in the School of Languages and Literature at Shri Mata Vaishno Devi University, Katra, Jammu and Kashmir. The title of her Doctoral thesis is *The Writer as Hero and the Hero as Writer: A Comparative Study of Hero in the Selected Plays of Rabindranath Tagore and Wole Soyinka.* She has attended various National and International Conferences, Seminars and Workshops and contributed articles to several journals. She is associated with the Editorial Board of *Literary Confluence: A Global Journal of English and Cultural Studies.*
17. **Dr. Ratan Bhattacharjee** is the Chairman of the Postgraduate Department of English; Dum Dum Motijheel Collge, Rabindra Bharati University. He is the Executive Member in the International Advisory Board of International Theeodore Dreiser Society, USA. He is basically a poet, and very popular one with his bestseller bouquet of fabulous love poems, *The Ballad of the Bleeding Ballads.* His other stories, articles and poems are published in numerous journals and magazines in India and abroad. He was associated with the Indian Association of American Studies (IAAS) as a member of the Executive Body and now he is the Founder Director of the newly inaugurated Dattani Archive and Research Association (DARA), Kolkata. He edits the Journal VIEW, 'Voices of the Indian English Writers' and another International ISSN journal 'Literary Confluence'. His papers have been accepted for the International Conference at Romania organized by the University of Craiova. He has to his credit nearly five books on

British and American literature, nearly 650 articles and 200 poems and short stories in English.

18. **Dr. Sohel Aziz** (M.A, Ph.D, UGC-NET) is an Assistant Professor in Raj Kumar Goel Institute of Technology, Ghaziabad. He has done his Ph.D on Harold Pinter from Aligarh Muslim University, Aligarh. He has presented several research papers in different national and international seminars. He has special interest in modern and post-modern drama, fiction of Indian and British literature and literary theory.
19. **Jyoti Arora Sharma** (M.A., B. Ed, UGC-NET) is an Assistant Professor at the University of Delhi and is currently teaching at the Equal Opportunity Cell of the University of Delhi. She completed her B.A. Honours English from Delhi University and M.A. English from Jamia Milia Islamia, New Delhi. She is a creative writer and also a member of Shakespeare Society of India. Her teaching and research interests include Diaspora Literature, Postcolonial Literature, Indian Writing in English, Early Twentieth Century British Literature and British Romantic Poetry.
20. **Suruchi Sharma** (UGC-NET) is an Assistant Professor in R.K.S.D. College, Kaithal, Haryana. She has done her P.G. from K.M.V. College, Jalandhar, Punjab. She is pursuing Ph.D from NIMS University, Jaipur. She has presented her papers in many national and international seminars and conferences. Her papers have been published in national and international journals and seminar/conference proceedings.
21. **Kusum Kanger** is an Assistant Professor in B.A.R. Janta College Kaul, Kaithal, Haryana. She is a Ph.D Research-scholar in NIMS University, Jaipur. She has earned her M. Phil from Kurukshetra University, Kurukshetra. She has presented and published her papers in many national and international seminars and conferences. Her papers have been published in many national and international journals.
22. **Shankar Lal Seemawat** is a Research-scholar at the Department of English, University of Delhi. He did his B.A.

in English Honours from University Rajasthan College, Jaipur. He obtained his M. A. from Jawaharlal Nehru University, New Delhi in 2013. He has presented papers in many conferences and seminars on diverse themes like Subaltern Studies, Indian Writing in English, Peace and Ethics Studies, Indian Literature in Translation, Afro-American Literature and Indian Diasporic Studies.

23. **Sushil Sarkar** is an M. Phil Research-scholar at Visva Bharati, Santiniketan, West Bengal. He is a guest lecturer in English in DDE, RBU, Sukanta Mahavidyalaya, Dhupguri Study Centre. His areas of interest are Indian English Literature, Post-colonial Studies and Cultural Studies.

24. **Tuhin Majumdar** (UGC-NET & JRF) has been empanelled to join Khatra Adivasi College affiliated with the University of Burdwan as an Assistant Professor. He has completed his M.A. from Banaras Hindu University and he is pursuing Ph.D in Graphic novels from the University of Burdwan. He has rendered his services as an Assistant Professor in English Language and Technical Communication in Hooghly Engineering and Technology College. He has published papers in various peer-reviewed national and international journals. He has also presented papers in many esteemed institutes during seminars and conferences.

25. **Bijender Singh** [M.A., M. Phil, UGC-NET, SET, HTET, MPHW (Male), Shastri, Arts & Crafts Teacher Course] is an English Lecturer in Govt. Sr. Sec. School, Hatt, (Jind), Haryana. He is a poet, creative writer, editor and ardent researcher. He writes both in English and Hindi. He has published a few books and many research papers.

26. **Nandini Maity** has completed her M.A. from the University of Burdwan. Clearing NET, she is pursuing Ph.D in Comics from the University of Burdwan. She is serving as an Assistant Professor in English Language and Technical Communication in Saroj Mohan Institute of Technology. She has authored a few scholarly papers which have been published in various journals.

She has presented papers in many seminars and conferences also.

27. **Mohini Gurav** is an Assistant Professor in Department of English, GMD Arts, BW Commerce and Science College, Sinnar, Nashik, Maharashtra. She has been working in the teaching field for the last 18 years. She is also a Ph.D research-scholar at Mumbai University. She has presented papers at international and national seminars/conferences in India. Her reviews, interviews, articles and research papers have been published in many journals of repute. She has creative bent of mind and few of her poems are published in an anthology entitled "Scaling Heights" edited by Gopal Lahiri and Kiriti Sengupta.
28. **Priti Sharma** is a former Assistant Professor of English in Lingaya's University, Faridabad, Haryana. She has taught Communicative English and Literature to various branches of the university. She has six year teaching experience. She has done her Masters from Ravenshaw University. She has done B. Ed and C.T.E (Certificate in Teaching in English). She is being published in reputed International Journals and books. She has been awarded the first prize in All Orissa Inter college literary competition for writing English short story. Her areas of interests are Creative Writing, Indian Writing in English, Dalit Literature, Indian Diaspora, Linguistics and English Language Teaching.
29. **Dr. Parmod Kumar** is an Assistant Professor in the Faculty of English at Indira Gandhi National Open University, New Delhi. He has done his doctoral research on the domestication and insurrection of marginalized voices in Indian English Literature. He edits an e-journal Struggle/Sangharsh also which puts to centre all academic and social issues related with Dalit Discourse. He has been a proud recipient of Australia India Council Fellowship and has worked extensively on the perspectives in indigeneity in India and Australia.